VOICING SOCIAL CONCERN

• The Mass Media • Violence • Pornography
• Censorship • Organization • Social Science
• The Ultramultiversity

Otto N. Larsen
University of Washington

Afterword by William R. Catton, Jr.

UNIVERSITY
PRESS OF
AMERICA

Lanham • New York • London

Copyright © 1994 by
University Press of America,® Inc.
4720 Boston Way
Lanham, Maryland 20706

3 Henrietta Street
London WC2E 8LU England

Library of Congress Cataloging-in-Publication Data
Larsen, Otto N.
Voicing social concern : the mass media, violence, pornography,
censorship, organization, social science, the ultramultiversity /
Otto N. Larsen ; afterword by William R. Catton.
p.   cm.
Includes index.
1. Mass media—Social aspects—United States.
2. Communication—Social aspects—United States.
3. Social sciences—United States.   I. Title.
HM258.L357   1994   302.23—dc20   93–48776 CIP

ISBN 0–8191–9437–9 (cloth : alk. paper)

 The paper used in this publication meets the minimum requirements of
American National Standard for Information Sciences—Permanence
of Paper for Printed Library Materials, ANSI Z39.48–1984.

-TO-

Dan, Erika, Chloe, Andrew, Elizabeth
(and any other grandchildren that may follow)

iii

Contents

Three Memorable Mentors

Afterword

Preface

A professional career takes unpredictable turns. When the journey consumes more than four decades, many vistas are recalled. Here I want to recount mine in a somewhat novel way. This volume presents a collection of talks that I delivered in places around the world, principally in the United States, but also including sites in Denmark, Argentina, and Canada.

The content covers social, political, and professional issues that I encountered as a teacher, researcher, advisor, administrator, and public official. The issues are addressed with varying shades of curiosity, analysis, vexation, or preachment.

In most cases, I tried to convert research ideas into a pertinent message of interest to intelligent people beyond those regularly met in a circle of peers with technical specialties. That effort often departed from theoretical concerns to engage troublesome civic issues and problematic professional arrangements. The troubles and problems persist today. Thus, we are still perplexed by sex and violence in the mass media, by parochialism in our professional associations, by misunderstanding of social science as science, and by role confusion in higher education.

In probing these topics, I discovered how perceptions emerge as potent realities in the power games that play out both on campus and in the broader realms of public policy. This is an irritable fact about human communication, a point that I tried to underscore in a number of presentations.

Every professor has a specialty. My fortune, in and through sociology, was to become known as an analyst of the mass media and as a missionary for the discipline. These traits mark this manuscript.

As an analyst, I always tried to post ideas on how we might advance understanding of the direct and subtle effects of mass communication. It was fascinating to look for ways to link media outcomes to public policies.

As a missionary, I enjoyed the challenge of attempting to advance public comprehension of the promise and the performance of sociology in particular and social science more generally.

On the occasion of giving the early talks posted in this book, I was proud to be introduced as a sociologist. Later in my career, I deemed it even more rewarding, and actually more consistent with career-long dispositions, to be identified as someone who worked to enhance the perception and to advance the reality of the scientific legitimacy of all the social and behavioral sciences.

The introduction to each section of this volume provides biographical notes on the evolution of interests and the impact of cultural heritage. In his generous *Afterword*, William Catton adds penetrating clarity about such matters. Clearly, while I embraced the need for dispassionate inquiry, I was not reluctant to advance value preferences born out of a humanistic legacy.

These accounts also reveal a trait I tried to mask. In preparing for a podium, I invested in "planned spontaneity." With a full script in hand, including tall tales built in, there was security enough to proceed. Other outbursts might reflect genuine spontaneity; fortunately, or otherwise, these are lost for the record.

For more than forty-years, my family has had more than forty occasions to assert, "You talk too much." Recently, I discovered that I actually defended this disposition years ago when the first sentence of my doctoral dissertation compounded the trait by proclaiming, "Man, the talking animal, not only talks, but he talks about his talking."

That I enjoyed agitating air molecules occurred to me again when, as a retirement exercise, I sorted through boxes in the basement and uncovered a musty hoard of scripts, lectures, transcripts, notes, and tapes. To review and to organize this material was more fun than to codify the research on which some of it was based. The absence of footnotes and tables did not seem to detract from important information, strong argument, and serious intent, even when cast in a presumed satirical cloak.

As I sorted out memorabilia, eight themes emerged. They now encompass the thirty-three talks selected and presented here as chapters. The time and place of the initial oral delivery is also recorded.

With the exception of a few minor editorial adjustments, the content presented here is the same as prepared and delivered for each forum that I was privileged to address in the time that spans some forty years.

Reading, of course, is not the same as hearing. In the pursuit of being effective and successful in the oral forum, serious intent can be peppered with light, if not outrageous merriment. I found myself remembering audience reactions. There were tense moments; but, on the whole there was hearty response. To impart information and to spark enjoyment was satisfying. More memorable were those moments that aroused serious intellectual curiosity and a disposition to act on it.

That's worth trying to reach out for again.

This time, print will also accommodate my desire to leave a record for our grandchildren. Some of their communicative skills have already exceeded mine. But maybe this benchmark will kindle additional effort, and thus, I trust, be of service to them and to their offspring.

By the same token, since the inception of each chapter is dated, every reader will be able to assess what progress, if any, has been made in coping with the concerns posted from that time forward to the present date. In many instances that exercise will confirm how difficult it is to advance understanding of social concerns but how necessary it is to maintain the effort.

Communication

Communication is the most significant social force in the long career of human-kind on earth.

One can but marvel that eons of evolution brought forth creatures that share thoughts of remote ancestors as well as of each other. Each generation struggles to understand the fundamentals of the exchange. At stake are matters of continuity and change in the social order. As modes for transmitting meaning multiplied and became more efficient, the evaluation of the mass media came to the fore.

Pure intellectual curiosity did not launch my professional interest in mass communication. Personal economic needs, coupled to chance factors, brought me to an apprenticeship on research projects in this area.

The graduate school environment that I entered after World War II sparked with opportunities for empirical studies of various media forms. Research moneys flowed in from private and from public sources. Thus, state and city government alarmed about violence in comic books funded assessments of content to identify offending material; the Curtis Publishing Company, interested in showing that their *Saturday Evening Post* was more influential than *Life* magazine, funded audience studies requiring sociometric research on status linkages in total communities; and the Air Force, committed to instruments of psychological warfare, funded large-scale studies of message diffusion from air-dropped leaflets.

These projects afforded exciting opportunities to construct and use tools of observation and data analysis. Questionnaires, attitude scales, sampling designs, interviewing techniques, and statistical measures became matters of great curiosity and considerable challenge.

My first effort at an interview in the field was a memorable learning experience. The potential respondent, a burly man whom I beckoned from behind seemingly impenetrable barriers, actually threw me off his porch. Strong recollections also persist from discovering the impact of question wording and ordering, from observing the power of probability sampling, and from learning how to terminate, as well as to initiate, an interview.

There was gain from exercise in first-hand data collection. The yield included a special sensitivity to the fragility of findings, to the necessity of verification, and to the challenge of generating new and testable hypotheses.

Other graduate students of my cohort pursued opportunities in demography, criminology, organization, or race relations, but I found myself midst comic books, diffusion studies, and public opinion polling. This provoked irritation among peers. Unlike the study of gangs, drug addiction, or prostitution, the study of television, movies, or magazines raised charges of trivial pursuit. Students of the media seemed to enjoy their work just a bit too much.

More seriously, it soon became apparent that the mass media had a significant capacity to convert conditional statements of complex findings into simple accounts. Sociologists needed models of clarity. But, when news reports distorted findings and contested the fundamental worth of inquiry, we harbored resentment. Nonetheless, events sustained curiosity about media effects and the cost and consequences of what to do about them.

I first confronted some powerful dynamics in the interaction of media and public when working with a Mayor's Committee on Comic Books in Seattle in 1947. That inquiry led to a an act of civic censorship where 50 crime comics were banned as elicit material. Later, even greater complexities were confronted when I served a Presidential Commission on Obscenity and Pornography from 1968 to 1970

So, for me, puzzles about communication persisted over several decades. Moreover, public interest in media matters never retreated. Accordingly, I have had many opportunities to assess the state of knowledge, to confess the limits of the same, and to address new challenges on the horizon.

This orientation was incubated early as evidenced in the first four chapters in this section under the rubric of "Communication." It was extended, and tested, under even more trying conditions as should be apparent when, in successive sections, the focus shifts to violence, pornography, and censorship.

Chapter 1

Trying to be Effective--
Vying to be Successful

Davidson Anthropological Society, University of Washington
February 6, 1963

The channels between disciplines, especially those concerned with communication, should be open and active.

That ideal is rarely achieved. Disciplines tend to get addicted to their own language systems and often are tangled in the web of their own information networks. To penetrate these is to open the possibility of learning from one another.

Let me congratulate the anthropologists for sensing this possibility. It is not surprising that they would organize a public symposium to challenge a linguist, a sociologist, and an engineer. I do not refer to their demonstrated capacity to endure hardship as they forage about in far-distant cultures. Rather, I have in mind their scientific self-concept. However specific they are in dealing with data, anthropologists proclaim that their ultimate general goal is to be a coordinating science.

That idea disturbs some sociologists. They harbor similar aspirations. This, however, is not the forum to revisit ancient intramural controversies. Otherwise we would have to try to resolve the priority of the cultural egg of anthropology over the societal chicken of sociology.

Instead, for tonight, let us merely be grateful to our friends from anthropology who by hosting this occasion invoke the principle that good intentions must have a structure in which to operate if communication is to be achieved.

When sociologists approach communication, what is the focus? Some elementary definitions might help locate the touchstone of communication in the ore of sociology.

Sociological Focus

Sociologists formulate and test generalizations about the form, process, and consequence of inter-human behavior. Social organization and social structure are central concepts. Organization refers to recurrent and coordinated relationships among interdependent persons or groups. Social structure refers to a network of social positions that is assigned relatively fixed tasks, responsibilities, and avenues of communication. To achieve certain objectives, all groups and societies arrange their activities into a social structure.

Social structure was not invented by sociologists. Long before the term "sociology" appeared, groups shaped patterns that we now call traditions, folkways, and norms. People must have been talking sociology ever since they talked at all. Order emerges from communication. Communication is basic to any social system. It is the fundamental means of establishing consensus and bringing about social unity. It is the key to the question of how stability and order are achieved midst continuing requirements for flexibility and change.

What, then, is meant by communication? The concept refers both to an interactive process and to an end product. All of us are engaged in acts of communication, but not all of these efforts result in communication. That is an intriguing distinction.

The shaping and transfer of meaning involves a dynamic interchange. Participants are simultaneously both senders and receivers. Analytically, we may freeze the frame and state that communication has been achieved when meanings embodied in a message are conveyed to persons in such a way that the meanings received are equivalent to those which the initiator(s) of the message intended.

In a communicative act, then, when the intended expression and the received impression coalesce, then communication may be said to be effective. Correspondence is usually a matter of degree. Feedback is the major mechanism for ascertaining how effectively it has been achieved.

Other problems remain.

Consider the distinction between effective and successful communication. When expression and impression correspond, communication has been effective. When the expression is received and is evaluated favorably, the encounter is successful.

When I assert, as I sometimes do, that "sociology is a science," you may get the message exactly as I expressed it. That would be effective communication. However, if you evaluate this assertion unfavorably, as some misguided souls are apt to do, then communication has not been successful.

Not all social encounters involve both informative and persuasive intent. Various social roles engineer consent with different emphases. A preacher wants to be both effective and successful. On the other hand, a professor wants to be effective without necessarily striving to be successful. That is, professors want students to understand a point of view, not necessarily to subscribe to it.

But other outcomes are possible and, curiously, even tolerable. It is quite possible, for example, to be ineffective and still be successful. To make this important point, and to lighten the mode of this presentation, please bear with me as I challenge your imagination with the following story.

Communicative Encounter

Several hundred years ago the reigning Pope became alarmed over the growing number of Jewish people in Italy. After consulting the College of Cardinals, he decided to issue an edict banishing all Jews from Italy. The Jews were stunned by this act; after all, most of their families had lived in Italy for centuries and they regarded it as their home.

Accordingly, they sent a delegation to the Vatican to protest. The delegates appealed to the Pope's scholarly nature. They pointed out their cultural contributions, the high value placed on learning, and the loss that Italy would sustain if the edict remained in force.

The Pope was impressed. Nevertheless, the order could not be canceled out of hand. Therefore, the Pope proposed a three-pronged "test." He said that if the delegation would send him their most distinguished scholar, they would, through signs and gestures, engage in communication. No words would be spoken. If the results were satisfactory, the edict would be canceled.

Returning to the Ghetto, the community selected their most

learned Rabbi, a dignified little man, bent with age, whose hair and beard were white as snow. On the appointed day, they took their scholar to the Vatican's ornate audience room. There they met the Pope, surrounded by Cardinals in their elegant robes, and the test began. The Pope made the first sign--he held up one finger. The rabbi replied by holding up two fingers. Upon seeing this, the Pope smiled and the delegation felt that all was going well.

The Pope's next gesture was a large sweeping one in the shape of an arc with the right hand and arm and with one finger extended. The rabbi replied by holding his left palm in front of him and vigorously tapping it with his right index finger. At this, the Pope smiled and positively beamed. The Jews began to relax.

The third and final gesture by the Pope was made quickly. He reached into his gown and pulled out an orange which he held up for all to see. The rabbi responded without hesitation. He reached into his tattered robe and pulled out some matzo, the unleavened bread eaten by Jews during Passover.

The Pope responded enthusiastically and threw his arms around the rabbi while triumphantly asserting, *"You have sent me a learned man indeed, the Jews can stay in Italy forever."*

As soon as the delegation departed, the cardinals gathered around the Pope excitedly asking for explanation of the conversation of gestures. The Pope explained. *"Well, first I said, 'There is but one God'* (hold up one finger) and the rabbi replied, 'But don't forget the Son and the Holy Ghost' (hold up two fingers). *A brilliant theological response."*

The Pope continued. *"Then I said, 'God is everywhere'* (sweeping gesture) and the rabbi replied, *'Yes, but he makes his presence known to us right here right now.'* (tap palm with finger) *A keen deduction."*

Then the Pope concluded, *"Finally I said, 'But God made the earth round', and I held up the orange to convey that meaning. But then the rabbi replied: 'Yes, but for our purposes, he made it appear flat right here' and he held out his matzo as a reply. A brilliant scholar. We need such people in Italy."*

Meanwhile, the rabbi and his contingent arrived back at the ghetto and everyone rejoiced in the outcome. Finally, they asked him to recount the trial and the rabbi explained:

"Vell, the Pope said, 'You be getting out of Italy or I'll be poking out your eye' (holding up one finger). *"And I said, 'If you do, I'll be poking out both of yours'"* (two fingers). *"Then the Pope said, 'All the*

Jews have got to be getting out of Italy' (sweeping gesture). *And I replied, 'Hell no, we'll be staying right here'* (palm tapping). *Then the Pope pulled out his lunch, so I pulled out mine!"*

Apocryphal?

Yes, but this yarn clearly signals how communication can be successful without being effective. Real life provides similar instances. Teenagers professing love, or diplomats pleading their case, are likely to engage in communication that is ineffective but yet successful. This also happens to professors as when students fail the course but claim they got a lot out of it, enjoyed it, and agreed with everything that was professed.

But other combinations are possible in this four-fold model. Thus, the cold war is partly a matter of ineffective and unsuccessful communication and partly a matter of effective but unsuccessful communication. Perhaps as long as the latter fusion outweighs the former, wars will remain cold rather than heat up. Stability and peace, however, surely will require continuous communication that is both effective and successful.

Directions and Issues

To a sociologist, then, communication is a pivotal concept. We explore the conditions that give rise to kinds and degrees of communication in order to appraise how they affect social arrangements and the behavior of persons. This requires an assortment of tools including participant-observation in families or gangs, controlled experiments in small group laboratories, and sample surveys in whole communities.

Current inquiries begin with questions such as, how does variation in leadership status, group size, and physical arrangement affect the achievement of consensus? Or, how is the diffusion of information and the decision to adopt an innovation related to status integration? Or, as the size of a community increases, what happens to the degree of interest that people take in public issues?

Such inquiries both grow from and nourish a varied curriculum involving classes on the sociology of language, knowledge, public opinion, and mass communication that nestle among other standard topics on groups, stratification, and organization.

At this stage, the study of mass communication is propelled more by practical questions than by mature theoretical conceptions. This reflects the explosive growth of the media themselves. All over the world more and more people are spending more and more time in exposure to the mass media. This fact alone prompts controversy over whether the media enhance political involvement and cultural creativity, or induce apathy, indifference, and standardization and thus constitute a mechanism for the manipulation of the masses and the concentration of power.

Many people liken the media to a giant hypodermic needle. In the hands of a few skilled operators, the needle persistently pecks and plunges away at the passively poised body of the masses, whose response is direct and immediate. This conception motivated early research. It assumes that society is an atomized mass of disconnected individuals where there is a direct stimulus-response relationship between the sending and receiving of mass media content.

However, current research illuminates limits to the power of the media. Interpersonal linkages mediate impact. Group structure intervenes. Selectivity in attention, perception, and response arises out of stimulation from organized social process rather than merely from the personal interests of isolated individuals.

The major demonstrated impact of the mass media is a reinforcement of attitudes and behavior. That conclusion flows from research directed mainly toward short term effects.When impact over time has been studied, different results will likely emerge. This prospect is underscored by growing evidence that the use of the mass media goes far beyond the intent of the mass communicator.

Moreover, media impact on individuals is not necessarily the same as that achieved, even simultaneously, on the collective level. Thus, reinforcement of the attitudes of individuals can also yield collective polarization. Accordingly, a force that is conservative for individuals could be radical for the collectivity when polarization induces conflict, the incubator of change.

This general commentary on communication and sociology should now close. Perhaps through questions and discussion we can end the evening by being both more effective and more successful.

Chapter 2

Comic Books and Creative Leisure

University of Copenhagen, December 18, 1959

Age, whether young or old, can provoke problems for all of us.

It is a pleasure to share a rostrum here in Copenhagen with my American colleague, Professor Gordon Streib. Though we are of the same generation, our focus today reflects an age-gap. I am going to talk about a medium mainly pointed toward children, while his interest directs us to the problems of the aged. Perhaps, in the end, some theory of the middle range will bring us together in the ecumenical spirit of this festive, annual Christmas seminar.

As we approach the holiday season, it might be well to reflect on matters of leisure, a concept strongly sensed though not easily defined. Nearly everyone prizes leisure, and wants more of it, even though when we get it we are not always certain how to use it. Therein lies the problem of creative leisure, a concept that is sharpened by contrasting it with the idea of recreation.

Recreation is behavior distinguished chiefly by the degree to which it is an end in itself; a free and pleasurable act not impelled by a delayed reward or by any immediate necessity.

Creative activity, on the other hand, is effort directed toward the production of objects or values containing an element of design or invention that lead to something else. Thus, in the crystallization of mental and physical free-time energies, something new has been added. And if it is a creative act, this "something new" becomes a kind of "cultural capital," usable in the production of further capital.

Creativity can yield either hard or soft-ware. That is, the product can be either material or symbolic--artifacts or mentifacts--as when some of us carve objects for games from wood or wax, while others are moved to manipulate or modify the rules or the strategy of games.

Clearly, you and I , as academics, are mainly in the "mentifact camp." We are symbol creators. Sometimes we compound matters by producing symbols that stand for nothing else but other symbols. This is called deep thinking.

Since we are always in a thought mode, the implication is that creative leisure is not our problem, but a predicament for others. More precisely, it is often perceived to be the problem of the younger generation, the category that always seems to be wasting time. You've heard that message. The patriarch inevitably proclaims that "Things are not what they used to be." To which the insolent but bright youngster replies, "Nor have they ever been."

So let us consider the plight of the younger generation--the children born into an age bursting with concerns ranging from inner self to outer space.

Time Absorption

At the outset, there is a numerical fact sometimes called the population explosion. Not only are there more children now than ever before in history, but there is less excuse for having them now than there ever has been. Where once children were an economic necessity for work in fields, mines and factories, today, in the western world, at least, they are a social luxury, born either from a consciousness of status or an unconsciousness of modern contraceptive technology.

To some degree, children today are the displaced persons of a crowded culture seeking to have and yet not to have them. One senses this in the growth of elaborate means to absorb large blocks of available time. Thus the increment in pre-nursery schools, nursery schools, kindergartens, and summer camps. As for regular schools, while there is much complaint about them, few parents are unappreciative of their capacity to perform custodial functions.

Despite these efforts, children seem to have more time than parents have time-absorbing techniques. Perhaps it is not too cynical, then, to suggest that underlying the problem of creative leisure is the matter of how to control the biological activity of adults. That is a topic I can't deal with on this occasion.

In the meantime, the children are with us. And what are they doing with those large blocks of time that have not been committed to approved organized exercises? The answer in large part is that they are absorbed in mass communication--going to the movies, watching television, and reading comic books.

Comic books? Am I serious? Yes, indeed. The ubiquitous presence of this curious medium merits attention.

Significance of Self-Regulation

Just five years ago in 1954, 100 million comic books were sold every month in the United States. What did that mean? It meant that comic book sales reached over one billion copies per year, or an expenditure of about one hundred million dollars--more than was spent for the entire book supply for elementary and secondary schools for one year, and four times that of the combined book purchasing budgets of all public libraries. If the vast market for second-hand comic books were included, expenditures would be considerably higher.

Today, the market has been cut to about one-half with about 50 million comic books sold monthly. This cut is due largely to competition from television, but it also is influenced by restrictions placed on content through industry self-regulation. The evolution of the latter form of control should be of particular interest to sociologists.

Where did this medium come from? How did it gain its prominence? What are its prime messages? What responses did they evoke? Let me sketch some answers to these questions.

The technique on which the comic book is based dates back to drawings by the cave dwellers, but the full innovation is relatively recent. In its present form, comic books sprung from the womb of newspaper comic strips in the mid-1930s. Thus the comic book today is only about 25 years old.

As with many technological innovations, including all the mass media, the appearance of comic books was marked by anxiety and resistance. Most of its brief life span has thus been spent in "stormy adolescence" where the medium has been charged with abetting all possible forms of delinquency.

While it may not yet have grown up into full professional maturity as measured against any set of artistic standards or standards of social responsibility, the comic book has, in America at least, reached a stage where it is tolerated, if not fully accepted. This toleration is due mainly to complex interaction between the medium and the opinions of important publics.

Ferreting out this relationship and observing how it contributes to the institutionalization of a popular art form is the central focus of my inquiry. This involves observing the interrelationship of forces in the production, distribution, and consumption of this medium as well as responses generated by critics, the government, and by other media. The resulting interaction produces the unique American process of generating and then resolving controversy.

Soon after it emerged, the comic book became a subject of bitter contest. Through the influence of opinion leaders and the efforts of voluntary associations, comic books were banned in some communities, burned in others, and the distributors were boycotted in numerous local areas in the United States.

Action at the grass roots level prompted politicians to launch a full-scale congressional investigation of the comic book. The threat of restrictive federal legislation led the industry to form a trade association, to adopt a code of good practices, and to engage in self-regulation.

Ultimately, grass root's action prompted politicians to launch a full-scale congressional investigation of the comic book. The threat of restrictive federal legislation was a factor in leading the comic book industry to form a trade association, to adopt a code of good practices, and to engage in self-regulation.

Self-regulation is a product of perceived public opinion. It is also the characteristic way that the American mass media have responded to threats of intervention from governmental bodies. Thus each case of its development symbolizes the continuing dialogue in free societies on the relationship between the freedom of expression and the security of the social order.

This approach to the comic book, then, becomes an analysis of the way in which the forces of public opinion are mobilized and maintained to suppress or restrict expression that is believed to have the capacity to undermine various kinds of authority and order, or to have undesirable effects in relation to what is considered to be the common good. Perhaps this is but a more abstract expression of the problem implied in the inquiry into the relative creative and recreational power of the comic book. In any event, let us describe some other characteristics of this medium that have given rise to the consideration of the comic book as a social as well as a sociological problem.

Nature of Medium

First, what is this medium that is called "books" by the children, "pamphlets" by the printing trade, and "magazines" by the Post Office which accords them second-class mailing privileges?

A comic book is a printed form which in words and colored cartoons tells action-oriented stories from a wide variety of settings ranging from inner earth to outer space involving all kinds of characters from little animals to superhuman beings.

The average book will contain four complete stories in the brief space of about 33 pages involving about 42 cartoon-frames per story. Complex plots with subtle shadings do not evolve in such a limited space structure. From the first picture, there is action and movement, all in color. Stimulus leads quickly to response without the intervention of complex cause and effect considerations. This elementary structure is the key to why the comic book has become a mass medium of communication. For mass it has become.

In 1938, there were about 60 different comic books published. A year later, there were about 160, and this figure was more or less maintained until after World War II. Then the number increased until, in 1954, one could buy upwards of 500 different comic books from the newsstands at one time.

These are approximate numbers for commercial comic books, the bulk of which sold for ten-cents each. These, however, were not the only comic books available. Others, produced and given away by corporations, churches, government and political parties, conveyed special-interest messages. Thus one can today read comic books with stories attacking racial and religious prejudice, or proclaiming the virtues of the free-enterprise system, the importance of cooperatives, the necessity of welfare policies, and how to become a stockholder in a corporation. One can also read the life-stories of Jesus Christ, Harry S. Truman, Thomas Edison, Paul Robeson, Pope Pius XIII, James Roosevelt and Booker T. Washington.

Audience

But, who reads comic books anyhow? The short answer is nearly all children read them regularly and many adults are in the audience. A national survey of comic book readership showed that in the age categories between 6 and 11 years, 95 percent of the boys and 91 percent of the girls read comic books regularly. That means reading between three and four books per week.

Another national survey in the United States indicated that 25 percent of adult high school graduates and 16 percent of adult college graduates regularly read comic books. Twelve percent of the nation's school teachers were also regular readers. Clearly, while nearly all children read the comic book, this medium is not merely a child's toy. Adults get into the act, too. The significance of this is that it complicates attempts to control the distribution and sale of comic books. A dilemma emerges; how do we protect children while safeguarding the right of adults to read matters of their own choice?

Patterns of Content

What gains all this attention? Some attempts have been made to characterize the patterns of content presented by this medium. In 1954, we secured copies of the 351 comic books being sold in Seattle during a three month period. These books contained 1,325 stories, 9,013 pages, and 55,859 frames. They also provoked a long summer for testing the eyesight.

The content was analyzed by specified criteria. Story types and other units were classified with high degrees of reliability (the main client and supporter was the Governor of the state who was concerned about the portrayal of violence).

In this particular sample, there were three main types of stories: 35.4 percent were of the humor type involving mainly the Walt Disney characters such as Mickey Mouse and Donald Duck. Crime stories were second in prominence, accounting for 27.5 percent of the total; and third, 20.6 percent, were romance stories. So, humor, crime, and romance stories were the big three of comic book content. Let's summarize a few other findings from this content analysis concerning particularly the latter two categories--crime and romance--the story types most likely to elicit complaint and generate controversy.

Crime Comics

One out of six frames in the total comic books studied involved the portrayal of a violent act, defined as a scene in which someone is the recipient of damaging physical action. Three-fifth of the violence took place in the crime comics, the category that constitute slightly more than one-fourth of the sample. Some other findings included that:

♦   Law and order is maintained in crime comics mainly by supernatural and superhuman heroes.

♦   Real law enforcement officials are discriminated against in the amount of space they receive.

♦   Law officers are ineffective in apprehending criminals. They must depend on chance or aid from fantasy characters or the criminal culture itself.

♦   No emphasis is placed upon careful, routine investigation or scientific police methods.

♦   The police depend upon physical strength in apprehending criminals. They must be very strong and capable of great physical feats.

♦   If chance factors and supernatural-superhuman beings are eliminated from crime stories, criminals would not be caught. To this extent "crime pays."

Romance Stories

What role-models, values, and norms come to the fore in the romance stories, the category that accounted for about one out of five of the stories studied? Six points sum up the main themes.

♦   Romance stories dealt with pre-marital and marital problems, with the pre-marital stories dominating in a ratio of about four to one. Without exception, pre-marital stories upheld marriage as a desirable end for young couples. On the other hand, none of the marital stories presented marriages as a happy relationship. It would seem, then, that the most exciting and interesting time in life is before marriage and that such pleasures end when marriage begins.

♦   In the pre-marital stories, love is portrayed as the only requirement for a successful marriage. And physical attraction is the basis for love.

♦   Romance stories suggest that there is one and only one right mate for each individual. If one waits long enough, he or she will come along.

♦   Virtue is always rewarded. The story endings always support this ideal. However, in considering the sequence of events, if chance or unexplained factors were ruled out, virtue would not always be rewarded.

♦   Sex is hinted at less by the pictures and more by the sequence of events (the brief time from initial contact to total embrace) and the language used to describe embraces.

♦   There are two kinds of men in romance stories. The first are those glamorous, physical types, rough and uncouth as they may be at times, who can provide considerable physical stimulation. And second, there are those men who are suitable for marriage. They do not attract physical interest.

Controversy

Such patterns of content stir public concern. What might comic book imageries, repeated as they are, have to do with shaping attitudes or fomenting acts? Does the visage of villains and the depiction of heroes, for example, involve role definitions that tend to create conflict more than they facilitate consensus?

That question probably resonates with this audience. One does not travel far in Copenhagen, Stockholm or Oslo without observing that Scandinavians are committed to consensus, while they believe that Americans are deeply afflicted with conflict.

If not via comic books, certainly the intrusion of American television into Scandinavia has aroused intense interest in effects along the conflict-consensus continuum. Empirically, more is known about media content than is known about media impact. The gap magnifies feelings. Where research is short, controversy is long.

The controversy over comic book effects has been long, indeed. "Experts," including child guidance counselors, psychiatrists, librarians, and sociologists, freely issue arguments and opinions, many as colorful and superficial as the comic books themselves. A summary of commonly registered views underscores this point. You will note that while they are emphatic, there is nothing systematic about them.

Negative Claims

The critics of comic books usually include the following negative points in their indictment:

♦   Comic books over-stimulate the unstable child and exert a powerful adverse effect upon the uncritical minds of all children.

♦   Comics make criminals and criminal acts attractive and also supply details of crime techniques.

♦   Comics make children and many adults impatient with good literature and its method of presentation. Their production freezes out the production of good inexpensive children's books.

♦   Artwork, printing, and color are frequently of such poor quality as to be physically injurious to the eyes of the reader.

Positive Claims

In contrast, the defenders of comic books usually make the following positive points in support of the medium:

♦   We should not judge all comic books by a small proportion that might be controversial.

♦   Anti-social behavior results only if the reader is neurotic, disturbed, or unstable in the first place.

♦   Comic books act as a catharsis and provide a release for aggressive behavior.

♦   The public can exercise freedom of choice in its selection of reading material. Any form of censorship creates more problems than it solves.

♦   A child may ascribe delinquent behavior to a comic book that he or she has read, but such explanation cannot be considered scientific evidence of causation.

Conclusion

So goes the rhetoric. Neither side presses a case for the comic book as an instrument for creative leisure. The critics argue that while reading the comic book may appear as simple recreation, the consequences of exposure are complex and damaging to personal and public health. The defenders dismiss, for lack of evidence, notions of adverse impact and they seem to characterize exposure as harmless recreation with only an occasional reference to the possibility that it might serve aspects of creative leisure.

An investment in serious research on the possible short and long-term effects of this medium is likely only if the controversy continues to heat up in the public arena. I should mention that only a few studies now available resemble inquiries that we would recognize as research. Among the findings are:

◆　Children perceive selectively as they go through cycles of exposure to content. At the pre-school period they start with the little animals and they close out a career of heavy exposure during the late teenage period with the vigorous fantasy figures.

◆　The impact of images varies markedly depending on whether the child is more peer or more parent oriented.

◆　This medium can be quite successful in adding words to the vocabulary of the child. In fact, fairly standardized and somewhat complex meanings get attached to those seemingly primitive grunts and groans like "Aaagh," "Eeek," and "Whack" that regularly punctuate expression in the comic book world.

Clearly, the approach to effects, whether on the individual or social level, is as yet quite primitive. There are prospects for advancement. To the extent that the comic book is recreation to the child, it tends to disturb the creative leisure of the parent. Accordingly, that can also become a force for stimulating research by sociologists.

Chapter 3

From the Flow of Information to the Adoption of Innovation

Danish Sociological Society, Copenhagen

January 27, 1960

A puzzle arises from the fact that this is the second sociological society that I have had the pleasure to address in Scandinavia.

The first was at Lund University in Sweden. From that, and from tonight's experience, I perceive a possible cultural difference in the approach of Swedes and Danes to a visiting American sociologist. In Sweden, I talked first, and then we had something to eat and drink. In Denmark, I note that food and libations come first.

You may entertain your own interpretation of this observation. Perhaps a difference in folkways signals a difference in national traits. Do Swedes and Danes actually differ on matters of prudence and risk taking? You appear willing to reward speakers first and then chance it that they will have something to say. On the other hand, maybe you merely want to insure that part of the evening will be a success.

Whatever the meaning, the present arrangement will, perhaps, avoid one aspect of my Swedish experience. In Lund, we had reached the question period only to have a response postponed because food was on the table. After fine food and drink, mainly the latter, no one could remember the question.

Now that we have imbibed, I'm not sure I can remember the substance of my intended talk. Perhaps a few ideas will spread out as we go along. Yes, that was it, the spread of ideas, the flow of information, the adoption of innovation, and research thereon.

The Web-of-Mouth

If there is anything as important as an idea, it may be its diffusion, particularly if it leads to a change in behavior. How does this take place?

Take the immediate case. Each of you made a decision to come here tonight. This bit of personal recklessness was actually a complicated social act--the end product of a diffusion process. To be sure, the act may have varied for each person but common elements were present and they led to predictable results. This, of course, is a way of describing the general function of any communication system. Which is to say that through communication we achieve the consensus essential for the building of a social order.

What elements in the communication system led to the social order constituted here tonight?

To start, there must have been an innovator, sometimes called an "opinion leader." To organize a meeting like this calls for skills usually formalized into the role of the president, or the program chairman, but often informal influentials lurk near the throne with ideas for social innovation.

After the plot is hatched, the idea has to be encoded and transmitted over some channel of communication. How did you first hear about the meeting? Perhaps you caught the message through some special form of mediated information flow, like a mimeographed news-bulletin. To perceive such a message, relevant attitudes must come to the fore. This is the basis of the well-documented principle of selective attention and perception in communication. If you got the information in this selective way, it means that you, too, might have served as an opinion-leader, or at least an opinion lieutenant, in the two-or-more-step flow of information.

More likely, however, you probably received the information when someone told you about it. This we may call "the web-of-mouth" effect. Webs give rise to interesting sociological queries. Did the message travel up or down or the status ladder to reach you? Did status considerations influence what you did with the message, either in terms of further communicative behavior, or in terms of the decision making process?

By pursuing such questions we could unlock the mystery of your presence here tonight. What I really intend to imply is that diffusion studies are not an end in themselves. Rather, they are a way of empirically approaching general sociological problems about decision-making, the power structure, and social change.

If we were to undertake a serious diffusion study of the present situation, we would have to consider not only those persons present but also those who heard the message and didn't appear tonight, as well as those who did not hear the message even though they were eligible to be here. Since we dare not pursue these missing links, we'll drop the illustration right now and, instead, pursue the content of the dignified literature on diffusion.

Linkages

For some time, the effects of mass communication have captivated my interest. It is now hard to believe that when I first came upon this area, a bit more than a decade ago, the dominant assumption was that society is an atomized mass of disconnected individuals for whom there was a direct stimulus-response relationship between the sending and receiving of media content. Research proved these assumptions false. We rediscovered the primary group, or how interpersonal relations intervene to mediate and modify the impact of the mass media.

With this emphasis, came a rise in diffusion studies, many of which focused on the linkage of interpersonal and mass media networks. I have pursued the flow of information in a variety of settings including scenes of natural disasters, incidents of collective delusion, and the spread of the news of the death of prominent persons.

The mass media are important in early notification of events. It should also be emphasized that in no instance was all the diffusion accounted for by the mass media alone. Interpersonal networks always account for an important proportion of "first learning," let alone the reinforcement of curiosity, further information seeking, and the creation of concern.

There is not much one can do with certain messages, such as those about the death of prominent persons, except talk about them. Other messages, however, suggest other modes of behavior such as to buy or not buy a television set, to vote for or against a proposed law, or to try or not to try a new drug, a new fertilizer, or a new dance step. How do mass media and interpersonal channels enter into the adoption of such innovations? That is the level of my current interest, one that I want to mull over here tonight.

I am now preparing some work on the social itinerary of technological change here in Denmark. I want to analyze the diffusion and adoption of television. Preliminary to this, I have been revisiting earlier studies, including some of my own, to appraise possibilities in the challenging realm of innovation adoption.

A review of the literature is, of course, an essential stage of the research task. I would like to share with you some observations from recent rummaging about in the storehouse of knowledge that brings us into contact with various traditions of research on diffusion. These observations will provide some answers to questions implied thus far in my comments, and also, I trust, raise some new questions, all of which I hope we can remember when we come to the question period.

New Clues from Old Research

The study of social diffusion can bring an investigator close to the core of sociological phenomena--the observation of interaction over time. When these temporal observations include a noting of the spread of any given item over specified channels of communication and through some delimited social structure, then, following a definition offered by Elihu Katz, the four essential criteria of a diffusion study will have been satisfied.

In a recent concisely written book, Georg Karlsson, our Swedish colleague, reviews a large body of observational data on the flow of information and provides a brilliant demonstration of how empirical studies can be used to introduce realistic probabilities into formal diffusion models.

Included in the factors that Karlsson found to be associated with the way information is diffused is the geographical distance between persons, the social distance between them, the motivation to transmit information, the perception of the message by the contacted person, the degree to which the message fits into the attitudes held by the recipient, the attitude of the reference group, the credibility of the source, and the way in which the message is changed in transmission.

That is a considerable inventory of concerns. But, yet other factors provide gist for the model-building mills. Let me focus on some of special concern for my current work on the adoption of Danish television. These, of course, ultimately feed into the effects of mass communication because they deal with the early phase where people are confronted with the decision of whether or not to have anything to do with the medium. There is evidence to suggest that the pattern of decision here, influenced as it is by continuing social factors, could become the incubator of the later and more complex effects of television viewing.

Rural sociologists, geographers, and more recently students of mass communication, have devoted considerable effort to deciphering the communicative elements and mapping the social pathways that lead to the adoption of an innovation. Despite the speed at which some innovations apparently spread through a population, all people do not adopt it at the same time. In the complex diffusion and decision-making process that starts with the establishment of awareness of the innovation and ultimately leads to some degree of adoption, there are leaders and laggards, and there are even some people who hold out to the bitter end.

A few studies have been concerned with identifying and comparing the characteristics of early and late adopters of an innovation, or of comparing adopters with non-adopters. Some of these comparisons are made in a context where one innovation, or one class of innovations, is traced through a single social structure--as when Katz compared the early and late adopters of seed corn among farmers with the early and late adopters of a new drug among doctors. The latter effort led Katz to conclude that what we now need is a comparative study which will trace different innovations, variously classified, as they proceed through given social structures. In my forthcoming work along the border between Germany and Denmark, I will attempt a variant of this idea--the tracing of the same innovation through various social structures for the purpose of observing the emergence of the key adopter categories.

Adopting Television

When a major technological innovation first appears, there is a period of active definition, or norm formation, in which the relationship of the innovation to the established features of the environment is worked out. Following the introduction of the innovation, the producer begins to share this process of definition with an growing number of consumers.

In the case of television, this means that the mass communicator begins to take his audience into account, either directly or indirectly. The early adopters of television may be important, then, not only because they are instrumental in influencing others to become adopters, but also because this influence could include broader definitions of the meaning of television, how it should be used by whom and when, content preferences, etc. These definitions may be directed not only at the remaining potential adopters, but may also be available for perception by the mass communicators themselves.

Thus it would appear that early users have an unexcelled opportunity to be influential not only in the diffusion, but also in the process of definition that accompanies the introduction of an innovation.

Accordingly, I believe, it becomes particularly important to examine the characteristics of those persons who accept an innovation early to try to gain some understanding of the selective processes that led to their pioneering behavior. I expect this idea to be especially interesting when we examine it in the context of majority-minority cross-national relationships such as we intend to explore among Germans and Danes down on the border.

To do this we need a set of adopter categories. The work done in 1958 by Everett Rogers on agricultural technology marks off an early-late continuum into five categories each of which has arbitrarily been assigned a percentage of the maximum adoption of a given innovation.

The *innovators* are defined as the first 2 1/2 percent to adopt a new idea or practice. They are followed by the *early adopters*, the next 13 1/2 percent; the *early majority*, the next 34 percent; the *late majority*, the next 34 percent; and finally by the *laggards* who are the last 16 percent to accept an innovation.

With the adoption of agricultural technology, some fairly regular continua emerge. Thus, as you move from early to late adopters you also move from the highest to the lowest in social status, income, education, size of farm, specialization of enterprise, extra-community social contacts, formality of the sources of information, and in attitudes toward scientific experimentation.

Apart from the general applicability of this model, about which Rogers makes no claims, this formulation focuses attention on the first-stage of the adoption process and suggests that it is a more differentiated than heretofore suspected.

Rogers acknowledges that innovators might possibly influence the early adopters, but he emphasizes that the early adopters exert more leadership than any other adoption category. The explanation is that the innovator, embedded in cosmopolitan traits, is not concerned with fitting smoothly into the social relationships of the local area, whereas early adopters are more closely integrated into the neighborhood or the local community.

Detecting the Diffusion Process

What happens to the outcome as one or the other of these two types gain relative prominence? The contrasting characteristics attributed by Rogers to the innovators and the early adopters form a pattern similar to the characteristics that Elihu Katz found in his study of the adoption of a new drug by doctors. Two distinct diffusion processes emerge. Integrated doctors have characeristics comparable to elements in the early adopter type noted by Rogers, while isolated doctors and agricultural innovators are similar.

I get excited about such findings, tentative as they might be. The implication is that when a social structure consists of a population whose members resemble early adopter types, then the innovation will spread earlier through the community and the resulting diffusion curve would be of the accelerating form which represents a "snowballing" of interpersonal processes where adoption proceeds as a function of the proportion who have already adopted.

On the other hand, to the extent that a social structure is characterized by innovator types, the result would be an individual process, uninfluenced by interpersonal communication, represented by a linear line of growth resulting from some stimulus operating at each time period so as to influence a constant, not an accelerating, proportion of those who adopt.

The constant rate of adoption may occur for two reasons. First, the relevant social structure may not be well-integrated. Second, although the social structure may be well-integrated, the early adopters in that network may react differently to the definition of the innovation provided by its adoption by the innovators. In either case, the rate of adoption undergoes no significant acceleration.

Where does this speculation lead? Whereas Katz relates the shape of diffusion curves to the interpersonal versus individualistic processes, I would now like to relate them to the initial stage of an adoption process where innovators and early adopters operate. The questions for exploration then become:

Do variations in adoption curves reflect variation in the relative role of innovators and early adopters?

In what ways is this relative role evidenced and illuminated by differences in the characteristics of people who are innovators and those who are early adopters? and

In what ways does this relative role predict the form and the extent of the remaining diffusion patterns?

About twenty-two percent of the households in Denmark today have television sets (as compared with about eighty-six percent in the United States). Given your excellent statistical record system, I am about the find out who these Danes are, and when they first "adopted" the set. In a few months, if you ask me to return, I will let you know all about innovators and early adopters in Denmark, and whether that distinction makes any sense, or makes any difference.

The readiness with which innovations are accepted into a society depends on their similarity to established elements in that culture. It is unlikely that Danes will for long resist the temptation of television. That innovation will open cultural borders, particularly to Germany, and perhaps that will help explain the current resistance, and the slower pace to its adoption here than elsewhere.

It also makes the research task that I have outlined more feasible and much more interesting. Everybody with a television set now is either an innovator or an early adopter. This leaves the challenge of estimating who will follow, and who, among Danes, will be numbered among the interesting category of laggards or non-adopters.

Whatever the outcome, I don't think the lag will last long. Television has ways to capture and even captivate an audience.

Chapter 4

How Good are the Polls?

Adult Education Lecture Series, University of Washington
October 27, 1964

Pollsters are risk-takers.

If the election polls are wrong here in 1964, the resulting ridicule and criticism will make practitioners of the craft yearn to return to the relative silence and safety of the period that followed their disastrous 1948 predictions.

After that failure, you may recall a storm of public concern. Scorn led to investigation and to statistical soul searching. Some sensitive pollsters felt that the negative response was out of proportion to the magnitude of error. One prominent social scientist said the reaction reminded him of the conversation that took place in London between two charwomen during the blitz bombings of World War II. One said to the other, "Isn't it dreadful? The bombs fall and they explode, and they blow you into middle of maternity." And the other responded, "Aye, and the worst of it is you'll never know who done it!"

Following the failure of the polls in 1948, the Indiana legislature rose for one minute of silent meditation in memory of Dr. George Gallup. The late Professor Samuel Stouffer called that a great tribute, particularly since it came from the same body that about 100 years earlier tried to simplify arithmetical operation by decreeing that pi should equal 3.14, and no more.

But this is 1964, and we ask again, how good are the polls? If the word "good" kindles partisan passions, then those of you who are

Democrats should think that the polls look mighty good right now, while those of you who are Republicans are bound to question that judgment.

What about you Independents? If nothing else, you have probably turned to technical questions about surveys merely to take your mind off what appears to be the most dismal and disgusting presidential campaign in the history of the republic. However, as a student of public opinion, and a part-time practitioner of polling, I do not come here to provide escape for Independents any more than I come to provide cheer for Democrats or solace for the Republicans.

I am not responsible for current poll results, but I can try to speak responsibly about what they report. You may find this analysis more objectionable than objective. Perhaps you will sense that this topic lends itself to a treatment not unlike that attributed to our colorful Secretary of State, Victor Myers, when he is challenged to explain how he stands on the liquor question.

After weighing the evidence, Myers reportedly says: "Well, on the one hand, rum is a demon. Drinking leads fathers to desert families. Drunkenness causes crime and brings slaughter to our highways. Whiskey dulls the brain, hardens the arteries, and corrodes the liver. But, on the other hand a cocktail before dinner does relieve tension, inspire conviviality, and heighten sociability. And, of course, there is always the danger of snake bite. Furthermore, the liquor industry does support many jobs in the state, and taxes from liquor benefits medical research." The Secretary then concludes, "So you see, on the liquor question some of my friends are against liquor and some are for it, and me--I'm for my friends."

With that, dear friends, let me first note what the polls are saying about the 1964 election.

Current Poll Results

For once, all polls now report essentially the same thing. Up to this point in the current presidential campaign the vast majority of Americans favor Lyndon Johnson and his policies over Barry Goldwater and his policies.

All polls, Gallup, Harris, Roper, Democratic or Republican, and even the informal pop-corn sales indicator in theaters, and the responses from barber shops across the country, point positively in the LBJ direction. Moreover, they have done so since the candidates were nominated. Two things stand out: (1) the width of Johnson's margin, and (2) the stability of this margin over the past two months.

To be specific, let us trace the numbers from the American Institute of Public Opinion, commonly know as the Gallup Poll, in its four reports made since the nomination.

The first Gallup report in late July showed Johnson receiving 59 percent, Goldwater 31 percent, and 10 percent undecided. Following the North Vietnam PT boat attack in August--and at a time when international strife had replaced racial troubles as the nation's number one worry--Johnson's popularity rose to 65 percent, with Goldwater at 29 percent, and 6 percent undecided. The same outcome was found in September. The report from early October shows Johnson with 62 percent, Goldwater 32 percent, and 6 percent undecided. The final Gallup report prior to the election will come this weekend.

Recently a number of dramatic news events have surfaced. An allegation of homosexuality has moved one of the President's assistants out of the White House. In England, a new Prime Minister has moved into number 10 Downing street. In the Soviet Union, Kruschev has been booted out of the Kremlin. And in China, atomic energy has been unleashed for the first time. These events may have had some impact on public opinion, and yet the current national polls show little change in presidential preference. Tonight's *Seattle Times* carries the Lou Harris poll reporting Johnson 68 to 32 over Goldwater in the nation as a whole.

Do these consistent results signify that Johnson will win, perhaps even by a landslide? That certainly appears likely. But a number of cautions must be posted. First, there is always a possibility of a last minute shift.

Before 1948, it was accepted as a political axiom that votes are not shifted in the last month of a presidential campaign. The Gallup Poll learned the hard way that this is not true when, in 1948, it stopped polling in mid-October and failed to catch the swing to Truman in the final days of that campaign.

Since 1948, the Gallup Poll has interviewed right up to the Saturday before Election Day, and this has contributed to the Gallup Poll's record of accuracy. In 13 out of 14 national elections--the one exception being 1948--its final figures have pointed to the winning candidate or party. In the elections since 1948 the average deviation from election results has been reduced to less that two percentage points. However, a safe rule is to allow for a margin of error of four percentage points.

This weekend keep your eye on the margins reported in the final polls. If things do not change from where they have been in the past two months, Johnson should win handily.

Impact of Turnout

However, there is another reason for caution in interpreting survey results as election predictions. Polls register the expressed opinions of specified samples of the population at a given time. The science of polling has advanced to a point where this task is performed very well. But elections involve another factor, the matter of turnout, an element that is more difficult to anticipate via polling.

True, most polls involve screening questions so that only eligible voters end up in the sample. This helps. Some polls also use intensity questions to give weight to how strongly a person holds opinions about candidates and issues. This, along with probes into previous voting behavior, and into current participation in campaign activities, help yield estimates about the likelihood of turnout.

Such measures gauge the probability of turnout--but there is still room for magnificent margins of error. The facts from 1960 make that clear.

Four years ago Kennedy and Nixon attracted the largest turnout of voters in the history of American elections. Even at that, one-third of the electorate, or about 40 million eligible voters, did not vote. Add to that the fact that 10 million new voters are eligible in 1964 and you begin to see the challenge to prediction. Yes, at this stage both parties know that turnout is crucial. In their strategy, the Republicans would appear to have little left to hope for except differential turnout.

But here the polls are also informative. The Gallup Poll of October 7, 1964 indicates that the Republicans have been working harder than the Democrats at the "grass roots" level. Republican party workers have reached 7,100,000 households across the nation--either in person or by telephone--while their Democrat counterparts have contacted far fewer--3,800,000.

GOP "grass roots" activity exceeds that of the Democrats in all communities except small towns. Evidence gathered in earlier surveys indicates that grass-roots activity yields political rewards. Thus, during the 1960 campaign the Democrats outscored the Republicans in party effort at the local level. What, then is the message? It is that it is possible for political organization to make polling projections unreliable. It appears, as of now, that Republicans have been working harder than the Democrats to get out their own vote.

Other factors could work for a turnout to favor Goldwater--overconfidence on the part of the Democrats, for example. Potentially more significant, I think, is that in this year of "extremism" and sensitive issues such as race relations, and visceral issues such as morality, Goldwater's followers are more committed and more intense in their feelings for their candidate than is the following for Johnson.

What's more, weather is always a factor in turnout. Consider what might happen on November 3rd if a hurricane hit the East Coast, or a blizzard the Midwest, or a flood inundated California. I don't know if Republicans own more umbrellas than Democrats, but there is some evidence to suggest that come rain, snow, sleet, hail, hell, or high water, Goldwater's dedicated minions would be likely to trudge through to the polling place. Would Democrats be equally motivated? Most observers think not.

Another element in this whole equation is the fact that it does not take a majority popular vote to win an election. Clearly the Republican strategy around turnout involves focusing on selected states in the south, Midwest, and west.

Here, however, a counter consideration emerges from polling data. Regional breakdowns in all the polls show that Johnson consistently has been doing well in all areas of the country. More important, I think, is the fact that this has also been true around issues.

The Democrats have retained a wide lead in all regions in calling the issues, and in arguing major issues of peace and prosperity. In all sections, the Democratic party is seen as the best party to keep the country prosperous and to keep the country out of war.

Gallup has polled on these issues for 13 years from 1951 to 1964. Except for a brief period in 1955, the Democrats have consistently been chosen by a majority as the political party that people that people think would do the best job in keeping the country prosperous.

However, until 1961 the Republicans were thought of as the party most likely to keep the United States out of World War III. Since then the Democratic party has become the "peace party" on the American scene. And on this critical question the Democrats top score came at the beginning of this year's campaign--43 percent versus 20 percent for the Republicans, with 21 percent holding no difference and 16 percent no opinion.

There are other interesting poll results such as those dealing with the image of the candidate, new issues, etc. However, our assigned topic directs that we turn the balance of the time to the standards that are used to assess just how good the polls are.

Evolution of Methods

From the beginning of popular elections, people follow forecasts of the outcome before the votes are tabulated.

With respect to polling, two elections are of historical importance. The first is the election of 1936, the year that the modern pollsters emerged as prophets. The second is the election of 1948 when polling (with two rare exceptions), and other forms of prophecy, failed.

Straw votes of various kinds had been carried on for almost a century before the prognosticators of 1936 applied a more scientific mode of sampling opinion.

During that long period, straw votes were frequently inaccurate. For example, in the straw polls on candidates for the years 1916, 1920, 1924, and 1928 conducted by the *Literary Digest*, there was a plurality error of 20, 21, 12, and 12 percentage points in the predictions. On the other hand, the Digest was remarkably accurate in 1932, when the magazine predicted the total popular vote on the two major presidential candidates--Hoover and Roosevelt--within 1.4 percentage points.

But reputations based on straw votes fly like straw in the wind.

In the months before the election of 1936 the *Literary Digest* mailed over ten million ballots and 2,376,523 were returned. This was hailed as a large sample, one that was bound to yield reliable results. The *Digest* predicted a victory for Landon over Roosevelt. Their data indicated that Roosevelt would only get 40.9 percent of the vote. Then came the election. Roosevelt actually gained 60.2 percent of the vote. The gross error hastened the end of straw ballots, and also quickened the demise of the *Digest* as a magazine (robust competition from *Time* magazine was also a factor).

At the same time, the election of 1936 marked the appearance of a new band of budding election prophets. Numbered among this breed was George Gallup.

Two months before the *Digest* mailed out their ballots, Gallup predicted what the *Digest's* results would show. He came within one percentage point of their actual results. His analysis was based on the probable returns from the magazine's "incidental" sampling procedure. He argued that the *Digest* could not obtain a representative sample of the voting public from its mailing lists which were compiled from telephone directories (roughly 40 percent of American homes had telephone in 1936) and from automobile registration files (some 55 percent of all families owned an automobile).

Gallup was right. The *Digest* straw ballot of 1936 was a fiasco, its methods were subsequently discredited, and new types of surveys began to appear on the American political scene.

Gallup's own methodology employed a combination of mail ballots and personal interviews with subjects selected through quota sampling. This design selected respondents so that their distribution by characteristics such as age and sex matched that of the total adult population. Gallup's survey forecast that Roosevelt would win. While the prediction was correct, it underestimated the Roosevelt vote by 6.4 percentage points.

There is irony here. This successful prediction launched the Gallup poll. However, the findings were cast with the greatest degree of error ever posted by the Gallup organization subsequently, greater even than the five percentage points that marked the error in the 1948 polling prediction when Truman "upset" Dewey.

The 1948 election shook public faith in polls and even arrested the pollsters confidence in their craft. Presumptions of credibility were probably too high before the election and probably lingered at too low a level for too long a period after 1948.

But, ultimately, confidence in polling was restored as the survey research community mobilized to critically examined its methods. Commitments were made to better sampling designs, to extending the interview period up to elections, to more rigorous pre-testing of the wording of questionnaires, and so forth.

Basic research can be expected to yield additional technical advances over the next decades. A great deal has yet to be learned about how to accurately measure sentiments, attitudes, and opinions, and about how these are linked to behavior such as the act of voting.

Conclusion

On Tuesday we will have yet another test of how good the polls are. I expect confirmation of their growing ability to forecast outcomes.

For the longer run, I expect survey research to have applications far beyond elections. But election polling will continue to fascinate because there is an outcome against which the goodness of this instrument can be assessed.

Accordingly, I would not be surprised if politicians, for better or worse, became ever more reliant on pollsters in the future.

Now, there is a prediction!

Fortunately, I will have some time to run from it before I am required to follow in the footsteps of the *Literary Digest*.

Violence

If the mass media did nothing more but hold up a mirror to reflect reality, the content would be violent enough; but they do more, much more.

The media also create a vast fantasy world peopled with violent characters who intentionally do physical harm to one another. Beyond attracting large audiences, what is the impact of the portrayal of real and fictional violence?

Twenty-five years ago, I testified before the National Commission on the Causes and Prevention of Violence, chaired by the late Dr. Milton S. Eisenhower. I began my remarks by expressing uneasiness over how social scientists had approached the question of media influence. I wondered then, as I have in the years that followed, whether the right questions were being asked.

To be sure, research has not stood still since that time. Inquiry has penetrated much deeper into media performance and reception. There is now some evidence that television has the power to blur the distinction between public and private behaviors, to reshape group identities, to alter socialization processes, to undermine the exercise of authority, to merge gender identities, and generally to demystify the operation of traditional institutions. This range of possible outcomes reflects a concern with media effects that extends beyond the psychological level of impact on individuals.

On the individual level, the most common contention is that symbolic violence, whether portraying fantasy or reality, will arouse aggression, or through imitation, will increase aggressive behavior, harden persons to human pain and suffering, and lead them to accept violence as a way of life and as a solution to personal and social problems.

Let us stipulate that if media violence induces aggression in individuals this will be evaluated as an undesirable effect. However, what may be negatively evaluated for individuals, could, under some circumstances, be positively valued in a collective form.

For example, violence sometimes serves as a catalyst for desired social change as when alienated sectors of the population take recourse to violence and aggression to overcome blocks to social-economic achievement. A largely unexplored question here is the role of the media in schooling persons for such action either through the portrayal of fantasy violence or through reports of actual collective violence.

There are other dimensions. Effects may be direct or indirect, and immediate or long range. Whatever the complications, I suggest that it will be fruitful to look at violence in the mass media as a product of social forces flowing through intersecting channels that eddy around many persons, groups, and values in the total society.

Mass communication to most people simply means radio, television, newspapers, magazines, books, and motion pictures. Reaction to these media is often based on the assumption that their content, like acid rain or radioactive fallout, is being poured over a large population in a ubiquitous and inescapable deluge. This dramatic conception is actually too restrictive, both with reference to media structure and to the possible range of effects.

Broadly stated, mass communication refers to the relatively simultaneous exposure of a large, scattered, and heterogeneous audience to stimuli transmitted by impersonal means from an organized source for whom the audience members are anonymous. In this system, the source of information is a complex organization, itself a product as well as a potential molder of social forces. The central task of this organization is to formulate the content that is transmitted to the audience. Many roles interlock in this effort. Since there are alternative ways in which media content can be presented, if it is to be presented at all, and since the mass communicator is usually under considerable time pressure, the decision-making process is not a simple one. By grasping the elements involved, we are in a better position to assess accountability for bringing expressions of violence to media audiences. In particular, we must seek to know to what extent others outside the media--critics, government agencies, citizen groups, and the audiences themselves--impinge on decisions that shape media content.

Taken as a whole, the audience constitutes a "mass," large numbers of anonymous persons from all walks of life. But seen in terms of the ways they sense, interpret, and act on information about violence, the audience, though anonymous to the communicator, is embedded in primary and secondary networks--family, friends, work places, etc.--critical for understanding how media violence is perceived and acted upon.

The source and the receivers of media messages are brought together by impersonal transmission mechanisms (e.g., satellite, cable, video cassettes), but even the operation of distribution systems is influenced by social factors, as for example by the politics of deregulation. Furthermore, the linkage of source-distribution-receiver is forged in the culture of a particular society. Thus television is subject to a different political control structure in the United States than in any other country.

I first taught Sociology 443, Mass Communication, at the University of Washington in 1948. Four decades later, in 1988, I returned to repeat the class for the last time. My notes reveal that I rather consistently attempted to analyze mass communication as a social process and that I usually organized research materials around four themes:

♦   How issues emerge: the reciprocity of public opinion and mass communication;

♦   The problem of effects: individual versus social dimensions;

♦   The problem of control: censorship and the alternatives; and

♦   Research and social policy: how are they linked?

These themes underlie the presentation in this section on violence and in the next section on sex.

Sex and violence have long been perceived as either double delights or as the twin terrors of American mass media. They have a powerful capacity to attract large audiences. But they also stir heated controversy, create publics, and mobilize efforts to control media content.

While advances in understanding media violence have been made, even beyond those of my experience as reflected in the three talks presented in this section, methodological and substantive difficulties, particularly around the impact of long-term exposure, remain to be overcome before adequate knowledge will have the possibility of putting the issues to rest.

In other words, the vexation expressed over media violence in the

1960s has not, three decades later, been extinguished. Rather, its fury only shifts successively to each new form of media expression.

That fact makes revisiting old concerns something more than a visit to a museum. In the ruminations of the past, researchers may find clues to avoid old errors and to discover new truths.

Chapter 5

Dialogue on Media Violence

Governor Rockefeller's Conference on Crime, Astor Hotel, New York City
April 22, 1966

It is undoubtedly wise to place the topic of media violence at the end of a conference, particularly a meeting like this marked by so much harmony. Governor, this circumstance reminds one of the Irishman who walked up to his host and said, "This a grand and glorious party. Let's start a fire."

I recently tried to imagine what sparks might fly when a sociologist, a psychiatrist, and an economist got together to discuss media violence. To give that hypothetical dialogue some credence, I edited it around selected statements from a single publication from each of three distinguished experts, Joseph Klapper, a Ph.D. in sociology, currently directing social research for the Columbia Broadcasting System; Frederick Wertham, a New York psychiatrist; and Dallas Smythe, formerly Chief Economist for the Federal Communications Commission and now a professor of economics.

We are fortunate to have two of these authorities, Dr. Klapper and Dr. Wertham, here on this panel today to address the very subject matter in question. Realism can now reject, or correct, my conjecture. I only wish I had included a psychologist so that the views of Professor Leonard Berkowitz, who is also here today, might have enlivened my speculation. Now, however, he can proceed unencumbered by attribution.

My task is to set the stage for genuine dialogue. I will do this by citing the imagined conversation because I believe it will frame critical issues on our agenda today. We need to address what is known, what needs to be known, and what constitutes knowing about the effects of media violence. Moreover, this opening will give two colleagues a chance to set the record straight--I know that our host, Governor Rockefeller, uses and appreciates that phrase. Here, then, is a script that will, I believe, echo in our later exchange. Of course, I have let the sociologist lead off:

Sociologist: There is no doubt that violence is frequently depicted. However, even if there is a trend in media content, it does not indicate that any particular effects are therefore more or less likely to occur. Actually, nothing is known about the relationship, if any, between the incidence of violence in media programs and the likelihood that it will produce effects.

Psychiatrist: If, as you say, there is nothing known, we are scientifically in a bad way indeed. As I see it, we are confronted in the mass media with a display to children of brutality, sadism, and violence such as the world has never seen. At the same time there is such a rise of violence among our youth that no peace corps abroad can make up for the violence corps at home. Social scientists say that the test of science is prediction, and I predicted fifteen years ago that more and more brutal violence would be committed by younger and younger age groups. Now it is a matter of common knowledge.

Economist: Can it be proved that particular television programs or comic books are prime causes of delinquency? The problem children you have studied appear to be media addicts who are affected by cumulative media violence. However, you also indicate that delinquency arises from a complex of factors, including economic and social conditions of the environment.

Psychiatrist: It makes no difference in our stage of knowledge if a cause is not "immediate" but remote, not "primary" but indirect. What is important is that without this contributing factor the harmful effect would not have taken place, or at least not in that form. In mental life, all contributory factors have to be regarded as causal. My clinical studies of over two hundred unsolicited cases lead to the conclusion that children are getting more and more tele-directed. As a result there is a loss of emotional spontaneity and a distortion of natural attitudes in the direction of cynicism, greed, hostility, callousness, and insensitivity expressed in over acts, in fantasy, and in dreams.

Sociologist: You mention only a few of the specific fears about media effects; some of those who fear the effects of violence seem unsure of what specific consequences might follow, only that they are undesirable. Others fear that such material elicits direct, imitative behavior--that an otherwise normal child may commit crimes after seeing them on television.

Psychiatrist: I have seen it in my clinical studies.

Sociologist: This presupposes that the media have a "hypodermic needle" effect. Research does not support this. Others say those media depiction's of violence constitute a school for delinquency, teaching methods of crime, or that the media will have a kind of trigger effect that operates in situations of reduced moral resistance. Finally, there are even those who believe that media violence has beneficial effects by providing a kind of catharsis of antisocial drives.

Economist: To my knowledge there is no research evidence to support any of these charges, but my hunch would be that no child exposed to mass media content in large doses is unaffected by it. Certainly, from our content analysis of televised programs, one can conclude that, except for doctors and the unemployed, characters are highly stereotyped, with some of the stereotypes presumably being dangerous if taken as models for viewer behavior.

Psychiatrist: I might point out here that although your empirical research may not prove that there are effects, neither does it prove that there are not. A number of books minimize or deny media effects and confuse the issue. So the home, which in pre-electronic times afforded the child protection, is now invaded on two fronts: by bad television programs that influence the children and by slanted books about television that influence the parents.

Sociologist: It seems to me that *Television and the Child* by Hilde Himmelweit gives some relevant evidence. She studied 1,854 children in England divided into viewers and non viewers and matched by age, sex, intelligence, social background, and other factors, to determine whether observed differences were the product of viewing or were pre-existing.

Psychiatrist: The children were not examined. They just filled out formal questionnaires. Furthermore, when this report appeared it was already out-of-date; the British screen had not yet become littered with dead cowboys. Moreover, it does not apply, then or now, to American children who are exposed to much more and worse screen mayhem. It is also a fallacy to think that findings are not scientific unless they can be expressed in a graph and in very large numbers. There is no substitute for a thorough clinical psychiatric examination of actual cases.

Economist: You are saying that you don't believe that they can generalize their findings from a large sample to the individual, but that you can generalize your results with an individual to the larger group.

Sociologist: Despite your objections, let's look at some of the British results; we may even find some support for your conclusions. First, they do find that some content may be frightening, on radio as well as television.

Economist: We must not forget the violence in documentaries, on news broadcasts, and perhaps even in sports programs.

Sociologist: True. However, Himmelweit did find that real violence is less likely to frighten children than is violence in fictional programs, but, on the other hand, real violence is more widely disliked. Virtually nothing is known regarding the duration of such fright or the ways, if any, in which it may affect children's concepts or behavior. The alleged effect on disturbed sleep, nightmares, and the like would appear to be evanescent.

Psychiatrist: Case histories in psychiatric literature...

Sociologist: Let me complete the summary. The degree to which children are disturbed appears to be related to the means by which injury is done. Shooting is not disturbing, but a knife attack may be. Violence that follows a conventional pattern, the outcome of which is predictable, such as is found in Westerns, apparently disturbs few children.

Psychiatrist: That pronouncement indicates the difference between the adult's offhand acceptance of what he thinks the child gets from television and the actual reaction of the child. It is a typical adult response, and is not how children see it. For example, the report states that if the victim who has been shot clutches at his stomach, that merely means to the child that he has been shot from the front! Many children have told me what it means to them: that the man is shot in the stomach because that is one of the places where it hurts most.

Sociologist: However, the study also shows that children are more sensitive to acts of verbal aggression than to actual physical violence. Sound effects are about equally as frightening as visual effects, and the child is more likely to be frightened viewing alone or with children his own age than when viewing with adults present. They also found that there was no more aggressive, maladjusted, or delinquent behavior among viewers than among non viewers.

Psychiatrist: As far as negative effects are concerned, this report centers on what is frightening or disturbing to the child. From a mental health point of view, these are neither the only nor even the most important bad effects. Furthermore, the study relies on statistics based on individual answers to questions, without considering the whole child.

Sociologist: While the media do not appear to be a crucial or primary determinant of behavioral tendencies, there are indications that violent fare may serve special functions for those who are already socially maladjusted.

Psychiatrist: The normal child is alleged to be invulnerable. It is not only the abnormal child, however, who can learn--and be seduced. Normal children are not inaccessible.

Economist: Certainly there have been studies, by Albert Bandura and others, which have shown that children in laboratory experiments exhibited greater aggression and inflicted greater punishments on others after seeing a film with violent content than control subjects who had seen a neutral film. Does this not cast doubt on the catharsis principle?

Sociologist: Perhaps. While we all follow with interest the newer laboratory studies, we will also continue to be curious about what happens when laboratory studies are translated into real-life situations where influences such as social norms and parental sanctions operate. Certainly we need to know more about the duration of any immediate effects.

Economist: I wonder if television crime programs and crime comics are being made scapegoats?

Psychiatrist: How do you mean?

Economist: Could it be that we are really fighting a threat to individual integrity from a technologically oriented society? Our mass media have the aspect of a one-way conveyor belt. In work, the individual has become a narrow specialist. In leisure time with the mass media, he seems to become a passive, receiving automaton. If adults sense that political apathy and a feeling of anomie relate to threats to their autonomy, small wonder they protest that passively sitting and watching television crime programs is not good for their children. Couldn't mass media violence also be a symptom of our general social life, and not a cause?

Psychiatrist: Something may very well be a symptom and at the same time a cause. This is no argument. Socially, mass media violence is a symptom; individually, it may be an operative cause.

Economist: Possibly our concern over television and children would lead to more significant results if it were focused on the effects that are precluded because certain kinds of cultural experience, being outside the orbit of cultural industry, are not being made available to children.

Sociologist: Himmelweit points out that violence programs take up a disproportionate amount of viewing time; this prevents the showing of more varied fare that could offer children a broader view of life.

Economist: What do we actually find on television? Do we find a world where men and women enjoy self-respect and freely accord it to others? Or, does television present a world peopled with characters so stereotyped as to lack diversity and who are portrayed merely as all good or all bad? We don't know, but perhaps the intuition of sensitive laymen--such as found in Parent-Teacher Associations--may not be wide of the mark.

Psychiatrist: Hear! Hear!

Sociologist: I rest my case with need for further research. Thus far, there is little evidence that media violence is a prime mover of behavior. The content seems rather to reinforce or implement existing and otherwise induced behavioral tendencies. For the well-adjusted, it appears to be innocuous or even to be selectively perceived as socially useful. For the maladjusted, particularly the aggressively inclined and frustrated, it appears to serve, at the very least, as a stimulant to escapist and possibly aggressive fantasy and probably to serve other functions as yet unidentified. I would also add that further information on the role of mass communication in the development of delinquency is more likely to come from the study of delinquency than from the study of mass communication.

Psychiatrist: We are asked to eradicate from our thinking the stereotype of the Big Media and the Little Me. This is far from being a wrong stereotype; the contrast between the immensely powerful mass media and the individual family and child is one of the most essential facts of our present existence.

***

This is a hypothetical dialogue. Let us now turn to the panel for a reality check.

Chapter 6

Violence May be Hazardous to Your Health

American Society of Newspaper Editors, Shoreham Hotel, Washington, D.C.
April 17, 1969

Preachers and Professors sometimes share common traits, particularly if they are father and son.

Many years ago my father was a preacher in a small town. He once told me about his communication problem. In preparing sermons he often felt that his message pertained more to people who didn't come to church than to those who did appear in his congregation. This did not imply that his parishioners were perfect Christians. It only meant that the special kind of hell that he wanted to raise seemed more suitable for persons absent than for the congregation present. Ultimately he abandoned the pulpit, partly because he grew weary of visiting the sins of the absent while nourishing the self-righteousness of those present.

I find myself in a somewhat similar situation today.

The special kind of hell that I want to raise might seem more appropriate for absentee television producers than for you newspaper editors. Whether justified or not, this is a common perception. In the current clamor over mass media violence the definition of the problem is largely drawn from images cast by the electronic media.

But the sins that emerge from Marconi may also be attributed to the progeny of Gutenberg. I suspect that this makes you uneasy. It should not translate into self-righteousness. You could hardly afford that. Recent research from the Lemberg Center at Brandeis University charges you with imprecise, distorted, and inaccurate reporting of violence in racial incidents last summer. Newspapers built myths about those events. For example, in treating sniper attacks, you found conspiracies where none existed.

But I do not come here mainly to preach, to seek sin, or to attempt to redistribute guilt. Rather, I take my primary task to be one of analysis; one that conveys some judgments from the current state of the social science understanding of mass media violence. In particular, I want to state some implications from what is, what is not, and what I think needs to be known about the individual and social effects that are linked to the manner in which the mass media portray violence.

Learning About Violence

Violence takes many forms. The kind of violence to which I want to direct your attention consists of those acts where persons intentionally use physical force so as to injure or kill other human beings, or to damage or destroy property.

Violence has both legitimate and illegitimate expression. The definition of legitimacy is itself in constant process. Later I will suggest that this is the area where mass media violence probably has its greatest effect, namely that of shaping and often extending the boundaries of the possible and the permissible for the acting out of real violence.

Unfortunately, we do not have very good indicators of how many persons are actually involved, either as perpetrators, victims, or mere onlookers to real acts of violence. Yes, we do know something about certain forms of violence from official crime statistics such as homicide and assault rates. Whatever the current reading of these figures, they reflect enough to arouse alarm. However, they do not record the full range of physical encounters--spanking, beating, slugging, etc.--that probably occur in society. Nor do they tap important areas of collective violence represented in riots, gang fights, and the like.

The National Commission on the Causes and Prevention of Violence, headed by Dr. Milton Eisenhower, has undertaken a national survey of how persons have experienced various forms of violence. When this report is issued, it will give us some better estimate of the situation. My own guess is that this survey will show that while violence of all types is found in all sectors of American society, the vast majority of Americans has never been involved even as observers of serious acts of real violence, let alone as instigators or victims.

If direct experience is not our teacher, where, then, do we go to school on violence? The answer, of course, is the mass media. And here the curriculum is crowded with violent content in both real and fantasy contexts.

One report to the Federal Communications Commission stated that between the ages of 5 and 14 the average American child has witnessed destruction of 13,000 human beings on television alone. Of bullets and bodies on TV we have had many counts, enough to tax the latest computer even without the grisly daily input from Vietnam. The pages of your newspapers are not exactly devoid of human carnage either, although you may be less likely to celebrate destruction in the mode of Western and Eastern fantasy thrillers.

The point is that while few of us have had direct experience with real violence, all of us have had copious contact with the symbolic form. By this means we think we come to know how acts of violence are in fact done, and who is justified in doing them. These materials also structure our views about what we think the actual level of violence in society is.

And what do we think? While we do not know from reliable data whether we live in a more violent world than that of our ancestors, it is clear that a majority believes that never has there been so much violence and, indeed, that we are experiencing a rising tide of brutal violence. That is our belief, and that is what we act on.

I want to call your attention to a letter in this week's *Time* magazine from a lady who writes "A commentary on the violent age in which we live was reflected in the question of our 6-year-old daughter while watching the funeral of President Eisenhower. She asked, 'Mother, who shot him?'"

Where do you suppose the little girl learned that? And note that the mother thought about this in terms of "the violent age." Well, beliefs are powerful, and many believe that we are experiencing that age.

An accompanying danger is the growing public feeling that events are beyond control, that the individual is powerless to affect the course of events, let alone the march of history. Meanwhile, back on television, the blood continues to flow from the pens of fantasy creators. For this reason, most of what I will now say about the effects of media violence pertains to the entertainment realm of television.

You, of course, are interested in newspapers. But you are also interested in what people are doing. Certain social facts, therefore, should compel your critical interest in television. Indeed, quite apart from motivation derived from competition for advertising revenue, I want to urge you to become more vigorous and responsible critics of television, just as you are of any institution in society.

Chicken or Egg?

A lot of violence is portrayed on television, and a lot of violence happens in the real world. Different people see different connections between these two facts.

In general, media spokesmen tend to see their content as being designed to reflect rather than to influence the real world. On the other side, critics, including anxious parents and politicians, tend to tun the problem around. Their concern is whether the violence of the real world is somehow aggravated, triggered, or caused by the mass media content.

Thus, a chicken-and-egg-like controversy seems to emerge. What comes first, the violent act, or its portrayal? Some of my colleagues opt for neither chicken or egg. They say the hatchery comes first. And of course they mean the cultural hatchery called society into which we all are born and where, through complex processes, human personality is developed. Obviously, many things shape that society. But few appear to have more prominence today than television.

We have all heard many characterizations of the television potential. Once a culture gets bound up in its circuitry, it is said that tastes take novel turns, new aspirations are forged, pressure for participation accelerates, the urge for immediate gratification mounts, and political action is transformed. Television, it is claimed, has spawned the "now" generation, one where instant awareness seems to produce contradictory blends of involvement and cool detachment, both of which can stir massive challenges to all that is traditional in society.

However conceived, the individual and social effects of television must depend in some way upon the pattern of content offered, the opportunities for access to the medium, and the use the audience makes of the exposure to the content.

Concerning these elementary points, numerous studies clearly support what has long been the contention of many concerned citizens:

♦   The menu offered by television is saturated with violent content including incidents of persons intentionally doing injury to one another--there is no argument about that, even from television;

♦   More and more people have ready access to the medium. For children, television occupies about as much time as school in their first 16 years of life, and

♦   For most persons, but particularly for the poor in American society, television is perceived as the most credible and believable source of information concerning what the world is really like.

In a way, these points add up to a statement of one kind of effect: television portrayals of violence attract large audiences. This, however, implies a much more difficult question: if models for violent behavior are repeatedly presented with few competing notions, and children repeatedly see such materials, what could be a more favorable arrangement for learning about violence, if not learning to do violence?

This critical question is easier to pose than to answer, unequivocally at least. Social scientists do not hold that the facts concerning the abundance of violent television content, and the frequency of exposure to the same, are, in themselves, sufficient to prove that televised violence induces violent behavior. But, nonetheless, we do have more conclusive evidence about the effects of media violence than some media spokesmen would have you believe.

Weight of Evidence

In my judgment, social science knowledge about the effects of media violence resembles medical knowledge about the effects of cigarette smoking. This means that while there is considerable controversy among researchers, and the issue is complex enough to warrant great investments in continued study, the weight of the evidence designates televised violence as a national health problem. I find cumulative research impressive enough to assert that we no longer need acquiesce in the conclusion that our findings from social science must support do-nothing policies about media violence.

If I am right, it is certainly time to post some health hazards about media violence, or at least to consider giving equal time to anti-violence messages.

What is the weight of the evidence? Without citation to source, without important qualifying conditions, and recognizing that we have better evidence on short-range than on long-range effects, let me quickly enumerate four key points.

♦   *Good intentions are not enough.* Material designed merely to be entertaining actually fosters a great deal of incidental learning. When television portrays people getting things done by violence and getting pushed around if they refrain from violent actions, it teaches the use of violence. It teaches forms of aggression by giving information about how to attack someone else when the occasion arises.

♦   *Portraying violence as justified is not enough.* Aggressive responses are more likely to be induced than reduced even when anxiety is minimized and violence occurs in a justified context. Thus in showing that "crime does not pay," by depicting the hero's successful and righteous use of violence against the "bad guys," the media are creating the very conditions most conducive to the instigation of violence. Remember, I am speaking from research findings.

♦   *Ethical endings are not enough.* When the villain is punished, this may keep viewers from reproducing villainy right away, but it does not make them forget how to do it. The ethical ending is just a suppresser of violence; it does not erase.

♦   *The catharsis principle has little support.* Observing media violence does not discharge in harmless ways whatever pent-up hostilities or frustrations the viewer may have.

These, and other points that could be cited from the research literature, add up to the following conclusion: repeated observation of media violence tends to reduce inhibitions against behaving in violent and aggressive ways or, to put it another way, it increases the probability that such behavior will follow.

Important as I think that the weight of the current evidence is, even more critical questions about effects awaits the attention of researchers. Let me sketch the challenge.

Beyond Triggers to Climates

We need to broaden our inquiries beyond a concern for whether media content directly triggers violent acts. We must also be concerned with how the media portrayal of violence might build a climate of attitudes, norms, and values as a condition that leads to, supports, or prevents the abandonment of violence in society. This might include investigation of the following kinds of questions.

♦   Does mass media content cultivate the acceptance of the idea that this is a violent world where there is nothing you can do but accept violence as the norm?

♦   Does mass communication tend to teach its audience that they live in the kind of world that they must take up arms against?

♦   Even if the mass media focus on violence does not instigate violent behavior, is there yet an opportunity lost in that the media do not help achieve abandonment of violence by the audience?

This level of questioning suggests research not unlike the study of the climate or the tides in the ocean. Such study may not tell us what you and I will do, or where we will go, but it can tell us in which way the cultural winds blow or the cultural tide flows. And much moves with that.

To put it another way, we must be concerned with what aspects of life, what values, and what means to goals, the informal schooling of mass communication is providing. Careful studies of television already reveal one dominant theme for all types of programs. What is that theme? It is that the end justifies the means; and violence is the most prominent means for achieving goals in all types of television stories.

Let me again emphasize that whether or not such messages encourage some persons to directly follow suit by engaging in violence may not be as important as the cultivation of the assumption that that's the way it is, even if done by others.

The larger point is that the acceptance of violence makes those who accept it a party to the occurrence of violence. It does this by making those who are inclined to engage in violence, act in ways they sense to be socially tolerated, approved, or even expected. This is why mass media images of violence are so important, I think, and it is a larger conception than the mere triggering effect. And since this includes news as well as the entertainment realm, let's also inspect that side of the ledger.

Role of the Press: Registers or Tribunes?

What most of us know and think about violence must in great part come from its portrayal in print and picture. Just as recent charges in reports such as that from the Kerner Commission have helped sensitize many persons to the subtle and pervasive forms and expressions of racism in society, perhaps the current muster over violence in media entertainment will result in new sensitivities to the subtle and extensive ways that violent practices and terminology have seeped into our culture, even where it is not relevant.

We all have a part in it; and we could all do something about it, at least on the symbolic level. As a small step, journalists could set the tone by reducing the use of violent terms to report nonviolent happenings. For example, when a governor vetoes some legislation, why do we have to read that he "killed the bill?" Politicians could help by finding alternative phrases to characterize "wars on poverty." One United States Senator recently asked me, "Professor, could you give us some ammunition so we could fight this violence thing?" And at lunch, Eric Hoffer, the folk philosopher, pounded the table and raised his voice to a fever pitch to proclaim that "We are not a violent people!"

To be sure, there are more important considerations. For a long time, the press has diligently recorded the incidents of violence that mar society. No one quarrels with the obligation of newsmen to mirror reality. But reality is more than the incident, or the act of violence itself. We all know that news processing is necessarily selective, and that there is a profound difference between reportage and journalism. However, Leo Bogart eloquently reminds us that "It has always been the journalist's task to weave information into its context, to show it as a part of the texture of its time, to unveil the drama beyond the outcropping of isolated facts, to see the shadows of future events cast by those of today."

But when the students stir on campus, or when the blacks revolt in the ghetto, what is the dominant story but an account of incidents of violence, largely isolated from antecedent conditions, conveying little understanding of either the root causes or the possible consequences of unrest.

For that matter, there may be little understanding on the other side of the routines and constraints on reporting, or the functioning of the media. But, uniquely to the other professions, you command the means to help us understand your problems, too.

On the news side, the irony, as I see it, is this: In this period of the greatest prosperity for newspapers in American history, with daily circulation up to over 61 million, with advertising billings at a record $5 billion, and where your industry is now the ninth largest employer in the United States, you are losing the attention and respect of significant sectors of the population today.

For the young, the black, the poor, you are perceived as having less credibility as basic channels of information than even your electronic counterparts. You are not seen as being responsive to the needs of a changing society. Indeed, you are in danger of becoming irrelevant.

I urge you to listen to the raucous sounds from the underground press, to the anguished cries from minority groups, to the surge of student dissatisfaction, which involves many more elements than those conveyed in the rhetoric of a handful of revolutionaries. They say you have no comprehension of their pleas for peace, peoplehood, and human equity now. And for our present concern, they are even saying that you don't dig violence.

In their eyes, you play up and misplace the incidents of violence. You confuse, or refuse to face, the issues that violence signifies. They contend you are false contenders to virtue because what you condemn in them you condone for the establishment, and profit from yourself. How do you answer the black student from Atlanta when he asks, "If I have to pick up a gun to defend my country, why shouldn't I do that to defend my dignity as a human being?"

These views need not be valid, nor widely shared, to be the potent force they are in the restless movements stirring in America today. Anxious pleas for "law and order," or simple old-fashioned editorializing from the point of view of your personal standard of morality, will certainly not break up the coalition of forces for change that has been nurtured by the torture of Vietnam and which is sustained by unfinished business here at home.

Whether anyone likes it or not, the press--all of us--will have to reckon with unrest, dissent, and protest, in both old and new forms, more in the future than we have in the past. How the mass media respond to the conditions that call for change, I think, could be decisive in determining the degree to which violence will be a part of the process of facilitating change.

These are complex issues. The claims about your performance in them that emanate from the restive sectors of society are strident claims. However you assess these claims, something else of note is happening to the general flow of information in America that also relates to media violence. It is the growing importance of television, not only as a mode for entertainment, but as a primary source of news.

As a basic news source, over recent years, newspapers have been holding their own, but television has been growing in importance, particularly for persons below the age of 30. In 1967, 55 percent of the public got "most of their news about what was going on in the world" from newspapers, but 64 percent got it from television (some people named several media). Six years earlier, newspapers were dominant as a primary source by 57 to 52 percent. Given the demographic fact of the continuing youth structure of our population, this trend to video as the window to the world is unmistakable and will likely continue. I see this as important for at least two reasons.

First, the growing attention to TV could involve increased exposure to incidents of violence divorced from an immediate accompanying contact with generalized interpretive accounts. Potentially, at least, print has a greater opportunity to elaborate the meaning of events by connecting facts that are separated in time and place; television flows in time and operates under greater constraints to be visually specific and concrete. Above all else, I believe that problem of violence in society today needs the critical interpretive perspective that the print media can in greater degree exercise. And let me add, I think you could by serving less as a register for TV activities and more as a tribune challenging their performance.

Secondly, the change in media exposure is important because the television experience, both from the manner of presentation and from the vagaries of audience perception, result in a blend of news and entertainment. So monumental is the mix that newsmen, whatever their professional dedication, inevitably become star-rank celebrities. We do not know what distortion results from Walter Cronkite being perceived as both a celebrity and a newsman, particularly since he seems only to be bringing us the war through the courtesy of a commercial sponsor. Not knowing, however, is no excuse for pretending that such communication practices are inconsequential.

On TV, the real and the fantasy appear in a kaleidoscope of violence in living color. Here we can see not only the gripping instant of the actual slaying of a Lee Harvey Oswald, and the shocking picture of the death of a Vietcong at the hands of the Saigon police chief, but an endless, and seemingly impersonal, beating and battering of persons, and a continuing clinical attention to mayhem as men do combat in every conceivable setting both on and off as well as in the center of this earth.

To be sure, you newspaper editors sometimes get involved in the same kind of mix. On April 9, in a leading metropolitan newspaper, there appeared a three-column story telling of the trial of a young man, age 19, accused of killing a boy, 15, on the streets. The heading read, "Slaying Suspect 'Heard It Was Wrong to Kill.'" The accused is quoted as saying, "Somebody said 'shoot.' It was kind of stupid, you know, but I did...I thought it was all rather cool, you know, with the cops chasing us and guns waving all around." The prosecutor then asked him, "If you were 'stoned' and I told you to shoot the judge, you'd do it?" The young man replied, "I don't know. It depends on what you wanted me to shoot him for."

This is a straightforward news report from the courthouse. But right next to that story, under a section called "The Arts Today," was a two column picture, ostensibly not an advertisement, of a movie star grimly pointing a dangerous weapon. Under the picture we read, "Michael Caine wields a machine gun and his most murderous look in his latest role as the protagonist of 'Play Dirty.'"

For some people, and perhaps more than just a few radical young people, this kind of mixture speaks directly to the charge that the media are hypocritical in their treatment of violence. As I see it, the basic issue is not the elimination of violence from the mass media. The case rests more on how rather than on whether it is presented.

In both news and entertainment realms, and even in advertising, we have a surfeit of raw incidents of violence and a deficit of materials plying an understanding of such acts. To be sure, conflict is news, and it is also an effective dramatic device. But even in reality, violence is not the only operating, let alone newsworthy, means to resolve human conflict.

I hope these remarks stir up at least one question.

Are you confident that the current practices of your newspaper have not contributed to the image of the world so prevalent among today's youth who want to smash it?

Chapter 7

What is the Question?
What is the Question?

Last Lecture, University of Washington
October 30, 1988

It is reported that Gertrude Stein's last words from her death bed were "What is the answer, what is the answer?" To which her friend, Alice Toklas, is said to have replied, "What is the question, what is the question?"

That exchange underscores what I want to bring to the ongoing distress about media violence. Answers depend on questions.

My thesis is that questions about the effects of media violence are too narrowly cast; they must be converted into a social-effects view. To do this, I will pose questions about effects in a framework of issues over the regulation and control of media content.

Simple curiosity about the effects of media violence is hardly enough to justify a serious penetration into this policy thicket. Neither is the fact that media violence often offends personal taste. I propose a more penetrating warrant: an inquiry into how media violence gets defined as a social problem to enter into the arena of public policy.

In travel to other countries one frequently encounters the view that Americans, paralyzed by ambiguous research findings, cannot see the obvious necessity for governmental action to control the portrayal of violence. Even though this solution runs counter to precedents in American law and custom, it continues to have support both inside and outside the United States. That, alone, is a powerful response to media violence.

Advocates of control tend to take one of three positions: (1) that which calls for direct government action to stop the flow of media violence; (2) that centering on increased surveillance, classification, and labeling of media material to facilitate individual selection and family regulation; or, (3) that which emphasizes placing pressure on the media to the end that they will exercise self-regulation over the presentation of violent content.

Today, we will examine how media violence gets defined as a social problem to prompt consideration of control options.

Pathways to Violence

Violence is not a simple concept. Harm, injury, or destruction might come about in a variety of ways, including:

♦   It can be self-inflicted and, if it results in total destruction, we call it *suicide*.

♦   It can happen when persons inadvertently stumble, or make an error in coping with some aspect of their environment, to result in what is called an *accident*.

♦   It can happen when the forces of nature suddenly sweep in on a community and produce a *natural disaster*.

♦   It can happen when societies set up means for recruiting, training, and dispatching organized units to use force in carrying out social and political policies. This we call *police or military action*.

♦   It can happen when one person attacks another with hand, fist, or weapon. Under some conditions this may simply be an exercise in discipline under parental authority. Under other conditions, total destruction is an act of *homicide*.

Every mode of violence can inflict great damage and be costly to persons involved. It is also obvious that not all acts of violence evoke the same response. The condition under which an act of violence is experienced is critical. How shall we think about that? Linkages are important.

If one is a participant, various role possibilities come forth. One can be the recipient of harm or destruction and thus be called the *victim*.

Or, one could be the initiator of the act and give, but not receive, harm and thus be called attacker, assailant, or *aggressor*. A person could also both give and receive harm as a participant without reference to how the act was initiated.

To know that one has been a participant in an act of violence opens the door for grasping: (1) How the act of violence was initiated; (2) What the response was in terms of retaliation and (3) How the act was concluded or terminated, and with what consequences. This broadens concern. The prime target becomes acts of social violence wherein persons deliberately do physical harm to one another.

At the same time, concern is extended from isolated incidents where weapons are noted and bodies are counted to the act as a social process involving elements of instigation, retaliation, and termination. In other words, if persons are participants, we would now want to know what they have done, or what they have seen relevant to how the act started, how it was responded to, and how it ended. It appears that the mass media provide more realistic models for initiating violence than they do for terminating it.

There are various ways to participate in acts of violence. Similarly, there are various pathways to observe forms of violence. A basic distinction is that between the direct and the mediated form.

To be "on the scene where the action took place," is different from reading about it or seeing it in the movies or on television, even though "first-hand" observation does not necessarily imply participation other than in the spectator form.

The mass media are the prime generators of the spectator form. Mediated observation means that observers can be distant in space but not far removed in time from an actual incident. For example, television brings live war scenes and sometimes even catches a dramatic moment of interpersonal violence as when Lee Harvey Oswald was shot following the assassination of President Kennedy. On the other hand, media fantasy violence is not restricted by time and space dimensions, either for the creator or for the observer.

Actual violence can be directly experienced (as victim or assailant) or visually witnessed (with or without intrusion). Furthermore, the media portrayal of violence can either take real or fictional form, and each is subject both to direct observation or to indirect reception through message diffusion. Accordingly, we must ask:

♦ How, in fact, do persons experience violence in various societies?

♦ What elements in the population have participated in how many acts of violence?

♦ In what ways have they participated?

♦ How many persons have directly observed an act of violence but have not participated in one?

♦ How is the experience of participation or direct observation related to the way in which people observe, perceive, interpret, respond to, use, or are influenced by mass media violence?

♦ Do participants have less favorable or more favorable attitudes toward media violence than observers?

♦ Is there any significant difference between observers and participants in their responsiveness to counter-norms of nonviolence from media sources?

Controversy: Cause and Consequence

Paul Lazarsfeld, a pioneer in media research, once reminded us that the effect of television is controversial not because some people are against crime and others are for it; it is controversial because so little is known that anyone can inject prejudices or views into the debate without being proved wrong.

Yes, the absence of knowledge propels controversy. That is certainly the case over media violence. There is not much argument over whether sticks and stones can break our bones; the evidence is fairly convincing. However, we are not yet sure about words and pictures. Moreover, controversy takes different directions depending on whether the issue turns over the presentation of real versus the portrayal of fictional violence.

Fantasy violence from the entertainment realm comes first to the forefront of public policy debates, probably because audience concerns are more apt to involve children. If so, controls are presumed to be essential and, accordingly, are deemed to be politically viable.

Violence as news gets entangled in other complexities. Its repeated and superficial portrayal often prompts concern about impact that yields commentary on human nature, national traits, moral laxity, and other problematic dimensions. Moreover, pressures for controls quickly engage legal constraints involving constitutional rights.

Sociologically, then, one of the effects of mass media violence is to generate controversy over what mass media material might do to make society more violent, or to prompt people to be more aggressive in their relations with other persons. From such concern, argument readily branches out into the advocacy of controls. The question now arises, what merit comes from approaching the question of media violence through the doorway of effect-control controversies?

Social problems emerge in a context of controversy: opposing views are projected, persuasion processes are activated, organization is mobilized, and attempts are made to institutionalize power and authority to manage the condition in accord with preferred values. The pertinent questions become:

♦   How does mass media violence emerge as a public issue?

♦   To whom does the condition appear troublesome?

♦   What social mechanisms operate to force the issue to points of policy decision?

♦   What possible solutions are available?

♦   How are they initiated and processed?

♦   What actions have been taken?

♦   How are they sustained after the public loses interest?

♦   What other consequences do institutionalized controls have beyond affecting the portrayal of media violence?

These questions prompt us to identify how public opinion is generated, molded, expressed, and impressed on policy decisions concerning the presentation of violence--in this case, a policy to define the social responsibility of the media themselves.

The Critical Entry of Public Opinion

We need to clarify the conditions under which public opinion commences to form through various exploratory ventures in collective behavior before it is registered in commitments to action. This directs us toward a research agenda where the analysis of media effects will be enhanced by investigating:

♦   How critics play a role in defining discontent by identifying what is "undesirable" and directing attention to the substance of violent media content.

♦   Why an inventory of relevant research is inconclusive about effects, partly because of varying conceptions of what constitutes evidence.

♦   How a dynamic opinion process involving a network of voluntary associations leads to control efforts by governmental agencies.

♦   How the mass media respond to controversy and threat of censorship with systems of self-regulation.

♦   How in American society, systems of regulation and control grow out of public opinion and are sustained by it in a delicate balance of social, political, and economic forces linked to some degree to developing knowledge of the effects of violence.

This agenda implies that sociological interest in the mass communication of violence does not confine itself simply to asking what persons do, or even why they do it; it is also concerned with the problem of why persons must do what they do. In other words, we are challenged to detect underlying factors that impose structural opportunities and constraints on mass communication with respect to the portrayal of violence.

Inciting Social Sensitivity

It is not a simple task to arouse publics and crystallize attitudes so that action will be directed against media violence. Why is that?

Most people are not particularly critical of mass media content. Routines of daily life do not ordinarily include effort to evaluate how the mass media bring the world of reality and fantasy to the household. Media exposure gets to be a deeply ingrained habit, the selective features of which tend to reinforce satisfaction more than they stir complaint.

The grip of this habit may first become visible through personal irritations that arise with a burned-out television tube, a substituted program, a newspaper strike, or with the failure to find the morning paper on the porch. In moments like these, persons become aware of media dependence. This condition is not a fertile base for the nourishment of social concern over media performance. Nonetheless, displeasure does arise. When it does, individuals may cancel subscriptions, fail to show up at the box office, or write letters and make telephone calls to register complaints.

From personal irritation and individual acts collective action can arise to cope with media performance. Thus, boycotts are organized, legislation sought, censorship called for, and books banned or burned. What triggers such strong actions?

In the American system of mass communication, complaints, whether thoughtful or not, can be the beginning of a communicative process that may ultimately register impact on the decision as to what content the media will offer their audience. No one argues with the following empirically based assertion: more and more people are spending more and more time in exposure to media content. Anything that compels so much attention inevitably calls forth acidic reflection.

In this climate, critical publics can emerge from previously unquestioning populations.

Guided as they are by economic considerations intimately tied to audience size, the media are acutely sensitive to audience feedback. If complaint generates controversy, and if controversy generates consensus, then the probability of influence and the possibility of change is maximized.

In some instances, complaint can also be effective apart from a real consensus. The media are prone to over-generalize certain registered reactions. Voluntary telephone calls, for example, are often mistaken for a general, representative trend. Complaint, then, whether selective or representative, has a significant energizing potential. For this reason it is important to identify its place in the interactive media-critic-public system.

Complaint, as a forerunner to controversy, is a definition of a problem that may generate discontent, but does not uniformly arise from discontent.

Criticism and complaint about the mass media rarely emerge in an unguided, spontaneous fashion. Since the media cater to a mass audience and attempt to satisfy the largest possible number of persons, it is not surprising that complaint does not generally originate as a full-blown grass-roots response. Initially it is, rather, the reaction of a select, articulate minority. Collective concern is generated by persons who know how to formulate indictments in clear, sharp, normative terms to specify how media content is a threat to venerable values. Where do we look for such persons?

The work of the mass communicator is routinely subject to the appraisal of fellow professionals, and the often biting responses of inter-media critics such as book, television, and motion picture reviewers. While these reactions spark concern for artistic, technical and professional matters, they do not automatically incite sensitivity about broader social issues. This requires that criticism be projected from a wider base of social values where media performance is posed as a threat to these values. Such indictments are most likely to flow from sources external to the organizations of mass communication.

The response is not automatic in American society because some unique value clusters come into play. One is aversion to censorship (prior restraint by government). Another derives from a deep cultural experience with violence extending back to frontier days. Throughout American history, some forms of violent behavior have been sanctioned. Indicators of public fascination with violence are all around us: the popularity of professional wrestling, football, and ice hockey; the booming Christmas sales of toy weapons; and the attraction of both real and fictional accounts of war and crime.

While the media whet the taste, any would-be-critic ultimately recognizes that the appetite is rooted in deeper American experience, if not in human nature. At the same time, other value clusters (e.g., concern for the welfare of children) can provide a cultural counterbalance. The context in which media content is received, affects both the possibility of controversy and the manner in which it is formed and expressed. Equally important is the role of persistent action-oriented critics who gain power as opinion leaders depending on:

♦   Their professional status.

♦   Their access to a platform or medium to amplify and spread arguments.

♦   Their linkage to sources of organized response from voluntary associations.

♦   The ability of such organization to mobilize community concern, to activate political investigation, to spur threat of legal sanctions, and to promote a boycott of the media.

In patterned sequence, these elements have emerged to direct pressure against most forms of American mass communication. A feedback chain is forged: critics speak; opinions are amplified; local groups pick up the argument; voluntary associations mount crusades; "legions of decency" appear; "clean up" campaigns are organized; distributors of content are challenged; petitions circulate; politicians are alerted; authorities testify; resolutions pass; and government intervention is threatened.

The evolution of criticism into effective public opinion through a maze of controversy, protest, publicity, community action, legislative investigation and, finally, media reaction, has been analyzed with respect to the motion pictures, the comic books, and the broadcast media. In each case, the feature that finally compelled the media to react in some visible and tangible way was the threat of restrictive intervention by government agencies.

Regulation and Control: Public Participation

How can the public respond to an articulation of alarm about media violence? One way is for citizens, either individually or collectively, to boycott the media, or the sponsors of their content, that offend their sensibilities. The economic structure of American mass communication makes the media particularly sensitive to this kind of action.

So far, however, large sectors of the American audience have not turned away from the media because they portray violence. The reasons are undoubtedly many and mixed. Most persons like what they get from the mass media, in part, perhaps they are not aware of possible alternative fare. Others do not approve of the content, but may not know what can be done about it. They ask, how to protest and how to identify media offenders? Such identification requires exposure to the media and some kind of continuing surveillance in order to know when and of what to disapprove.

Some advocates of surveillance encourage parents to establish a "personal watch society" to protect children from media violence. These can merge into neighborhood networks and community groups to monitor media content and to lobby for stricter regulation. American society has seen a number of instances where media watch organizations evolve from existing voluntary associations (e.g., PTA, churches, lodges, etc.) to become active forces for evaluating, grading, labeling, and in some sense "censoring" mass media content.

The action of citizen groups has altered media content. The reduction of violence might well be applauded; but it does raise other questions. What danger lurks from the power of an organized minority to set standards for the majority? Could these standards institute rigid conformity that would damage freedom and impair creativity in a pluralist society?

Regulation and Control: Government Participation

Government is often turned to as the final arbiter of controversy and the ultimate source of solutions to pressing social problems. However, while government has direct power to deal with the plentiful array of real violence in society, its responsibility for the presentation of media violence is still under contest. Should government measure out the quantity of violence that will be tolerated?

There are two possible responses, one involving the *control of the deleterious*, and the other the *promotion of the desirable*. Thus, theoretically, the machinery of government could be invoked directly to censor media content, or it could be employed, directly or indirectly, to encourage the media to perform in accord with standards widely conceived to serve the public interest.

Government intervention could range from the threat of investigation, to the offer of license preferences, mailing privileges, subsidies, or tax discounts. Simply stated, government could carry a stick, or offer a carrot. Given the array of legislative, judicial, and administrative features from local to federal jurisdictions, the possible points of penetration, either with power or with influence, are many and complex.

Technically, regulation by government may occur in accordance with the doctrine of *prior restraint*, involving prohibition of certain expressions, or the doctrine of *subsequent punishment*, involving a penalty after the expression.

The first amendment of the constitution forbids the federal government to impose any system of prior restraint. Clearly, the Founding Fathers did not envisage government as the Great Cultural Mother regulating the spheres of communication by universal decree. As a result, an American tradition of outspoken opposition to government monitoring of opinion and expression has emerged. That opposition asserts that while ideas may be dangerous, the suppression of them by government is fatal to a democratic society.

Despite law and tradition, there are constant efforts to test and redefine the limits of free expression. The first arena where such action becomes generally visible is a congressional committee room. Here, members of congress, prompted by pressure from constituents or from organized special interests, investigate alleged abuses of free expression by the mass media. This activity--sometimes characterized as "government by raised eyebrow"--ironically gain's potency when, through the media, media excess is exposed to cutting public complaint.

A strong public response encourages the committee to threaten the presumed offenders (e.g., the purveyors of violence) with formal, punitive action. Sustained public exposure has been a key factor in forcing the media to engage in self-regulation. Adverse publicity about media performance is probably a greater factor in affecting media adjustment than is the threat of legislation. Why? Because no one has found a way to overcome the real difficulties in formulating legislation that would set government standards for policing content in ways that would be constitutional.

The result is a loosely defined system of exposure and threat that links the public to the media through government. Sociologically, this is something less than a regime of law. Rather, it is a changing blend of public and private interests common in many sectors of American life and perhaps inherent in any pluralistic, democratic society. It is a highly flexible arrangement, with neither side wishing to run the risk of completely clarifying its responsibility for limiting media content.

From this situation, both sides derive some positive power, and each must adjust to the margin of doubt. Prodded by the public, government agencies prod the media. The pressure is cyclical, with sharp peaks of protest and broad valleys of indifference. The system often seems to perpetuate either dead center mediocrity or an evasion of responsibility.

Accordingly, the search for alternatives goes on. Not everyone is content to let the question of governmental participation in regulation and control rest on a wavering mechanism that induces media self-regulation. Instead, mindful that formal censorship through prior restraint by government is not constitutional, they advocate that government could yet effectively participate in controls. How? By formulating standards to regulate the portrayal of violence and other controversial content; by requiring the media to regularly defend their performance with reports that will receive unrelenting publicity; and, by imposing on the media an obligation to study the programmatic needs of their audiences.

Thus, from time to time, concerned parties urge Congress to set up some kind of public body that would not have the power to censor but would have the authority to expose, complain, praise, and exhort--to perform with respect to the mass media the watch-dog functions that the media presume to exercise against other institutions that serve the public interest.

This controversy will continue. Clearly, the First Amendment was not the last word on the subject of governmental participation in the regulation and control of mass communication.

Regulation and Control: Media Participation

The media can and do regulate and control the violence they portray. In the first place, they make selection decisions in the creative process. Such decisions are, in part, a product of audience response that can lead to pressure mounted by the public and by the government.

The form, scope, and continuity of media performance depend as much on the clarity, consensus, and force of public opinion as it does on production innovations internal to the media themselves. This means that the responsibility for violent content rests not alone with the media but resides importantly in the relationship between the media and their audience.

This fact generates special response by both parties. The mass media are naturally responsive to the interests, tastes, and habits of a numerical majority. They sense these in a number of ways. For example, the media assess what "sells" by measuring preferences through polling devices and rating schemes. They also receive, tabulate, and review letters and telephone calls, some offering innovative ways to control violence. For instance, one mother wrote to the Federal Communications Commission saying that she knew what to do with all that violence on TV: "Why don't you let those fellows use live bullets?"

Most important, however, is media response to criticism from forces linked to political power. The reaction follows a pattern: after a defense of performance in the name of a "free press," and after denouncing the evils of censorship, the media become "sensors" to take on functions of "censors"" themselves as each medium develops an internal system of control.

Self-regulation means that a communication industry taxes itself to establish an organization to police itself. One of the first steps is to formulate a code to guide the creation or restrict the presentation of certain types of content. Fidelity to the code is policed before the content is released, and conformity is symbolized by a "seal of approval."

Finally, to extend recognition of control efforts, and to head of the kind criticism that gave rise to them in the first place, the media mobilize a continuous flow of public-relations efforts. As a result, for a time at least, controversy over the excess use of violence subsides. A wavering equilibrium thus emerges between the force of public opinion and the powers of media policy, as each side of the interaction adapts itself to the other.

Self-regulation is not unique to mass communication. Many industries, professions and occupations engage in similar activity. However, the media would appear to have a particular advantage over their counterparts in fulfilling one of the peculiar functions of self-regulation. Given their vast, built-in resources for launching information campaigns, the media can do a more thorough and expert job of image-building and self-justification than can others engaged in self-regulation. Sometimes they disarm critics through co-optation. Thus, it is not unusual for religious and civic organizations who have been in the forefront of opposition to media violence to suddenly find that they have generous access to media channels for their own special "public interest" messages.

Accordingly, to assess self-regulation, it is necessary to probe behind the image-building process of media public relations, and even to go beyond the testimony of former critics such as the "watch-dog" committees of voluntary associations. Appraisal of self-regulation must consider not only the presence of widely heralded media codes and current changes in them, but also the manner of their use and the effects of their application.

Administering codes involves a "gatekeeper" to screen media output through a sieve of moral, political, marketing, and other specifications. Occupants of this key position bear such titles as Network Editor, Continuity Acceptance Director, Code Administrator, or Review Board Chairperson. Formal requirements guide the work of such agents. However, their interpretation of media performance is also influenced by informal working relations and expectations that arise in daily practice. Further research on the relationship of formal requirements and informal arrangements would clarify the merit and cost of bringing the attributes of self-regulation under closer governmental supervision.

Conclusion

Self-regulation has evolved to sense public taste and tolerance. It is also used to blunt criticism of media performance. It places highly specific powers in the hands of a few to decide the limits of what the many shall experience through mass communication. Before this mechanism is discarded in the interests of absolute free expression, or before it is brought under more stable and impartial auspices in the interests of controlling the flow of media violence, its workings should be thoroughly explored and pondered.

Whether such cycles ultimately evolve into satisfactory policy adjustments will depend on a better knowledge of effects, a clearer conception of alternative mechanisms of control, and a sharper understanding of how the two are linked.

Research directed toward such ends is a demanding labor, a continuing, hopefully cumulative, and highly self-critical enterprise. Scientific researchers must ask, "How do you know, and how can I come to know this too?" Thus research on the effects of media violence involves not only the conduct of particular studies, but a continuing dialogue between researchers on the shortcomings of studies, the feasibility of alternative strategies, and the necessity for the fresh pursuit of new leads.

I hope that some of you will be intrigued by the challenge and will proceed to enter this world of research.

Today we have explored a maze of matters that, if nothing else, has yielded a plethora of questions. *What is the answer? What is the answer?*

Gertrude Stein is not the only one who has departed without a reliable substantive response.

You can help remedy that condition for future generations.

Obscenity and Pornography

A President of the United States propelled me into probes on pornography.

An unexpected call from the White House asked me to join a Commission on Obscenity and Pornography. I was told that President Johnson was looking for qualified people who had experience with relevant research, but that he did not want persons who had already made up their minds about policy judgments.

I responded by asking if this meant that the Commission was free to move with the data and was not being formed merely to support a predetermined position.

The answer was an emphatic yes, and I was given names of prominent persons (including Charles Keating and Frederick Wertham) who were not being put on the Commission because they had publicly committed themselves to a particular view on the issue of controls.

With that assurance, I accepted the appointment.

Up until the first meeting of the Commission in July, 1968, a meeting held at the Institute of Sex Research at Indiana University, where they have the second-largest collection of erotica in the world (the Vatican is alleged to have the largest), my direct contact with sex-oriented materials had been limited to occasional inputs from peer groups, the mass media generally, and the usual exposure one gets in military barracks or from wartime enemy leaflets.

As a sociologist who had taught in the family field, I was generally aware of problems in sex-socialization but I had not done any research with erotic materials. However, I came to the Commission after having served as a consultant to another national commission, the one on violence headed by Milton Eisenhower, where I became convinced that violence on television was indeed a national health hazard.

As a result, my initial stance was open to the idea that pornography, too, might merit the alarm of an organization like the Citizens for Decent Literature. However, I was also mindful of the constitutional rights of free expression. A dilemma loomed.

From July, 1968 to October, 1970, it was my duty as a member of the Commission to think about these questions, to organize relevant empirical research, and to agonize about how the findings might inform policy choices posed for us by the Congress of the United States.

As it turned out, more than research was involved. Political influence drifted in from the Nixon White House. This was my first entry onto the stage of a national political theater. The experience became useful a decade later. After the commission concluded, I had many occasions to record my impressions in public forums including appearances on radio and television both locally and nationally. Media interest never lagged. And neither did that of colleagues, students, associations, church groups, librarians, and so forth.

The five following entries provide an account of my encounter with the volatile concerns provoked by words and pictures on sex. The fundamental issues are still with us. In the 1980s, another federal commission (the Meece Commission) went over the ground again. This time, moral indignation and legal posturing marked the center of effort. But just as in the case of our emphasis on empirical research a decade earlier, the Meece emphasis had little impact on the market. The explicit portrayal of sex has not yet been dampened.

Technology, however, has shifted "hard-core" presentation more to the privacy of the home, via video cassettes, thus altering the political press for controls.

Nonetheless, the portrayal of sex continues to vex vast sectors of society. The possible linkage of symbols to changes in actual sex behavior exacerbates concern. Thus, the rise in teen-age pregnancy, harassment, rape, and AIDS, inevitably provokes additional alarm about media responsibility. Work on causation must continue. It seems unlikely, however, that even a successful effort in this direction will completely resolve the issue of how to control words and pictures about sex in American society.

Chapter 8

Predispositions on Pornography

Commission on Obscenity and Pornography, Washington, D. C.
October 16, 1968

We have accepted an awesome responsibility.

Since I have been designated to chair the Panel of Effects, I thought we ought to share views, if any, on the puzzling problem of how to pose the problem of effects before we get down to the serious task of designing a program of research.

Let me lead off with a few thoughts. If nothing else, this will leave a primitive record that will be fun to glance back at after our actual work is completed.

Conceptual Confusion

In visits to the library I find there's not much on the effects of pornography, at least as derived from empirical studies. There is a variety of fascinating statements wrapped in considerable conceptual confusion. I think it is fair to say that the literature is littered with efforts to come to terms with the meaning of "pornography." A stunning array of jurists and journalists, doctors of medicine and divinity, sociologists and semanticists, psychiatrists and postal officials, have tried to bring precision to this term, as well as to such allied concepts as "obscene," "patently offensive," "hard core," and "prurient." So meticulous have been these pursuits that D. H. Lawrence once referred to them as involving "the splitting of pubic hairs."

Somehow, given our mandate from Public Law 90-100, sooner or duty is "to evaluate and recommend definitions of obscenity and pornography." In the meantime, this panel will have to develop some rather explicit operational definitions for research purposes if we are to follow the mandate "to study the effect of obscenity and pornography upon the public, and particularly minors, and its relationship to crime and other antisocial behavior."

While on the matter of the general mandate, let me emphasize how important one other feature is for the direction of our specialized efforts. Recall that the work of all panels, ours included, perhaps critically, is supposed to enable the Commission "to recommend such legislative, administrative, or other advisable and appropriate action necessary to regulate effectively the flow of such traffic, without in any way interfering with constitutional rights."

Accordingly, I believe we should try to consider options of control as we design directions for inquiry on effects. As we have told our students, the form of the question generally shapes the form of the answer. Now I know that control options will be addressed by other panels and we must try to integrate our efforts with their work. Given the division of labor, and the time frame for completion, that is not going to be easy.

Impact of Content

In a general sense, I assume that pornography has to do with someone creating symbolic materials that presumably will arouse some erotic response in the eye of the beholder. I would then suggest that the individual and social effects of such symbolic materials must depend in some way upon the pattern of content being offered, the opportunities for access to such content, and the uses that audiences attribute to their exposure to such materials.

Concerning these elementary points, as several of you know better than I, numerous studies clearly support what has long been a contention by concerned citizens: the menu offered by the general mass media, let alone the channels that specialize in sexual content, is heavily saturated with symbolic materials designed to stimulate erotic responses, if only to serve commercial purposes. In addition, more and more people have ready access to both the general and the specialized media of mass communication. In a way, these points add up to a statement of one simple kind of effect: the portrayals of sex, by both general and specialized forms of mass media, attract large audiences.

However, as we all know, the facts concerning the abundance of erotic media content, and the frequency of exposure to the same, do not suffice to prove that the media modify attitudes, values, or actions, let alone induce sexual behavior that clearly has antisocial consequences.

As such questions are usually expressed, they can hardly be unequivocally answered. Indeed, many of the questions that concern us most intensely involve both fact and value-judgment. More than this, their answers depend on relations between different kinds of facts, and on connections between these relations and certain value-judgments implicit in the thoughts of the questioner.

It is relatively easy, I think, to catalog the portrayals of sexually oriented materials in the media. This is not to say that reliable, systematic, content analysis can be done overnight by just any casual process of observation and classification. However, assuming quality findings, it is more difficult to relate such tabulations to the traits of consumers. It is still more difficult to show that such a relation is one of cause and effect, and if this can be established, it still remains to evaluate the effects produced. When any one of these steps is omitted, or seriously flawed, no firm decision can be made regarding the desirability of continuing or changing existing means of regulation or control.

Nexus of Effects

The principal point is simply this: the demonstration of effects through careful, objective research, as valuable and necessary as that may be, will not automatically shape the policy to solve the presumed problem.

The ultimate utility of effect studies for guiding policy decisions will, of course, depend not only how well they are done, but on how they are formulated. If they are merely directed toward an assessment of the power to induce erotic responses that are linked to some conception of antisocial consequences, the Commission will yet confront difficult decisions. Consider the following provocative possibilities:

♦   It may turn out that obscenity cannot corrupt. Even if it can, we may conclude that the family is better suited than the law to insulate the young and, failing that, to inform them that pornography is not within the sphere of adult society's approval.

◆   If obscenity can corrupt, we may decide that its corruption is a price worth paying. We could still opt for the position that our socity forbids any restrictions on ideas, since the law serves society, not the individual.

These are strong ideas, perhaps too strong for some of our colleagues to contemplate, but, nevertheless, worthy of consideration as we plan effect studies. That effort, I believe, must embrace not only the direct and the indirect, as well as the immediate and long-range social impact of exposure to erotic materials, but must also try to incorporate a concern for the social effects of attempting, by governmental action, to stem the flow of such materials.

Could we devise studies comparing the effects of prohibition versus the effects of permissiveness? I'm not certain, but I urge its consideration. Let me sketch some notions from my interest in collective behavior to underscore the prospect.

One of the consequences of a relatively unregulated flow of words and pictures about sex is to sustain a state of public contest and controversy. This, in turn, has consequences. Contentious dialogue can be functional for a society undergoing rapid change. For example, controversy leads to concern, and that concern can be a more sensitive indicator of the changing alignment of needs and norms on matters pertaining to sex than any legal structure involving centralized administrative surveillance and the application of prior restraint.

Furthermore, community concern can mount effective pressure on the sources that produce such materials. Indeed, the market mechanism may itself be one of the most proficient instruments of social control yet devised. A hard-headed examination of the developments in other countries could provide data for testing such a notion.

In sum, one hypothetical option, located at the extreme libertarian end of the policy continuum, namely, recommending no intervention by Federal governmental mechanisms, does not necessarily mean an abdication of responsibility for regulation and control. Indeed, it may actually implement, rather than inhibit, more effective mechanisms, because it may tend to place responsibility where the changing action is--among the sub-culture of consumers and in the community of the concerned.

One of the possible effects of formal intervention is to displace and dampen such activity, i.e., to pass on to a government agency that which, particularly in the case of sex-oriented materials, is operationally always a matter of individual choice and family values in a context of changing community norms.

But, rather than argue the case, the point here is that an exploration of policy options is a desirable antecedent to shape a program of research on effects relevant for ultimate recommendations.

We should not pre-judge Commission conclusions, but merely try to anticipate likely control alternatives so that we can develop, while there is yet time, data on effects necessary to assist a rational, and responsible, policy recommendation. At a minimum, I think we ought to request that the Legal Panel and the Positive Approaches Panel share with us, as soon as possible, their thinking about control options.

Chapter 9

The Anatomy of Pornography
University of Calgary
February 17, 1971

Human beings aren't the only social species to engage in communication, nor in sex.

How, then, are we unique? Humans alone invent and transmit words and other symbols in language systems. The product is culture, which includes values and involves rules prescribing what should or should not be done.

In few areas of human activity has there been greater sensitivity to values and more rigorous exercise of rules than in the realm of human sexual behavior.

All known societies devise rules to regulate actual sexual conduct, such as invoking prohibitions upon indecent exposure, fornication, or sodomy. Little wonder, then, that as media technology developed, so, too, did concern for how sex was portrayed and conveyed.

The problem is clear even if the answer is not: how much do the media reflect and how much do they change values and behavior in the sexual realm?

Today, all around the world, there is heightened interest in this question. Everywhere, traditional rules governing sex expression are challenged. Messages about sex have become more open, more explicit, and more abundant. In great measure, this is what is meant by the "sexual revolution." Words and pictures on the subject have long been with us, but advancements in technology have brought a torrent of explicit sex material to the market place.

The public portrayal of sex raises serious esthetic, moral, social, and legal questions. Are such words and pictures offensive? Are they harmful? Do they lead to crime or delinquency? Sexual or non sexual deviancy? Severe emotional disturbances? Do they debase and dehumanize social relationships? Are they a threat to the moral fiber of a society? Is censorship desirable? Can it be effective? These concerns are commonly expressed about materials that are called pornographic or obscene.

But, what is meant by these terms? Is everything called pornography also obscene? Can something be obscene if it not pornographic? Unfortunately, reference to either common speech or to legal language does not provide a clear-cut answer. What, then, are the key issues concerning the definition of terms?

One is the scope of distaste. For some, the public portrayal of sexual activity is in and of itself obscene. But even this view has difficulty line drawing decisions. What is meant by sexual activity? Does it begin with nudity, and if so, of what degree? And does public display include medical and health magazines and journals?

Sometimes the issue turns around whether the focus should be on the *intent* of the communicator as opposed to on the *response* of the audience. Thus some say that material is pornographic or obscene if it is designed to lead to sexual arousal. For others, however, the critical test is not a matter of intent but a matter of *impact*. Does the material actually lead to sexual arousal? If so, is that enough for a designation of obscenity, or must sexual arousal be shown to lead to something else?

While it may be uncomfortable to talk about such matters, it is obviously easier to raise questions than it is to devise adequate means for gaining answers. Complications arise. Consider, for example, the concern over arousal. Arousal can be measured physically, chemically, and psychologically. But, conceivably, under some conditions explicit sexual material may not lead to sexual arousal while non-sexual materials may. Would it then be appropriate to attach the concepts of obscenity and pornography to both sets of phenomena? And if the answer is yes, would identical sets of controls be appropriate? Complications arise from the fact that there is a long list of non-sexual items, including foods, types of clothing, and music which have a demonstrated capacity to elicit sexual arousal in a considerable sector of society.

Other factors thwart the achievement of consensus. In public discourse, obscenity and pornography are often used interchangeably to denote disapproval of any type of explicit sexual material.

However, pornography is not generally employed in legal assessments. Obscenity, on the other hand, while sometimes used to refer to such things as violence, pollution and war, is more frequently employed as a legal concept to denote prohibited sexual materials. The obscenity issue, then, usually turns around what words and pictures shall be prohibited. Where and how, for example, shall the line be drawn between "erotic art" and "hard-core pornography?"

For laws to be respected and to serve as effective restraints on expression, unambiguous definitions are called for. Yet, despite resolute effort by judges, librarians, lawyers, psychologists, sex educators, criminologists, and postal officials, no one has yet devised a precise and generally accepted definition of obscenity and pornography. Many would agree with a justice of the Supreme Court who declared that while he could not define "hard core pornography" he knew it when he saw it.

Thus, the United States seems to have reached certainty through individual perceptions while simultaneously being perplexed over a social and legal definition of obscenity and pornography. How did we arrive at this contradictory condition? A brief reach into definitions across a broad span of time provides a sense of how it happened.

Evolution of Restraints

Sex has not always been at the center of concern over what forms of public expression should be restrained. Dismay over sex is antedated by alarm over political and religious expression which dates back, at least, to ancient Greek and Roman times. In both places, sexual licentiousness was tolerated in drama. So, too, was bawdiness during medieval times in Europe when it was apparently quite acceptable in ballads and even in religious works. In 15th century England, with the printing of books on the rise, censorship was directed against seditious and heretical works, not against sexual matters. But a change was in the offing.

Under the influence of Puritanism in the early 17th century, proceedings were launched against the use of profanity by actors on the stage. The end of the 17th century in England brought the beginning of long-term governmental concern with the morals of the public in the sexual area which culminated in the Victorian period. A Society for the Reformation of Manners, which blacklisted persons guilty of "vice," was formed under royal patronage and Queen Ann issued a proclamation denouncing vice.

However, it wasn't until 1868, in Queen v. Hicklin, that an authoritative judicial definition of "obscenity" was adopted. The Hicklin case involved an anti-religious pamphlet with sexual content. The full citation to the publication described it as *The Confession Unmasked, Showing the Depravity of the Roman Priesthood, the Iniquity of the Confessional and the Questions put to Females in Confession.* In finding the publication obscene, the court held that the test was "whether the *tendency* of the matter charged as obscenity is to deprave and corrupt those whose minds are open to such immoral influences, and into whose hands a publication of this sort may fall."

The Hicklin case made it clear for the first time that works might be prohibited as "obscene" solely because of their sexual content, and not because of their attack upon the government or upon religious institutions.

The first obscenity case in the United States occurred in 1815 in Pennsylvania. There the court found the private showing for profit of a picture of a man and woman in an "indecent exposure" to be a common law offense because it was in violation of the public decency. In 1821, the publisher of *Fanny Hill* was found guilty of obscenity in Massachusetts. The first federal obscenity statute in the United States was part of the Customs Law of 1842. It prohibited the importation of "indecent and obscene prints, paintings, lithographs, engravings and transparencies."

Despite these legal stirrings, there was little enforcement in the United States of either state or federal obscenity laws during the first 70 years of the 19th century. This situation changed significantly after 1868, largely as the result of the efforts of Anthony Comstock. At that time, the New York legislature, at the urging of the YMCA, among others, passed a law against the dissemination of obscene literature. Comstock, a grocery-store clerk, began to investigate violations of the 1868 act by local retail dealers and to report them to prosecutors.

Later, Comstock became the chief Washington lobbyist of the Committee for the Suppression of Vice. In 1873, Congress responded by broadening the restraints against the mailing of obscene materials. Comstock was made special agent of the Post Office in charge of enforcing the federal law and he vigorously pursued these duties.

By the end of the 19th century, the federal government had prohibited the importation and mailing of obscene matter, and at least 30 states had some form of general prohibition upon the dissemination of obscene materials. The basic definition of obscenity used in both federal and state laws was the Hicklin definition borrowed from England. There was, however, increasing judicial dissatisfaction with this general definition. Through the years, the Supreme Court had appeared to assume the validity of these prohibitions as evident from their writings in other areas. It was only in 1957, however, in the case of Roth v. Unites States that the court ruled directly that broad obscenity prohibitions had a constitutional basis.

With Roth, the Supreme Court ruled that obscenity was not protected by the First Amendment of the Constitution. It then remained for the Court to set down guidelines for identifying obscene material. Three major tests emerged from various court decisions. Something would be judged obscene if:

♦   The dominant theme of the material, taken as a whole, appeals to a prurient interest in sex, and if

♦   The material is patently offensive because it affronts contemporary community standards regarding the depiction of sexual matters; and if

♦   The material lacks redeeming social value.

This trio of terms formed a somewhat porous barrier. All three tests must coalesce before material could be deemed obscene for adults. In other words, if the material could pass only one test, it could not be judged obscene even if it failed the other two. Thus, if a book, magazine or movie was found to have prurient appeal, and found to be patently offensive, it still would not be legally obscene if it was also judged to have redeeming social value.

In other rulings, the Court established special situations under which obscenity could bring convictions. These included the sale of obscene materials to minors; the obtrusive presentation of materials through public display; and, pandering by promotion or advertising that emphasizes sexually provocative aspects of material.

The search for clarification went on. In the years following Roth, there was considerable contest over the meaning and application of the three standards determining obscenity. The Court issued several qualifications. What appeared to be an absolute position gradually evolved into what might be termed variable obscenity. Simply stated, this meant that what is obscene for one group may not be obscene for another, and what is obscene in one place may not be obscene in another. Thus rulings emerged to indicate that materials not obscene for adults may be obscene for minors; material not obscene to the average person may be obscene for special groups such as homosexuals--and would be adjudged obscene if it were directed to that group. In addition, material that is obscene if offered for public distribution may not be obscene if it remains in the privacy of one's home.

Was the meaning of obscenity being clarified? The Roth test clearly rejected two elements present in application of the Hicklin rule--the examination of only isolated passages or excerpts in judging the obscenity of an entire work, and the focus upon the effect of material on particularly susceptible persons. Importantly, Roth required examination of a work as a whole to find whether its dominant theme is obscene, and it required that the obscene effect of a work be judged by its effect upon the average person.

Furthermore, under the earlier Hicklin rule, the test of obscenity was whether the tendency of the matter was to deprave and corrupt. Under Roth, however, material dealing with sex may not be deemed obscene in a general statute unless it appeals to the prurient interest, and that, in turn, was defined as material "having a tendency to excite lustful thoughts."

It is not difficult to imagine why the prurience criterion seemed vague and highly subjective, and why, despite all the other efforts to clarify the legal meaning of obscenity, uncertainty and confusion persisted. Furthermore, confusion is compounded because the Court has not yet settled the question whether the community by whose standards offensiveness is to be determined is a national community, whether it is the state, or whether it is the locality where the distribution occurs.

There is also disagreement over the precise role played by the social value standard. A plurality (not a majority) of the Justices has ruled that unless material is utterly without redeeming social value it may not be held to be obscene; a minority of Justices would permit a small degree of social value to be outweighed by prurience and offensiveness. Moreover, the Court has not authoritatively defined what social values are redeeming, although it has suggested that these may include entertainment as well as the more firmly established scientific, literary, artistic, and educational values.

The struggle to gain clarity has not yielded satisfaction. Vagueness remains. Subjectivity leaves law enforcement officials, courts, juries, and the general public uncertain about what is and what is not obscene. This also means that publishers, distributors, retailers and exhibitors have difficulty knowing in advance whether they will be charged with a criminal offense for distributing a particular work, since their understanding of the three tests could easily be at odds with that of the police, the prosecutor, the court, or the jury, who, in turn, may be at odds with each other.

Congress Creates a Commission

Mindful of the persistent definitional problems, and motivated by a judgment that found the traffic on obscenity and pornography to be "a matter of national concern," the Congress of the United States, in 1967, passed Public Law 90-100 to establish an advisory commission to undertake four specific tasks:

♦   With the aid of leading constitutional law authorities, to analyze the laws pertaining to the control of obscenity and pornography; and to evaluate and recommend definitions of obscenity and pornography;

♦   To ascertain the methods employed in the distribution of obscene and pornographic materials and to explore the nature and volume of traffic in such materials;

♦   To study the effect of obscenity and pornography upon the public, and particularly minors, and its relationship to crime and other antisocial behavior; and

♦   To recommend such legislative, administrative, or other advisable and appropriate action as the Commission deems necessary to regulate effectively the flow of such traffic, without in any way interfering with constitutional rights.

In 1968, the President appointed 18 members to the Commission. Included as commissioners were men and women with backgrounds in law, religion, psychiatry, and librarianship as well as from the fields of sociology, criminology, and mass communications.

A highly trained technical and professional staff was recruited to guide scores of research efforts including surveys, quasi-experimental studies, analysis of rates, investigations of organizations, controlled experiments, content analyses, and international comparative inquiries. Research studies were undertaken through contracts in universities and other research centers. In addition, the full commission undertook four full days of public-hearings that involved testimony from representatives of a variety of national organizations. The financial cost for the entire commission effort was approximately

$1.7 million.

In September 1970, the Commission issued a 646 page final report containing findings, conclusions, and recommendations. Almost 40 percent of the volume reported separate statements of members, including dissent from the recommendations of the majority. Nine additional volumes of technical reports were also produced. By these means, the Commission sought "to broaden the factual basis for future continued discussion." It acknowledged, however, "that the interpretations of a set of 'facts' in arriving at policy implications may differ even among men of good will."

Findings

Many findings were produced as complex problems were approached by research for the first time. For example, the Effects Panel drew on 39 studies in reporting the conditions under which specified types of sex materials were, or were not, apt to evoke physiological, attitudinal, judgmental, and behavioral responses.

There were also findings bearing on the constitutional criteria defining obscenity. The results confirm the difficulties in applying the three-part Roth test. Several studies found "arousal" and "offensiveness" were independent dimensions when applied to sexual materials; that is, material that is offensive may or may not be arousing, and material that is arousing may or may not be offensive. Only a restricted range of material seems capable of meeting both of these criteria for most people.

Further, there was little consensus among people regarding either the "arousal" or the "offensiveness" of graphic sexual depiction's of such items as female nudity with genitals exposed, heterosexual intercourse, or oral-genital intercourse. Moreover, judgments vary among different groups: males differ from females in their judgments of both "offensiveness" and "arousal"; the young differ from the old; college-educated differ from those with only a high school education; frequent church attendees differ from less frequent church attendees.

Further complications arose from findings about "social value." In the national survey of American public opinion, substantial portions of the population reported socially valuable effects from exposure to the most explicit sexual materials. Thus, about 60 percent of American men felt that looking at or reading such materials would provide information about sex, and about 40 percent reported that such an effect had occurred for themselves or someone they personally knew.

Further, about 60 percent felt that looking at or reading explicit sexual materials provided entertainment, and almost 50 percent reported this effect upon themselves or someone they personally knew. In addition, half of the adult male population reported that looking at or reading explicit sexual materials can improve sex relations of some married couples, and about a quarter of the sample reported such an effect on themselves or on someone they knew personally.

Fewer women reported such effects, but 35, 24, and 21 percent respectively reported information, entertainment, and improved sexual relations in themselves, or for someone they personally knew, as a result of looking at or reading explicit sexual materials. In addition, two controlled experiments reported more agreeable and enhanced marital communication and an increased willingness to discuss sexual matters with each other after exposure to erotic stimuli.

This battery of findings suggests that there is enough acceptance of very explicit sexual materials on the American scene to make it difficult to conclude that such works are entirely, or almost entirely, without social value for all adults.

Recommendations

The Commission concluded its work with a majority of members supporting ten recommendations--four of a non-legislative nature, and six pertaining to laws. In brief, the Commission recommended:

♦ That a massive sex-education effort be launched (ten features of which were described).

♦ Continued open discussion, based on factual information, on the issues regarding obscenity and pornography.

♦ That additional factual information be developed (research by federal agencies was encouraged).

♦ That citizens organize themselves at local, regional, and national levels to aid in the implementation of the foregoing recommendations.

♦ That federal, state, and local legislation prohibiting the sale, exhibition, or distribution of sexual materials to consenting adults should be repealed (nine supporting reasons were stated).

♦ That states adopt legislation prohibiting the commercial

distribution or display for sale of certain sexual materials to young persons (a model law dealing with pictorial material was offered).

♦   Enactment of state and local legislation prohibiting public displays of sexually explicit pictorial materials.

♦   Support for federal legislation controlling the mailing of unsolicited advertisements of a sexually explicit nature.

♦   The enactment of legislation that would permit prosecutors to proceed civilly, rather than through the criminal process, against suspected violations of obscenity prohibition (a model declaratory judgment law was described).

♦   Against the adoption of any legislation which would limit or abolish the jurisdiction of the Supreme Court of the United States, or of other federal judges and courts, in obscenity cases.

Reaction

When the Commission's report was issued, press accounts focused on the recommendation that called for the repeal of laws involving consenting adults. Denunciations followed. President Nixon called the report "morally irresponsible." It was also condemned by an overwhelming "sense of the Senate" vote in Congress. Later, however, more than twenty national organizations--church, educational, library, and publishing groups, formed a coalition to deplore the initial negative reaction. They asked for a serious study and debate of the report.

The controversy enhanced public interest in the report. A number of publishers reprinted the government version and offered it for sale. One publisher even added illustrations. This brought that publisher to trial under a charge of violating federal obscenity laws. Ultimately, he received a five-year prison term, not for publishing the report, but for failing to properly label envelopes containing a brochure advertising his illustrated version.

Conclusion

Several countries are reevaluating their obscenity laws. Recently an official commission report in Denmark resulted in the repeal of that country's adult obscenity legislation (with juvenile and non consenting exposure restrictions being retained). A similar recommendation has been made by commissions in Sweden, England,

and Israel.

However, as the American case indicates, there is a great distance between the recommendations of a commission and the repeal or enactment of legislation. If this distance is to bridged in America, it will come only after a more controversy. Three things appear to assure that controversy will go on:

♦   The continuing problem of defining what society wants to mean by obscenity and pornography;

♦   The ready availability of explicit sex materials; and

♦   A renewable curiosity and concern about items one and two.

Chapter 10

Should Pornography Laws be Repealed?
University of California, Riverside
February 9, 1971

The title of this talk is designed to arouse your attention. Other aspects of arousal will be discussed later.

The question posed deserves a direct answer. Yes, I believe that obscenity laws should be repealed. How did I come to this conclusion? Not without anxiety. Not without controversy. Consider first some possible predisposing experiences.

Predispositions

I recently worked for more than two years on the Commission on Obscenity and Pornography. One does not come to such service without baggage. In my case, I was neither a "mossback" conservative nor a "knee-jerk" liberal, although each strain could be found in my past. Thus, my father was a Lutheran minister--but he was also from Denmark. This may have put me under unique cross-pressures. Also entering into my acceptance of the assignment was the fact that as the father of four children, and as a grandfather, I had an intense interest in the health of our society and the shape of its future.

But there was another predisposition in my approach to pornography. I became convinced, as did the majority of the Commission, that we must enter our work with an inquiring mind that would seek objective facts relevant to a full range of control options, and that we would only commit ourselves to the charge of recommending public policy after such facts had been developed and assessed. We were charged by law to do research, research was clearly needed, and I wanted to see where the research led before attempting to shape policy recommendations, an act also required by the law that specified our mandate.

Policy Recommendations

What, then, was the result of two years of hard work and agonizing appraisal--other than having a pie thrown in my face at a public hearing by a man from the Underground Press, and having President Nixon label our efforts as a "disservice to the nation?"

The most visible outcome came when I joined with a majority of the Commission (12 out of 17 participating members) to recommend that federal, state, and local legislation prohibiting sale, exhibition, or distribution of sexual materials to consenting adults *should be repealed.*

That conclusion sparked prominent headlines in the nation's press, even though it was only one of ten proposals offered--five of which were also in the legislative field. The latter included laws to restrict sale of pictorial material to juveniles, and laws to control the mailing and public display of explicit sexual materials. But, in the political arena, and in the press, subtraction and addition did not carry the same weight The proposal to delete a control prompted excitement; the proposals to add controls were lost in the initial defining outburst.

The reaction to the issue of the rights of consenting adults, was, and I believe should continue to be, one of marked public interest and concern. Before summarizing the Commission's reasons for that recommendation, let me ask, how far does it actually depart from current practice in the United States? The short answer is, "not far."

About five months before the Commission drew its conclusions, the Supreme Court, in a unanimous decision around the Stanley case, moved a far step in support of the idea later expressed in our recommendation.

Speaking for the Court, Justice Marshall said, "If the First Amendment means anything, it means that a state has no business telling a man, sitting alone in his own house, what books he may read or what films he may watch.Our whole constitutional heritage rebels at the thought of giving government the power to control men's minds. The First Amendment protects a man's rights to satisfy his intellectual and emotional needs in the privacy of his own home, even if he satisfies them by watching obscene movies."

Subsequently, a district court in Boston held that adults have a similar right to view whatever they wish in movie theaters. Wrote federal Judge Bailey Aldrich, "If a rich Stanley can view a film in his home, a poorer Stanley should be free to visit a protected theater."

But it is not the legal issue alone that we are discussing. Courts make rulings and they change rulings as justices come and go. Ultimately, I believe, this issue will be resolved, if at all, not in court house but in the community of the concerned. And certainly, as we have seen in the case of our report, for a book to be "banned in the White House" only insures that more people will read it than otherwise would have been the case. In other words, we are dealing with a complex social issue which, while it can be turned to political ends, actually transcends the machinations of politics in a free society.

Basis for Conclusion

How, then, did the Commission come to the conclusion that there is no warrant for continued governmental interference with the full freedom of adults to obtain, read, or view whatever words and pictures they wish? Nine considerations entered into the majority opinion. Let me briefly characterize each of them:

♦   The Commission undertook 39 studies on the effects of exposure to sex-oriented materials; 14 of these were controlled experiments which supply data bearing on the difficult question of causal linkages. While all the research is conditional and has important limitations, the weight of the evidence suggests that explicit sexual materials do not play a significant role in the causation of social or individual harms such as crime, delinquency, sexual or non-sexual deviancy, or the promotion of severe emotional disturbances.

♦   Adults, particularly college educated males in their thirties or forties with above average social-economic status, are the dominant users of sex oriented materials. Young adults and older adolescents are not a large part of the market. Furthermore, some adults use these materials as sources of entertainment and information, and there is evidence that for married couples use of this material facilitates constructive communication about sexual matters.

♦   Society's attempts to legislate for adults in the area of obscenity have not been successful. Grave practical matters of enforcement flow from the highly subjective nature of legal standards concerning (a) an appeal to the *prurient interest* of the average person [arousal is highly variable by content of presentation and by characteristics of observers]; (b) materials that *patently offensive* in light of community standards [offensiveness is highly variable for both sexual and non sexual materials, and community standards are constantly in flux]; and, (c) reference to materials that lack redeeming *social value* [people with varying characteristics attach value to sexual materials with great variability, indeed they attribute both positive and negative value to the same material].

♦   A carefully drawn national probability sample of American adults showed that as of 1970 a majority favored the view that adults should be legally able to read or see explicit materials when they wished to so if negative effects are not demonstrated.

♦   Apart from the problems of legal vagueness and subjectivity, consistent enforcement of even the clearest prohibitions upon consensual adult exposure would be very costly in terms of law-enforcement resources.

♦   American traditions embedded in the spirit and letter of our constitution tell us that government should not seek to interfere with speech and communicative rights unless a clear *threat of harm* makes that course imperative. No such harm was demonstrated from our research.

♦   Whatever the arguments about protecting youth, it seems wholly inappropriate to adjust the level of adult communication to that considered appropriate for children. Indeed, the Supreme Court has unanimously held that adult legislation premised on this basis is an unconstitutional interference with liberty.

♦   There is little reason to believe that a lifting of restrictions on adults would result in a greatly expanded market for these materials. The evidence is that long-term consumer interest is relatively stable.

♦   The availability of explicit sexual material is not the only or even one of the most important factors influencing sexual morality in America. Attempted governmental regulation of moral choice can deprive the individual of the responsibility for personal decision which is essential to the formation of genuine moral standards. Such regulation would also tend to establish an official moral orthodoxy, contrary to our most fundamental constitutional traditions.

Such, then, were the major lines of reasoning that led a majority of the Commission to recommend repeal of obscenity laws pertaining to adults. You may, or may not, find the reasons sound, logical, consistent, or compelling.

Clearly, when the data were in, I, as one Commissioner, had to decide on matters of policy recommendations, and I did. Reasonable persons, and even unreasonable ones, can and will disagree with those policy points. But at least, at long last, the discussion can now proceed informed by facts instead of merely being motivated by fears. And this leads me to a final observation, one that is perhaps best characterized as a matter of sociological speculation.

Speculation

One of the possible consequences of the repeal of present laws restricting exposure to sex materials is to sustain a state of public controversy about such symbolic content. I would argue that, in a number of ways, such controversy might be a good and useful thing for a pluralistic society such as ours. Controversy stirs concern, and the nature and extent of that concern can be a more sensitive indicator of the shifting alignment of social needs and social norms on matters pertaining to sex than any legal structure involving centralized administrative surveillance of words and pictures.

Furthermore, public concern can mount profound pressure, allowing for local adaptations, on the production and distribution of sex materials. The market mechanism may itself be one of the most effective instruments of social control yet devised. Data from Denmark provides confirmation. Novelty wears off, satiation sets in. Commission research did produce evidence concerning the onset of satiation after repeated exposure to sex-oriented materials.

In sum, many problems ascend when a society attempts to control words and pictures about sex by laws. Effective laws are difficult to devise. Even if they could be perfected, it may be unwise to employ them for fear that could be extended to other realms. The threat of censorship is real. Laws can also be counterproductive. For some, they may only serve as labels to heighten curiosity.

Finally, I would emphasize that recommending the repeal of certain laws is not a call for anarchy. The position that I am taking does not mean the absence of social controls. One of the major effects of legal intervention is to dampen informal social controls that are, particularly in this area, driven by family values and community norms. Today those norms are changing in the direction of tolerating a more open expression of sexual matters. While this inevitably involves risk from distortion introduced by pornography, it also provides the possibility for introducing more valid information and education concerning human sexuality.

For the most part, an interest in sex is normal, healthy, and human. Here it is not necessary to ask the government to bestow, in the campus slogan of the day, "All Power to the People" because they already have it. That trust, it seems to me, should also extend to the realm of whether or not to evince an interest in words and pictures about sex.

Chapter 11

Effects as a Factor in a No Win Game

68th Annual Meeting, American Sociological Association, New York City
August, 17, 1973

Pundits and politicians rarely agree. There are exceptions. I am about to note one.

Elizabeth Drew of the *Atlantic Monthly* once described participation on a presidential commission as a "self-inflicted hotfoot." When President Johnson confronted the congressional mandate to appoint the Commission on Obscenity and Pornography he asserted that "This is a hot potato in a no win game." Thus, the object of our attention today seemed destined to evoke a heated political temperature

What, in fact, was the molten condition of our commission? Let me give you my reading of the gauge as fired by the critical role of effect studies.

The COP was conceived in the Congress, born in the White House, and after twenty-seven months of life, was buried without honor by both parent institutions.

Now, three years later, it is clear that the third branch of the federal government is not interested in resurrection. In recent obscenity rulings, the Supreme Court bypassed evidence from the Commission. Indeed, the Court has made it less likely that empirical research will penetrate future policies and influence control procedures.

A serious social science research effort has thus been deemed irrelevant. The product was denounced by the Senate as "degrading" and rejected as "morally bankrupt" by President Nixon.

It is not known whether these reactions were generated with or without benefit of exposure to any or to all of the 3,250 pages reported in one general and nine technical volumes.

It is known that 109 people contributed to 68 separate studies that cost the taxpayers $1,743,000.

It can also be established that this Commission had more input from social scientists than any other commission in government history. Thus, we have a clear-cut case of the failure of a our disciplines to influence government policy.

More than that, research has had the opposite impact of that intended by the majority of the commissioners in their final assessment. Facts have not stilled fears. Laws are more likely to be added than repealed. There is now more rather than less resistance to the idea that empirical research is relevant for legislation or for judicial rulings.

Could it have been otherwise?

Effects as a Catalyst

Unlike other well-publicized commissions, the COP was not created in response to an immediate crisis, such as an assassination or civil disorder. Neither was it born because the President wished to mobilize support for programs, show concern about a problem, gain new policy ideas, or launch an educational effort. To the contrary, President Johnson was a reluctant participant.

The creation of an expert advisory body was, rather, an attempt by Congress to do something about an irritant that had divided it and had frustrated legislative action for some time.

Going back to the Gathings Committee in 1952, there had been hearings before various committees to vent alarm about pornography. Mail from constituents and pressure from citizen groups brought a flood of complaints about the "rising tide of smut."

Ironically, this torrent probably grew out of the freer flow of sex materials following the 1957 Supreme Court ruling that obscenity was not protected speech. In litigation over the meaning and application of standards for determining what is "obscene," ambiguity led to uncertainty, which, in turn, promoted the entrepreneurship that promoted the distribution of sex materials.

Congress was then caught in a cross-fire between constituents with complaints and members with constitutional uncertainties.Civil libertarians and moral authoritarians were in a legislative deadlock. Senator Karl Mundt said, "It seems to me we are facing up to the alternative of using the commission approach or doing nothing."

The break toward agreement came when the idea of scientific evidence on "effects" was embraced. Ironically, again, no Senatorial statement implied anything other than the evidence would surely show that obscenity had ill outcomes.

At this point, Senator Mundt, a key figure in the drive to control obscenity, added that "...a great deal of work has been done by sociologists and others in this field, and I would hope that with adequate staffing the Commission could come up with a consensus of the findings on this problem."

In October 1967, Congress passed Public Law 90-100. The requirement to study effects was a central and fateful step. Congress asserted that knowledge of the effects of exposure to explicit sex material was relevant for making decisions about the forms of control that a society might exercise over obscenity. That decision had powerful impact:

◆   It de-politicized the selection of commissioners;

◆   It influenced the hiring of staff;

◆   It gave direction to the work;

◆   It affected recommendations;

◆   It stimulated minority dissent; and

◆   It flavored reception of the report--whether by friendly or by hostile readers.

This feature of the congressional mandate was also a departure from precedent set in the interpretation of obscenity law. Two cases make this point.

In the landmark Roth decision of 1957, the Supreme Court held that the protection of the First and Fourteenth Amendments, with their requirement that harm or immediate danger of harm be shown in justification of a governmental prohibition, do not apply to the dissemination of the "obscene."

Furthermore, following the commission report in 1970, the Court stated that effects can be assumed and need not be proven by scientific inquiry. It is therefore now permissible for legislatures to act against obscenity on the basis of unprovable assumptions concerning effects.

This is a different approach to effects from that taken by Congress in authorizing the commission, and it certainly was not the principle that guided the commission in carrying out its mandate.

The Commissioners

The law required the President to appoint "...persons having expert knowledge in the fields of obscenity and antisocial behavior, including but not limited to psychiatrists, sociologists, psychologists, criminologists, jurists, lawyers, and others from organizations and professions who have special and practical competence or experience with respect to obscenity laws and their application to juveniles."

It is difficult to find out how these guidelines were translated into choices. The "talent hunt" described to me at the time of my appointment, and again recently by a Presidential assistant, involved a problem of omission more than anything else. This meant fending off organizations desperate for representation. For example, friends of Charles Keating, Jr., a prime lobbyist before Congress, worked hard to get President Johnson to appoint him. But even the influence of Senator Frank J. Lausche (D., Ohio), himself a prominent and outspoken antipornographer, was unavailing.

President Johnson did appoint an un-related Keating to the commission, a former Republican Senator from New York, Kenneth Keating, then a judge. Kenneth Keating resigned from the Commission in June 1969, when President Nixon appointed him Ambassador to India. His departure took from the Commission its only national political figure.

Nixon then made his only appointment to the Commission, Charles H. Keating, Jr., a Cincinnati lawyer and founder of the Citizens for Decent Literature. His arrival came when the Commission had been under way for one year. Procedures had been adopted, and the research program had been initiated.

Charles Keating took strong exception to procedures. He attended only three sessions of the Commission, each time briefly, during the remaining fifteen months. Even though he chose not to participate in work and deliberations, the final 646-page report of the Commission contained a vigorous 117-page dissent by Keating. In retrospect, his appointment by President Nixon is all the more remarkable because of Keating's general assessment of commissions carried in the final report:

So-called Presidential Commissions do not work. They never will. Such Commissions, in my opinion, are not a valid part of the American political system. The structure of the Commission on Obscenity and

Pornography was similar to that of other Commissions. This Commission was not responsible to anyone, either to the President who appointed it, the Congress which created it, or to the people whom the Congress represented. In the case of Commission on Obscenity and Pornography, with men such as Jack Valenti and Abe Fortas in key advisory roles in the Johnson Administration, it was more likely than not that the orientation of the Commission for permissiveness would be exactly opposite the orientation intended by Congress; namely for moral discipline and responsibility.

Keating spoke authoritatively about his own belated appointment: "The White House knew when I was appointed my interest was to control pornography. They didn't send me in as an objective observer."

Although it might not have been possible to select without reference to constituencies, Johnson's appointments did not, with one exception, have an apparent vested interest one way or the other about obscenity and pornography.

The exception was Father Hill, Executive Secretary of Morality in the Media, Inc., This he described as "the interfaith organization working to counter the effects of obscene material on the young, and working toward media based on the principles of truth, taste, inspiration, and love."

If other members had pre-existing commitments, they perhaps more closely resembled disinterest than anything else.

Geography and gender are easy to identify for the sixteen men and two women from fourteen states on the commission. Constituencies can only be inferred. Lawyers, professors, and clergymen were prominent, but even here there was overlap. One member was both a professor of broadcast film art and an ordained Methodist minister. Three other commissioners were ordained clergymen: one rabbi, one Catholic priest, and one administrator of a Methodist retirement home.

One-third of the commissioners had law degrees and came from positions as dean of a law school, chief judge of a state juvenile court, judge in a federal court of appeals, attorney for the Motion Picture Association of America (the only nonwhite member), businessman in the book and magazine distribution field, and state attorney general.

Three sociologists were appointed. Two were professors and a third was director of social research for a television network.

Two commissioners were medical doctors, both psychiatrists, one a professor and the other from the Menninger Foundation.

Of the remaining members, one was a professor of English, one a director of a university library, and one a vice-president of a book publishing company.

These appointments were mainly male, white, professional persons, none of whom were under forty years of age. A majority held graduate degrees and either were or had been professors or teachers in law, theology, sociology, criminology, English, communications, psychiatry, and library science. Several commissioners had been presidents of national bodies including the American Association of Law Schools, the American Library Association, the American Orthopsychiatric Association, the American Association for Public Opinion Research, and the American Society of Criminology.

This aggregation had a bent toward curiosities cultivated in an academic setting largely devoid of sophisticated sensitivity to Washington politics. No one was aware that Lyndon Johnson sensed we would be in a "no win game." Nor could it have been known that his successor, Richard Nixon, would virtually ensure a lost effort by appointments to the Supreme Court.

Effects as an Issue

Public Law 90-100 opened by asserting:

> The Congress finds that the traffic in obscenity and pornography is a matter of national concern. The problem, however, is not one which can be solved at any one level of government. The Federal government has the responsibility to investigate the gravity of this situation and to determine whether such materials are harmful to the public, and particularly to minors, and whether more effective methods should be devised to control the transmission of such materials.

The law also stated that "after a thorough study *which shall include a study of the causal relationship* of such materials to antisocial behavior" the commission was "to recommend advisable, appropriate, effective, and constitutional means to deal effectively with such traffic in obscenity and pornography." It was further prescribed that it was the duty of the commission "To study the effect of obscenity and pornography upon the public, and particularly minors, and its relationship to crime and other antisocial behavior."

This inclusion of effect studies was a thorn in the side of three commissioners. Despite ardent advocacy of the "rule of law," a minority report by Commissioners Father Hill and Reverend Link, concurred in by Charles Keating, Jr., asserted:

> The Commission has deliberately and carefully avoided coming to grips with the basic underlying issue. The government interest in regulating pornography has always related primarily to the prevention of moral corruption and not to prevention of overt criminal acts and conduct, or the protection of persons from being shocked and/or offended. We believe it impossible, and totally unnecessary, to attempt to prove or disprove a cause-effect relationship between pornography and criminal behavior.

In his dissent, Commissioner Keating elaborated views on effects as follows:

> The mandate of Congress was not simply to study the "effect" of obscenity upon the public and minors, but more complete: "... to study the effect of obscenity and pornography upon the public, and particularly minors, and its relationship to crime and other antisocial behavior...." I read the "relationship" study as being at least co-equal with the "effect" study. Further, I do not read this duty to study "the relationship (of obscenity) to crime and other antisocial behavior" to be construed so narrow as to require a "direct" cause-effect relationship. For example, in one case of a rape of a 12-year-old girl by a 20-year-old boy, a girlie magazine belonging to the suspect was left at the scene of the attack and was identified by the victim as being in the youth's presence at the time of the attack. The presence of the girlie magazine in the possession of the rapist at the time of the attack is warrant notice as a statistic giving evidence of the "relationship" of obscenity to antisocial behavior and bearing on the "rationality" of such legislation.

Keating claimed that when he submitted a memorandum calling for such a study, it was ignored. As a point of fact, it was not. A careful analysis of his proposal was made. He was provided elementary statements about evidence, proof, and inference in social science. That critique drew heavily from Samuel Stouffer's brilliant 1950 paper on "Some Observations on Study Design," which explained the advantages of a before and after study with control and experimental groups--the four-fold table model. That account included the following phrase pinpointing the problem with Keating's proposal, "Sometimes, believe it or not, we have only one cell."

Division of Labor

The Commission organized four panels to address legal issues, traffic and distribution of sex materials, effects of exposure, and positive approaches to control. Each panel had its own chairman (a judge for legal, the attorney general for traffic, a sociologist for effects, and a psychiatrist for positive approaches). The three sociologists huddled together on the effects panel, which had five members, all Ph.D.'s. Two staff sociologists worked on the effects assignment.

Each panel processed research, received interim papers, and produced a final report to the Commission. Commissioners were responsible for reading three panel reports besides the one they had worked on. As the deadline for decision approached, that was a heavy demand. The entire experience was much like entering an intensive two-year research seminar, having a two-week study period, and concluding with a two-day final examination.

The effects panel was deeply involved in the planning, development, and evaluation of the competitive bids for the Commission's largest study. This was a national probability sample survey involving face-to-face interviews with 2,486 adults and 769 young persons (aged fifteen to twenty). This study cost approximately $225 thousand and produced data used by all the panels.

The survey had three general purposes: (1) to identify the amount, frequency, and circumstances of the public's exposure to erotic materials; (2) to describe community standards and norms pertaining to distribution, consumption, and control of erotica; and (3) to collect other relevant data concerning the correlates of exposure to erotic materials.

Key findings of the national survey underscore effects as a factor in public opinion, which, in turn, had considerable influence, when coupled with experimental and other studies, on the Commission's final recommendations:

♦   When presented with an array of presumed effects, including those classified as "socially desirable," "neither clearly socially approved nor disapproved," and "socially undesirable," there were no presumed effects upon which more than two-thirds of the adult population agreed (The most widely held opinions, also supported by experimental studies, were that erotic materials excite people sexually and provide information about sex).

♦   People were generally far more likely to say that they had personally experienced socially desirable or neutral effects than socially undesirable effects. Persons who had envisaged undesirable effects rarely or never reported having personally experienced them, and were more likely to say they had occurred without reference either to themselves or to anyone they personally knew.

♦   A majority of American adults (59 percent) believed that adults should be allowed to read or see any explicit sex materials they wanted to.

♦   Two-fifths of American adults would change their views about restrictive laws, on one direction or another, on the basis of clear demonstrations that there were or were not harmful effects. Of these, about one-half would be inclined to sanction availability of erotic materials if they felt sure that such materials would have no harmful effects; on the other hand, eight persons in ten would oppose availability of such materials if they were convinced that such materials were harmful.

♦   Almost half the population believed that laws against sexual materials would be "impossible to enforce." If restrictive laws were to be passed, 62 percent would rather have federal than state or local legislation.

Research Strategy

The initial concern in the effects panel was directed toward specification of the stimulus and identification of possible effects. Ultimately, thirty-six possible consequences were identified and classified as harmful, neutral, or helpful.

The panel then formulated seven general research goals, outlined appropriate research designs, and examined feasible methods of inquiry. A variety of methods were judged to be responsive to goals.

A decision was made to employ multiple methods to complement and supplement one another. Thus, in a variety of settings, using a battery of effect indicators, the panel authorized surveys, quasi-experimental studies, studies of rates and incidence at the community level, and controlled experiments.

The experience of earlier commissions, and sensitivity to problems confronted in sex-oriented research, induced the panel to stress limitations in methods and findings, major problems not resolved, and suggestions for how these might be approached in the future.

Such references did not, and should not, ward off criticism from scientific sources. Perhaps these will overcome the mis-perception that the Commission found "no effects."

The panel report is replete with findings of physiological, attitudinal, judgmental, and behavioral effects, some commonly anticipated (e.g., arousal), some surprising (e.g., "calloused" sexual attitudes toward women decreased immediately after viewing erotic films and continued to decrease up to two weeks later). Many effects are suggested by simple correlation's, but the direction of the relationship was clarified by reference to controlled experiments.

After analyzing the pattern of results from thirty-nine studies, including fourteen controlled experiments, the panel summarized its conclusion in the opening statement to it its report as follows: *"If a case is to made against "pornography" in 1970, it will have to me made on grounds other than demonstrated effects of a damaging personal or social nature. Empirical research designed to clarify the question has found no reliable evidence to date that exposure to explicit sexual materials plays a significant role in the causation of delinquent or criminal sexual behavior among youth or adults."*

This statement became the most widely quoted excerpt from the entire Commission report.

Public Hearings

From the outset, some members pressed for immediate public hearings. Their request was not granted. The majority concluded that in the first stage of its work, public hearings would not be a likely source of accurate data or a wise expenditure of limited resources. The social scientists concurred. The judgment was to postpone hearings until data were at hand that could be illuminated in such a forum.

That decision gave rise to strain. Two commissioners finally could not tolerate delay. In February 1970, Commissioners Hill and Link conducted, at their own expense, a series of public hearings in eight cities. They described their witnesses as "a cross-section of the community, ranging from members of the judiciary to members of women's clubs." In New York, this approach produced twenty-six out of twenty-seven witnesses who "expressed concern and asked for remedial measures." Hill and Link concluded "that the majority of American people favor tighter controls." They used this impression to counter conclusions to the contrary from the commission's national survey.

In May 1970, the full Commission held four days of public hearings. Twenty-eight witnesses were heard in Los Angeles and thirty were heard in Washington, D. C. In Los Angeles, these included the mayor, a movie star (Charlton Heston), a police captain, a judge, and persons representing Planned Parenthood, the American Library Association, Citizens for Decent Literature, the National Council of Teachers of English, and Christians and Jews for Law and Morality.

The hearings in Washington voiced similar point and counterpoint. All sides presented earnest counsel, and appeared hopeful that the Report, still five months away, would support their positions.

These four days would have passed largely unnoticed had it not been for a bizarre incident toward the end of the last day. It merits reference only because it provoked an instant worldwide mass-media response that heightened the visibility of the Commission. From that day forward the Commission lost its treasured anonymity. More important, the incident spurred public speculation about the nature of the final report. Doors were now open to political definitions as the Commission moved toward the final day of judgment.

It is not my purpose to suggest that obscenity is as American as cottage cheese pie. However, the thought did occur to me on the afternoon of May 13, 1970, in the New Senate Office Building. That day Thomas King Forcade, coordinator of the Underground Press Syndicate and self-styled "self-ordained minister of the Church of Life," concluded his testimony by pushing a pie in my face.

This was dramatic. It violated the decorum of an official hearing. But it had a stronger offensive intent.

In a setting where the subject was how we shall or shall not communicate about sex, the incident rudely broke through the boundaries set for the "proper" discussion of that topic, even when the limits are stretched to accommodate the rawest reach of crude expression.

Five times Mr. Forcade ended paragraphs of testimony about "witch-hunts" and "McCarthy-like hearings" with a ringing epithet "Fuck off and fuck censorship!"

And at one point during a curious silent spell, a three-year old girl accompanying Forcade's forces came toward the podium and echoed the first half of his refrain. Not even the First Amendment lawyers on the Commission were equipped by precedent to respond to that outburst.

The pie came in response to my challenge of his allegations about "McCarthy-like" procedures. I resisted the temptation to respond with force. Midst clicking cameras, I informed him that he had not answered my question. He was puzzled and quickly turned to pass out leaflets bearing the message, "All Power to the Pie."

The newspapers found the spectacle irresistible. Only the *New York Times* quoted my prediction that the press would play it up and overlook the substance of argument from two days of testimony. Because the pie thrower had signaled the press ahead of time, there were pictures for the front pages, to be adorned with headlines.

I was variously identified as an "Obscenity Panelist," "Smut Prober," and "Pornography Fighter." The caption in the *Honolulu Star-Bulletin* read, "Cream Pie Was Cleanest Thing at the Hearing." The *Akron Beacon Journal* noted, "Yippie Witness Makes Custard Last Stand." Even the *New York Times* came through with "Pornography Commissioner Gets More Than an Eyeful of Cheesecake." One more hearing had become political theater.

A barrage of editorials and letters followed. A few applauded turning of the cheek, but most favored an eye for an eye and a pie for a pie. I was charged with being the kind of professor whose permissiveness had created the on-going wave of campus unrest.

The mail eventually subsided, but it picked up again after the report of the Commission was issued. Once again, the charge of permissiveness thundered through the postal system. This time, given my stance on the recommendations supporting the repeal of laws, it was not without justification.

Advice and Dissent

The moment of decision, if not truth, finally arrived. It came to pass in a remote Virginia site where the Commission met for two long days to review panel reports, to reflect, and to recommend in accord with congressional guidelines.

The first day was devoted to studying, questioning, and revising the four panel reports. The draft of the effects report received thorough scrutiny and discussion. Technical questions were pursued with vigor. The sociologists were back in the classroom answering questions on the meaning of crime statistics, control groups, probability sampling, correlation, interview-completion rates, and the like. Substantive findings were also highlighted. A consistent pattern did not support allegations of "harm" from exposure to erotica.

The focus shifted on the second day. Members expressed feelings and conclusions. Reference to research diminished. One sensed the appearance of outside reference groups. This did not alter the stance of sociologists with tenured positions in universities. In their policy role, it was easier for them to move with the data. Others moved too, but more selectively.

The commission chairman, William Lockhart, Dean of the Law School at the University of Minnesota, a recognized authority on constitutional law, had brought his experience to bear on the work of the commission. Even with the prominent presence of social scientists, it is unlikely that the commission could have stayed on an empirical track without his reasoned support and vigorous leadership. He resisted all effort to use money for public relations and opted, instead, to allocate funds to research. He read every article, research proposal, and report. By his example, it became clear that this was to be a working commission, not one that merely reviewed the work of others.

A positive appraisal of Lockhart was widely shared. However, not by Charles Keating who stated that Lockhart was committed to preconceived goals because "...although Professor Lockhart did not pay his current dues to avoid the telltale association, he is and has been, for all practical purposes, a member of the American Civil Liberties Union."

The chairman ignored the slur. He clearly was affected by the research on effects. Dean Lockhart had said that before he undertook heading the commission he had favored control of obscenity for both children and adults, but that the scientific studies of erotic material had changed his mind with regard to adults. He found the evidence "overwhelming" and concluded that "erotic materials do not contribute to antisocial behavior of any sort".

The sociologists were more cautious in their characterization of the evidence, but more radical in the application of it to policy.

I did not find the evidence "overwhelming," but rather convincing, or even compelling.This was strong enough to move me to a recommendation, shared with another sociologist, Marvin Wolfgang, that all existing statutes on obscenity and pornography should be repealed.

This stance was taken because we honestly believed that the weight of the evidence supported it. We also hoped it would counter the other extreme presented by conservative dissidents, thereby adding credibility to the majority position.

Ultimately, the entire two-year experience boiled down to ten recommendations approved by a clear majority, with dissents appended by various minorities. Six recommendations directly involved legislation; four did not.

The central non-legislative recommendation, the first listed in the Commission report, called for a massive sex education effort; ten characteristics of this proposed program were described. Although this recommendation received strong approval from many sources, including commendation from the magazine of the National Parent-Teacher's Association, most such responses were lost in the backwash of the initial negative official reaction to the report. Overlooked were proposals by the majority recommending restricting sale of pictorial material to juveniles and controlling the mailing and public display of explicit sex materials.

It was the fallout from one particular recommendation, approved by twelve of the seventeen participating members, that precluded public consideration of the aforementioned ideas.

That bomb was marked as follows: "*The Commission recommends that federal, state, and local legislation prohibiting the sale, exhibition, or distribution of sexual materials to consenting adults should be repealed.*"

Nine summary statements supported this recommendation, six of which drew directly form the empirical studies of the Commission.

The potency of this one recommendation, and the volatility of the even stronger position taken by myself and Wolfgang dominated official reaction and the media coverage.

One New York writer, Stanley Kauffmann, assessed the situation in dramatic terms. He called September 30, 1970, a red-letter day in American social history. He found the majority report published that day, a revolutionary document. He called the Lockhart report, and the Larsen-Wolfgang supplement, strong stuff. He suggested that they might even be "anti-American" because they put the central issue right on the line: the commission did not contend that pornography was desirable, but that the law could not deal with it satisfactorily. Moreover, he noted, the report implied that once obscurantist and provocative laws were out of the way, there would be more chance for the social changes already in motion to prosper. Accordinly, he concluded, the Lockhart report is just possibly "epoch-making, and it's an epoch that needs to be made."

Conclusion

Three years have passed. There are now more laws on obscenity, but also more explicit sex materials in more places in our society than ever before in our history.

Much of what was within the Court's reach to clarify is now passed on to the local scene. Recent rulings decentralize decisions. But old tests of "prurience" and "offensiveness" remain. "Redeeming social value" has been replaced by "Serious literary, artistic, political, or scientific value" in the trio of standards serving as a test of obscenity.

Confusion on criteria and definitions will persist. Controls will be more varied. New restrictions may heighten rather than dampen curiosity. Obscenity laws have a way of becoming a kind of government "Bad Housekeeping Seal of Approval."

Some states might be moved by commission recommendations. If they are, given the Court's guidelines, the argument will not be won by reference to social science data, which could, through a concern with effects studies, have altered the test for obscenity. That test continues on ambiguous grounds. Empirical proof or disproof of damaging personal or social harm is not relevant.

The ultimate loss from this effort was not the failure to adopt recommendations. It was the failure to demonstrate that empirical research on effects is relevant for policy research.

Chapter 12

How Far Can We Go?

Annual Conference, Magazine Publisher's Association, Palm Beach, Florida
October 20, 1977

The keynote of this conference requires an answer to the question, "How Far Can We Go?"

Your printed program indicates that this question will be directed toward every aspect of the magazine business. My assignment is both limited and large. I am to focus on how decisions are made concerning taste, the public's conscience, and the public's vulnerability.

Such a formulation clearly suggests that your editorial judgments are affected to some degree by publics that extend beyond your advertisers and farther than your immediate circulation lists. Thus it conjures up a vision of editors and publishers with their ears to the ground. This is a commendable posture in a democratic society. It does, however, leave other parts of your anatomy exposed for ready assault. I say that merely to emphasize that while listening to the public is a necessary stance, it cannot be done without risk.

In fact, effective listening requires special sensitivity. Since personal tastes can come to be defined (through the media) as a matter of social right and wrong, the public becomes important not only for its tastes but also for its perceptions of the tastes of others.

In this presentation, I intend to outline problems and findings concerning how publics may be taken into account when matters of taste are at stake. The question of deciding how to communicate about sex will receive special emphasis. Actual sexual conduct or behavior are more than simple matters of taste. Words and pictures about such conduct, however, clearly involve taste oriented decisions.

So we ask, which way is the pendulum swinging on such decisions, and why? Is the sexual revolution over, or has it just started?

My answer will constitute the climax of this presentation.

Taste: A Matter of Dispute?

I once had a teacher who ruled out certain topics proposed for discussion in her English literature class, including sex, religion, and politics. She drew limits with a ringing reference to a Latin proverb, "De gustibus non est disputandum" which she proudly announced meant that "On matters of taste there can be no disputing."

Later, we read *The Education of Henry Adams*. Here, in less somber terms, Adams expressed a similar perspective when he wrote, "These questions of taste. . . .need no settlement. Everyone carries his own inch-rule of taste, and amuses himself by applying it, triumphantly, wherever he travels."

Such private orientations can be satisfying. In fact, it worked quite well for me until I came up against an instance where private taste came to be defined as a public matter, as a social issue, and even as a moral concern.

In 1968, I was one of eighteen persons appointed by President Johnson to the Commission on Obscenity and Pornography, a minefield of opportunities to test matters of taste. After two years of effort, we issued one general report and nine technical volumes that recorded in detail 68 separate studies, 39 dealing with effects, that cost the taxpayers $1,743,000. In 1970, the report, including its ten recommendations, was delivered to the Congress and to the White House.

President Nixon immediately denounced the work as degrading and "morally bankrupt." There is no evidence that this judgment was generated by exposure to any or all of the 3,250 pages of information that the commission produced. I suspect, however, that matters of taste, or the perceptions of public taste for political reasons, were somehow involved.

Indeed, Nixon's absolutist position was reminiscent of what John Ruskin had written many years earlier. "Taste," he observed, "is the only morality. . . Tell me what you like, and I'll tell you what you are."

Nixon told us what we were, and he unleashed Vice-President Agnew to speak out against the immorality of it all.

On this matter, and perhaps on others that arose later in his administration, the President gave no indication of having taken counsel with a contrary position from the salty pen of George Bernard Shaw who, in his notes to *Caesar and Cleopatra*, stated that "A man of great common sense and good taste, meaning thereby a man without originality or moral courage."

No, the President, and many other Ruskinites, condemned the Commission and ignored most of its findings and recommendations.

Clearly, they were offended by our advocacy of the idea that consenting adults should have the legal right to exercise their tastes when it comes to reading or viewing sexual materials.

Reflecting on this experience, I have concluded that the old Latin proverb was wrong.

The modern version should read, "On matters of taste, there is nothing but dispute."

Role of the Media: To Reflect or to Shape?

Taste is not only disputed, but public taste is usually lamented. So it has been throughout history. Long before the development of the mass media, an ancient Roman, Gaius Valerius Catullus, in 50 B.C., captured a phrase that has been reiterated down through the centuries: "Oh, this age! How tasteless and ill-bred it is!"

In recent decades, the various forms of mass communication have each taken their turn at being charged as the chief propagators of this low state of tastelessness.

The merit of this allegation has been subject to scrutiny by the methods of modern social science. The results are rarely unambiguous. It is difficult to isolate causal factors. Clearly, more than the medium and the message are involved.

It would be convenient if we could place full responsibility for public taste on the creators of mass media messages. In 1807, William Wordsworth would seem to have it so when he wrote, "Every great and original writer, in proportion as he is great or original, must himself create the taste by which he to be relished."

There is, however, also a receiving component in the model of how communication works. It is complicated in its function. No one has described it better than Shakespeare did in King Richard II: "Things sweet to taste prove in digestion sour."

Whatever your conception of the process of communication, the theme of this conference implies unease about your possible role in shaping tastes if not the moral tone of society.

Even if your intent is merely to reflect what is going on, the implication is that you are not always comfortable with what your mirror reveals.

Put another way, I think "How far we can go?" remains problematic whether we believe that the public taste determines the media fare, or believe that the media fare determines the public taste.

This is the case because neither the chicken nor the egg came first, both were preceded by a cultural hatchery. That is, both the media and the public are subject to social norms, those shared understandings of what persons should or should not say or do under various circumstances.

The fundamental answer to "How far can we go?" has to do with the state of social norms, and our capacity to sense them.

Sex and the Media

By your raising the theme question of this conference, I now sense that some of you believe that others of you have already gone too far. That is, you may think that elements of the industry are pushing too hard against the tolerance limits of the community.

If I am right, now the problem begins to get sticky. "Going too far" probably yields mixed results. Sometimes it means good business. Take a possible case in point: the matter of profits for the magazine dealer. Here, no matter how far you have gone, you undoubtedly seek to go farther. According to the Audit Bureau of Circulation report for the second half of 1976, the total number of copies sold, and the total dealer profits for magazines, were up from earlier periods.

But issues around the public's taste, conscience, and vulnerability do not seep forth from these figures until we examine what engines of content drive this business success. The top ten Audit Bureau of Circulation magazine titles for the last half of 1976 were the same top ten that had appeared for the first half, but the arrangement of places had shifted. *Hustler*, formerly number seven, had moved up to number four in average dealer profits per issue--a matter of some $787,457 each month. Only *Penthouse*, *Playboy*, and *Family Circle*, in that order, ranked above *Hustler*.

What can we infer from this rank order? With one exception, the content of the four top magazines clearly suggests that sex sells, and also produces significant profits. It also implies that these materials serve widespread interests, if not needs.

There are many publics out there, some larger than others, some more influential than others, some more critical to our present concerns than others. This differentiation might be troublesome. Particularly so if more and more elements in your industry attempt to cater to the interests already being addressed by those currently at the top of the bottom-line success.

How far can individual publishing entrepreneurs go before they create a problem for the collectivity such as that represented by your Association?

That question arises because we sense the possibility of a threat to a delicate balance. It is possible that by serving one public by "going too far" you may alienate yet other publics. The ensuing contest could place the reputation of magazines in jeopardy as you are assailed by critics who proclaim that the entire industry is debasing human values.

The above scenario is about what has been going on in television. Now, to be sure, there are major differences between TV and magazines, including the fact that your audience has to be literate. But, nonetheless, both media forms are currently asking "How far can we go?" and each might learn something from the other about the public processes that influence content decisions.

At the moment, television has been propelled by powerful pressures from specialized publics to reduce violence in programming. We now appear to have less violence, but more sex, or as one TV Editor put it this week, "The result is TV as tease. Allusions to sex, or the illusion of sex, without the real thing. Silly sex. Sex as a sophomoric joke. Panting, heaving, potboiler 'passion.' And only occasionally, realistic sexuality, sensitively portrayed."

An NBC vice-president told the Association for Consumer Research last week that commercial television is still the "most conservative of the mass media on matters of sex." Like other executives, he says TV does not want to be a trendsetter of the "sexual revolution." He said that television lags behind prevailing sexual attitudes, and that TV tries to reach a compromise between those who want creative innovation and those who urge conservatism.

So, cautiously, television proceeds to fill the void left by reduced violence with a kind of "middle ground morality." In the process, they pass on the chance for frank expression on legitimate concerns about sexuality. Uncertainty about viewer response, and anxiety about how pressure groups might react, undoubtedly reinforces that decision.

That may be appropriate for a mass medium like television, but is this the way you want to answer, "How far can we go?"

I suspect not. And I want to indicate two basic reasons why you have the latitude for a more creative attitude. One of these has to do with social norms as reflected in the public perception of public beliefs. The other has to do with the link between attitudes and behavior in the so-called sexual revolution.

Public Perception of Public Beliefs

Neither ordinary public opinion polling nor the conventional approach to social norms around matters of taste bear on how far you can go. Something more is needed than merely the expressions of representative samples of specified publics as to their own preferences and attitudes.

We also need to know their estimates of what they think that others think, feel, or do in this same realm. The imagined or perceived views that people have of others is a significant factor in judgments and expressions of taste and conceptions of morality.

As important as perceptions are, their accuracy cannot automatically be assumed. Indeed, moral principles with relatively little support may exert considerable influence because they are mistakenly thought to represent the views of the majority. This, I realize, is a complex idea, but one of importance, and thus it requires a little more amplification.

On a number of social issues, we have research that affords comparisons between the actual and the perceived distribution of opinions. Two main trends emerge from analysis in this area. One is called "the looking-glass perception," or the belief that others think the same as oneself. The other is called "the conservative bias." Together they produce the paradox where the minority perceives itself to be the majority, and where the majority perceives itself to be the minority.

That pretty well describes much of the confusion we have today on matters of sex. And this is one reason why I believe you can go farther in this realm of communication with less risk than your perception may have led you to believe is possible.

But there is an even more fundamental ground and need for "going further" in a creative and responsible way, and here we must turn to a few ideas on the so-called sexual revolution.

On the Sexual Revolution

As noted earlier, television seems to feel comfortable when its content lags behind prevailing sexual attitudes. In this realm, there is another lag that needs to be considered as you ponder how far you can go.

Attitudes are rarely in perfect alignment with behavior. Indeed, behavioral changes usually precede attitude or opinion changes. This is surely the case in most aspects of the sexual realm today. Which brings us back to the opening question, is the sexual revolution over?

No, it is not over; we are barely half-way into three of its fundamental phases. Furthermore, the behavioral changes already wrought are probably more extensive than perceived public opinion allows or that general communication practices have yet revealed.

This is why I say that you have an opportunity to go farther in this realm than your present perceptions of opinions may have led you to conclude.

If the sexual revolution succeeds, one can foresee an America where we have the same kind of adult sexual pluralism as we have pluralism other areas. Will the country become as safe for sexual diversity as it has become for religious and political diversity?

My colleagues who study human sexual behavior have produced evidence to indicate that the first phase of the revolution is already past. This phase, dealing with non-productive sex, involved the rejection of the popular requirement that persons, male and female, must be virgins when they marry. By and large, they are not; and attitudes are catching up with that behavioral fact.

Phase two is where society is now. We are now in the middle of a struggle to define the role in society of homosexuality. The discussion, at least, has come out of the closet.

The third phase of the revolution is upon us, but we are not dealing with it forthrightly as yet. This phase involves the challenge to the viability of the family as we have known it. There are numerous indicators, including rising divorce rates, and changing sexual patterns. The majority of both married males and married females have now engaged in extramarital sexual relations.

Only 29 states today offer any kind of sex education in their school programs. If we are to survive the impact of the sex revolution as a society, more valid information about human sexuality will have to be made available earlier for nearly all segments of our population, surely beginning no later than with the adolescent stage of human development

Both personal and social health could depend on that.

Here, then, is your challenge.

You are in a position to provide clear, accurate, meaningful, responsible information about human sexuality.

The problems associated with sex today need the critical interpretive treatment that the printed media can perhaps do better than any other form of mass communication.

That far, at least, you can go.

Censorship

A censor, the dictionary informs us, is an official who examines books, magazines, movies, etc., for the purpose of suppressing parts deemed objectionable on moral, political, military, or other grounds.

My first direct exposure to the work of government censors came during a sabbatical around-the-world tour. Below are notes on this journey shared with professional librarians, committed antagonists of censors.

Discovering national forms of censorship brought into focus the power of the First Amendment of the American constitution. Until then, I had not fully sensed how unique, and how radical, the idea that "Congress shall make no laws abridging..." is on the world scene. One has to marvel that a decision made about two hundred years ago still stands so that the United States is the only country in the world that prohibits the government from exercising prior restraint over the expression of ideas--particularly controversial, distasteful, erroneous, and dangerous ones.

Does this mean we live in a country where the privilege of free speech is unbounded? No, after the fact of expression there can be adjudication and the application of sanctions as, for example, against libelous utterance. And, as noted earlier, obscenity is not protected by the First amendment of the constitution. Since that was first decided by the Supreme Court in 1957, legal contests have waxed and waned as authorities have struggled over defining and applying the criteria by which something shall be judged obscene. My first major opportunity to participate directly in the legal process came in 1971 when I was subpoenaed to appear as a witness for the defense in the case of the U. S. vs. Hamling.

Some excerpts from my testimony on the, then, three-pronged test of obscenity are presented here. Technically, the materials in question could only be deemed legally obscene if, when viewed as a whole, they: (1) appealed to prurient interest in sex; (2) affronted contemporary community standards so as to be patently offensive; and (3) lacked redeeming social value. Should any of one of these tests be judged not to obtain then that body of material is not obscene. Accordingly, the courtroom becomes the theater for competing authorities to argue the presence or absence of prurience, offensiveness, and social value.

To be engaged in this legal contest was a novel communicative challenge. The text of a full day's testimony revealed that, as one trained to find conditional probability outcomes from empirical inquiry, I was not particularly attuned to the rules of discourse and evidence practiced in the adversarial tradition. From this, I gained some impulse to pursue a better understanding of alternative modes of dispute resolution possibly embedded in the general relationship of social science to law (interests later satisfied in my work at the National Science Foundation).

The case was dramatic. I wouldn't have tried to avoid participation even if that had been possible. The challenge was conveyed by headlines in *The National Observer* (11 December 1971): **Can a Presidential Commission's Report Be Obscene? Justice Department Says Yes, in a Suit Against the Publisher of an Illustrated Version.**

The publisher had no connection with the commission. He simply took our non-copyrighted report (as Bantam Books had done earlier for its paperback version), reproduced its text, and added vivid photographs and etchings of explicit sexual acts.

The unillustrated Government Printing Office version sold for $5.50, and the new illustrated version for $12.50 (produced at the cost $1.59 each), with a printing of 100,000 copies. The publisher had also mailed some 50,000 copies of an illustrated flier with a statement asserting that the President's effort to suppress this information was an "inexcusable insult directed at every adult in this country." The graphic brochure was also charged with being obscene.

The outcome of this particular trial (posted following the testimony) notwithstanding, ambiguities of definition have, over the years, made for the relatively freer flow of words and pictures about sex. Accordingly, the issue of effects continues to erupt. However, the agenda for research is now quite different from what it was in 1970 when, curiously, two separate commissions were formed, one to examine media sex and one to examine media violence.

Today, there are interesting theoretical, as well as practical and political, reasons for examining these bodies of media content jointly. That kind of work is underway and, enriched as it is by cross disciplinary efforts, may yet change our whole view of the long-term impact of media presentations.

Had I remained a researcher, instead of moving into science administration, I certainly would have pursued the possible cross-over effects from exposure to the sex and violence content of the mass media.

The hypothesis that a sex behavioral outcome is more likely to flow from violent content than from sexual content is particularly intriguing. But other combinations are possible. Some complexities are identified in the speech I gave to the production personnel of a major American magazine.

Chapter 13

Censors as Sensors
Washington Library Association, Seattle
May 15, 1971

You librarians have a way of evoking strong memories.

I must have been about twelve when I first checked out a book from a public library. It was 1934. We lived in a town of 900 population. These were hard times economically, and that's why I remember the book, *Martin Eden* by Jack London. I also remember the library. It was a little old building located out back between the ice house and the fire station in Junction City, Oregon. I became fond of that modest place and, somehow, still think of it whenever I read Robert Frost declaring--

Some say the world will end in fire,
Some say in ice.
From what I've tasted of desire
I hold with those who favor fire.
But if I had to perish twice,
I think I know enough of hate
To say that for destruction ice
Is also great
And would suffice.

There are at least two reasons why it is a special treat for me to speak today. This conference has an attractive and powerful theme, "This is the Right(s) Year," one that recalls memorable events.

I am also honored to be in the presence of Judith Krug who directs the Office for Intellectual Freedom of the American Library Association. Her leadership has broken more ice and fought more fires in the struggle against censorship than anyone else in the country. I look forward to every issue of the *Newsletter on Intellectual Freedom* issued from her office.

Let me also say that I appreciate the support from the library community for the report of the Commission on Obscenity and Pornography.

The Council of the American Library Association on January 20th urged the Senate and the President of the United States to "reconsider their categorical rejection of this significant data and to encourage the dissemination and evaluation of the materials by the citizenry of the United States," and, further, the Council urged "all libraries to provide their users with complete access to the Report."

I will be happy to respond to any questions about the Commission. As you certainly know, not everyone subscribes to our recommendation that all laws prohibiting the sales, exhibition, or distribution of sexual materials to consenting adults should be repealed. Which brings me to my topic today.

I want to share with you my first encounter with real live censors. Last year on a sabbatical journey around the world, my wife and I visited 25 countries and confirmed a precious fact.

The United States is the only nation in the world where a constitution prevents the government from practicing prior restraint over words and pictures that are disseminated to the public.

What follows are sketches from a diary that I kept about the first ten places we visited. Some elements of these accounts go beyond our topic, but I know you'll forgive me for not censoring out a few notes on sociological tourism.

Notes from Fiji (January 31, 1970)

Fiji has a visible social ladder. At the bottom are native Fijians. Indians (from India), once the underclass, have worked their way up.

Newspaper in Suva carry movie ratings: A for 17 years and over; Y for 14 and over; and G for general.

Tracked down Director of Film Review Board, an optometrist, Dr. Aasghar. Not instructive.

Informative talk with Secretary of board, Waisele Naituku, Ministry of Social Services. Seven persons on Board. Appointed annually by government. In turn, they appoint Censor Board of five citizens to review films.

In 1968, 1,470; in 1969, 847 movies assigned ratings. Why decrease? See annual report to be sent. "Ulysses" rejected totally, mainly because of words. Review Board final authority, serves as appeal group from Censor Board decisions. Local mores and citizen judgments dominate work. Some guidelines employed. New law being drafted with sanctions against exhibitors.

Sex and violence both troublesome. Trend toward tightening violence and liberalizing sex, but not on U.S. scale. Fiji follows New Zealand lead on movie censorship. TV being explored, but adoption some time off.

Fiji good site for TV before-after research, but racial and ethnic conflict, political drive for independence, and impact of tourism calls for complex design.

Film Board Secretary Waituku, black, native, civil servant, moves film censorship. Organizes agenda. Keeps records. Hints of role complexity.

Some topics (mainly sex) elicit attempts to sense tolerance limits of community. Bending allowed.

Violence evokes paternalism. Even if public would tolerate, it would not be good for them.

Notes from New Zealand (February 2-7, 1970)

New Zealand imparts image of order, efficiency, courtesy, and cleanliness. Do signs of solid comfort also signal crashing boredom?

First perceptions of media in Auckland leaves matter unsettled. One TV channel. Broadcasts from about 2 p.m. to 11 p.m. Content like Denmark--variety shows, even a minstrel program.

Newspapers appear more American (deviant acts noted) and less Danish (no long essays or editorials). Big news Sunday was Saturday night "disturbance" at Rock-Festival with 5,000 people. Beer bottles thrown, 25 injured in melee following performance by Robin Gibb. Some arrests for nudity, too. Mauri youth particularly oriented toward hip culture.

Prior restraint by government actually exists. Check of telephone book led to first official I've ever met called "Censor" (D.C. McIntosh, Chief Censor and Registrar of Films, 7-9 Walter Street, Wellington, New Zealand). Friendly, fiftiesh, former civil-servant, gregarious Scot, censor for eight years. Authority from law. Uses it with vigor and pride. Conscientious, independent, proud. Glad he's not Chairman of a Board. Can make decisions by himself. Likes to innovate, as with segregated audiences. Whereas Australia banned "Ulysses," he worked out novel arrangement: husbands could see movie in one theater, wives in another.

On personal side, he seemed a bit isolated and lonely. Enjoyed taking us to pub for special beer. Said "Pubbing" was relaxation, along with growing flowers and herbs in garden. Invited to dinner at home with wife and her mother.

Idea of censor as "sensor" was born in conversation. He visits schools to "sense" trends. Notes limitations to principle. Censor must protect society from itself, as well as protect children.

Liberalizing trend in New Zealand with respect to sex, but still a protective approach. "Fig leaves" put over words and pictures in movie ads. Censor's general guideline is not to permit any public expression that would offend your wife or mother. Segregated experiment is indicative.

Stewart Perry, city librarian of Wellington, long standing member of the Indecent Publications Tribunal. Met in library, a pigeon gray building like the one in Des Moines, Iowa.

Ushered into office where Perry, a man from a J.Arthur Rank movie, offered tea, began eloquent monologue on legal history of literary merit in NZ. From "Who's Who" Perry had me pegged as Arthur Larson, distinguished lawyer from Eisenhower administration. Thus legal emphasis. Correction did not cool ardor for imparting information. Has written history of print censorship in NZ. Sent copy to Washington. Will research details later.

Invited for a drink. Home has stunning view of harbor, marks of good taste, and clear evidence of do-it-yourself repairs. We talked, marveled at view, the Victorian furniture, and moved to private study filled with memorabilia. Collects match-folders.

Certain sadness about "den." A retreat into boyhood. A sophisticated man of letters with access to all kinds of books was proud of the most miserable book shelf I have ever seen. I must read his book.

Met T. F. A. Shankland, Controller of Television Programs, New Zealand Broadcasting Company. One-channel government monopoly TV system. Contemplating second channel. Shankland hopes it too will be government owned. Argues government planning, not private competition, best insurance for diversity.

NZTV is not yet a national network, except for news. Three main cities do their own transmitting. Movies are circulated. For a time, movie-censor did film reviewing, but now TV does its own. Claims stricter criteria than movie censorship. Also grades programs for adults and children by hour of day. Popularity, political paternalism, and pragmatism mix to guide program reviews. Shankland has UCLA assistant for audience research--a kind of Nielsen service.

Struck by absence of contact between NZ censors from print, TV, and film. Busy people. Locked into closely guarded bureaucracies. Youth influence in NZ will likely liberalize censorial atmosphere as "old school" (British) managers die off. Evolution not revolution. Homogeneity, size, and rationality key factors. Also a lot of Danish-like self-satisfaction. Maori minority may yet become catalyst for change.

Notes from Australia (February 10-24, 1970)

Australia is like a trip to Canada. Cultural ferment from daily contest between impulses from Victorian England and inputs from commercial America.

Renewed contact with Austin Snare, Chief Psychologist, Australian Broadcasting Control Board in Melbourne. Directs audience studies, content analysis, etc. Staff includes bright computer specialist and eager young assistants with more talent than bureaucracy will let them exercise. Surveys go beyond nose-counting and popularity assessments. Before-after TV study in Darwin could be major contribution.

Early on, Austin introduced boss, Adrian Jose, Director of Program Services. Tension underlies relationship. Jose aspires to be Commissioner. Keeps tight control on reports, but offered copies, forwarded to Washington.

Talked to research staff about commission's work, polling possibilities, and effect studies. One idea took root: organize seminars around university people and build alliances to relieve isolation.

Train to Austin's suburban home. Two domestic passions: (1) golf; great club nearby, and (2) grafting fruit trees. Conversation reveals frustrated long-term civil servant heroically doing his time. Finds it difficult to link research to content decisions, except superficially.

Met Dr. Clement Semmler, Deputy General Manager of the Australian Broadcasting Commission in Sydney. Literary-type, sophisticated, a son at Cambridge, authored book on censorship (*For the Uncanny Man*), office has a spiffy, modern, New York CBS-look.

In principle, Semmler doesn't like censorship, but "has a job to do." Problem for TV is resources for creativity. Sees violence as stronger potential threat to society than sex. However, sex sparks quick reaction. When conveyed by parliament, makes job "touchy."

On February 12, spotted poster at University of Sydney library announcing protest rally against media censorship. Went to downtown meeting hall. Gradually, about 35 people gathered. Pimple-faced youth called session to order. Free discussion followed.

Liberal reform position--act only after considering consequences-- gave way to heated outcries: tired of debating, heard arguments against censorship, frustrated, fuck the opposition, do something now! What? Picket theaters. When? Now, but let's make it big with "Easy Rider" (which passed appeals with cuts) when it opens Easter.

Beginning of social movement? Possibly. Foul-mouthed, articulate participant turned out to be gifted movie reviewer for publication, *The Australian*.

Met Richard Prouse, Chief Censor, Commonwealth Film Censor Board, in Sydney. Just back from holiday. Busy, powerful, civil servant with self-proclaimed hard-shell from experience. A one-armed veteran of war. Prodigious note-taker. A Sergeant in charge of a platoon. Definition of task simple: sense tolerance limits of community. Avoid concern with morality or effects. How to perform task? I'm a pro. I know intuitively how to read "feedback." Not alarmed by rising criticism. I have weathered many storms. He acts like he acts with authority. Film cuts suggests that he does. Cooperative in providing data--some of best collected so far.

Met E. R. Bryan, Chairman, National Literature Board of Review, Professor in Department of Languages and Literature, Royal Military College in Duntroon. Fondly recalled experience as chief librarian at Canberra. His Board deals only with "print of merit." Customs handles magazines, newspapers, etc.

Key idea: We banned "Portnoy's Complaint," even though split-decision on literary merit, because had we not, we would, in effect, have been out of business. (Explain? May I quote you?) Yes. We could conceive of nothing beyond Portnoy. Would have broken limits of all limits. Precedent too liberal for present. (Are decisions permanent?) No. We sense changing public attitudes. Books are taken off taboo list after a year or two.

In Canberra, met Noel Sloan, Acting Chief Inspector, Literature Review Department of Customs and Excises, and also John Byrne, Acting Secretary. Playboy often banned after review. Covers put on Danish magazines. Minister sometimes call for samples. All externally produced material is checked; not domestic production--a local police matter. "Oh Calcutta" was banned from opening on stage in Melbourne. This office reviewed script.

General guiding theme: community norms. What is national tolerance limit?

Office really feels like center of censorship--different from film center. Why? Work on it.

Notes from Singapore (March 4-8, 1970)

Rich ritual and traditions of rural Bali prompts thoughts on human freedom.

But so does Singapore. Greatest urban conglomeration seen yet. Strong sense of community, purpose, order, and action. Integrated participation by all of all ages. City-state alive at any hour. Work, play, and life all together. Congestion, but not dirt or disorder. Population over 2 million. Most interesting people-in-city experience ever encountered--almost overwhelming. What's going on here? What price order?

Met Raymon T. H. Huang, Chairman, Board of Film Censors. Office in Raffles Place. Intelligent, correct, suave, cool. A Chinese bureaucrat on way up. Bored with film board; having mastered that, now conquering new world--tourism. In six months will decide career path.

Sex and hippies cut from films. Tolerance level liberalizing but changing slowly. Will never reach Danish case because of religious culture. Violence liked by audience. Censor cuts some. Chinese films extreme on violence. Careful watch on political content, communism closely checked and censored.

Met Lim Joo Hock, Permanent Secretary, Ministry of Culture at City Hall. In line for Prime Minister at one time. Now helps make policy in four ministries. Home in his Mercedes after stop to pick up 3rd-year medical student son at university. Good discussion. Articulates national goals. Settled on "vigorous" society. Drugs and hippies are threat. Movie "Easy Rider" banned. Recordings with drug messages banned (e.g., "Puff the Magic Dragon"). Understood censorship issues. Justifies application by special problems of integrating a multi-racial-religious city-state.

Talked with Mr. J. F. Conceicao, Head, Extra-Mural Studies Department, University of Singapore. Member of parliament. Knows

political ropes. Tour of parliament. Struck by youth of M.Ps and
Ministers. Hurt response to Singapore as paternalistic society. Prefers
pragmatic and progressive designation.

Notes from Malaysia (March 9-14, 1970)

Kuala Lumpur, hot and humid capital of tin and rubber nation of
Malaysia. Airport stunning architecture and total design. Nine million
population. Country proud of new identity symbolized by modern
buildings, including startling mosque.

Fred Lim, Director Audio-Visual Department of USIS, American
Embassy led to interview with Chairman, Film Censors Malaysia,
Hussain Maricar. Office in suburb seven miles out (cab, $1.25 U.S.).
Production manager national films prior to censor's job four years ago.
USIS personnel described him as a quiet, cooperative man, not very
competent, and probable beneficiary of graft in view of high style of
living--house, car. Proud of new Barracuda, large American car.

Film censor building and office modern, but not clean. With
coffee, very black, interview began, interrupted by constant calls for
files and receipt of mail. Powerful, political man. Has operating
authority over all films in a country where movies very important.
Also regulates TV. Has staff of 7 for movies, 3 for TV. Checked 700
films last year. Powerful also because obvious good rapport with
Ministry of Home Affairs.

Printed forms for deletions and banning. Sensitive subject matter?
Sex most common complaint. In movie "Wild Bunch," bosoms, not
blood, deleted. Taboo on TV kissing. Rod Steiger as "The Sergeant"
kissing a soldier cut because "homosexuality is against the law here."
Censor claims ambivalence about sex, however. Asks, what harm
could it really do? But since important people (older Muslims) in
community object, objection is honored.

Predicts gradual liberalization of sex standards, but culture will
never evolve into Danish permissiveness. Violence bad, too.
Interesting qualifications emerge. Cartoon and cowboy violence can
do no harm. That's entertainment. What we can cut or ban is gangster
stuff, urban violence, social protest violence. Model of effects says
direct imitation of contemporary scenes, not fictional historic scenes,
is danger.

Admires realistic technique of popular Chinese films--4 to 1 over
U.S. films. For example? Hands cut-off, fingers continue to wave; or,

head cut off and eye balls roll. Asserts we cut the worst out, because some would be offended.

American "Thomas Crown Affair" with Steve McQueen and Faye Dunaway banned for over a year. Now playing because community settled down after rash of crimes. Cut smoke-bomb scene. Too easy to imitate here.

"Easy Rider" banned. Ignited protest. Ban upheld by Review Board because "the government does not want hippies here." Guesses that Chinese might model after hippies, but Malays and Indians would not.

Other concerns? We don't show anything about communism. "Chairman" with Gregory Peck banned. We have to watch out for leftist ideas in movies from Hong Kong. Race and religion also sensitive. Checks closely to avoid stirring trouble between groups in Malay society.

He promises to mail list of banned films and sample of reasons. Expresses strong interest in labeling procedures. Asks how selective entrance to theater is enforced. Will develop Malaysian rating system.

Wants badly to visit U.S. Asks me to engineer letter from Motion Picture Production people to his Minister so United States Information Service will send him on tour via scholarship.

Here, as in Singapore, in contrast with Australia and New Zealand, censor is political agent for a government wanting to stay in power, insure stability, combat communism, and foster national development.

Technically, Malaysia since May, 1969 elections (where opposition gained unexpectedly--riots rescinded the election) is still under martial law (one hour of curfew remains). Context important. Information must flow in service of stability. Let people be entertained by film and TV, let them get official news, but let's not show violence in a context of political dissent, or show sex if it arouses religious ire.

A Note from Thailand (March 17, 1970)

Call from U.S. Embassy leads to Mr. Ridgeway, Director, Film Division, USIS, Bangkok. Unlike counterpart in Kuala Lumpur, Ridgeway obviously did not link closely to censors in Thailand. See Mr. Blamey who represents Metro Goldwyn Mayer and Columbia Pictures. Blamey reports a censor division in police headquarters.

His personal impression: Thailand restrictive on sex, more liberal on violence ("as in so many places") but some cuts made in violence. The sex thing is based on cultural--family and religious--traditions which, despite Bangkok's famed "massage" reputation, is conservative and conventional.

En-route to Burma, meet a young Dane--Jan R.--who reports he has "given up trying to explain Danish sex attitudes."

A Note from Burma (March 20, 1970)

Late night arrival, and quick thrust of dysentery, did not detract from impression that we had slipped a notch on the "modernity" scale in flying from Bangkok to Rangoon. Dawn, and visual inspection confirmed this. Rangoon reveals remnants of British-built structures. River rapid, temple splendid, but all midst filth, decay, disrepair.

Mass media include radio and newspapers both government controlled. No TV. Several well-attended movie houses on main streets. One showing James Stewart cowboy film, another a Kirk Douglas comedy. Judged by ads, native films did not look as violent as those in Bangkok or Singapore.

No evidence of erotica. Newsstands and bookstores conservative and education oriented. Society grasping for coherence and growth, under revolutionary government that only gradually "trusts" the people.

Notes from India   (March 22-25, April 3-4, 1970)

Forewarning on Calcutta: beware of riot, revolution, disorder. On arrival, media reports police "mopping-up," bombs found, troublemakers detained. Marxist coalition falls. City under national "Presidential Rule." Suburbs rumble. Truckloads of soldiers. Observation does not confirm city convulsed or paralyzed. More than a media event? Multitudes muddle on. And what multitudes!

City a startling visual experience. Cattle on streets, people sleeping, dying, eating, squatting, lugging, milling, standing, begging. Patterned chaos. Carnival spirit next day. Annual Hindu Holy day envelopes population with colored paints daubed on face, hair and dress.

No TV. Radio government controlled. Newspapers regulated. Indian, American, English movies booming and popular. Attend one show. Sydney Potier, "The Lost Man." Ads precede program, one for population control. Ads and movie shown only after official censor rating form flashed on screen.

Erotica readily available on newsstands. Soft-porn pictures. Magazines stapled shut prevents in-depth browsing. Modesty prevails. Hotel floor-show presents strip-tease artist. Breasts not revealed, except in case of male dressed as female.

In New Delhi, talked with William Miller, Minister Counselor for Public Affairs and Director USIS India. Produces newspapers, magazines (very slick) and journal, *The American Review.* Distributes to power figures, influentials, future leaders. Plagued by calls to explain American violence; not sex though, yet. Indian TV development being debated. Northern network planned first. NASA satellite possibility. But high illiteracy, low-technical skills a problem. Even radio not advanced, only 10 million sets now operative.

Met Harish Khanna, Ministry of Information and Broadcasting. Articulate, intelligent student of mass media. Violence a problem; liberalization on sex, but showing kiss still a taboo. Double standard for Indian and American movies. See his *Report of the Enquiry Committee on Film Censorship.* Doing book on mass media in India.

Met Cedric Biswas, Chief Film Section, USIS. Twenty years with USIS. Practical man. Opposes all censorship. Asks, how can five people determine what is good for public? (Easily, with government authority).

A Note from Nepal (March 25-28)

Air-Thai, with SAS pilot, flew over spectacular sight. High Himalayan peaks. Terraced valleys, browns and greens mixed in splendid splash. Then, Katmandu. Name signals special place.

King departing airport as we arrive. Band, soldiers, diplomats. Ceremony wobbles like B-movie. Haughty King in black Cadillac roars out of palace and speeds through poverty pockets. Jet to Expo in Japan.

Problem not mass media, but electricity. Newspapers cater to King and establishment. No TV. Some radio. One movie theater. No sex on newsstands. But displayed on Hindu temples, at base of large wood carvings. Fantastic array of erotic art. Men, women, animals in all combinations of acts. One guide explains functions as a "guard against lightning striking the temple." More likely fertility symbols. Check the literature.

Temples and pagodas abound. Pigeons and poverty too. Filth everywhere. Humans and animals intermingle. Beggars press from every side. Some small boys feign being crippled. Actual cripples everywhere. Tourist impact visible. Drugs. Language adaptation. Expectations shaped. Will cars turn Katmandu into another Bangkok asphyxiation alley?

A Note from Iran (April 5-6, 1970)

From air, Teheran, rimmed by stunning mountains, looks like a gray-brown lego-town on plains below mountains.

Strong images: Shah's presence, Mercedes cars, tree-lined boulevards, American pop culture, movies popular, men in dark suits twirling beads, little shops with machine lathes, American embassy looks Russian, university completely surrounded by fence. Locked in hotel elevator for hour. Let's get out of here. Newsstands carry explicit pornographic paperbacks, first sighting on journey. No chance to check with authorities.

Conclusion

So much for the trail of a tourist through a terrain of censorship, one that illustrates how inventive governments can be in controlling the media and repressing free expression.

I had to break off the trip about three times to hurry back to Washington to wind up studies and to participate in preparing the final report of the Commission on Obscenity and Pornography.

I suspect that what I had experienced in my first encounter with real censors was a factor in spurring me to recommend against any policy that would even come close to arming our government with the power of prior restraint over words and pictures.

Censors are real people with jobs that make most of them feel rather uncomfortable. The reason is clear. They must see everything, and then judge what others may not see. Since they claim they are not at risk, why should others be?

That thought haunts them. But the job also sustains them--right up until pension time.

Chapter 14

Prurience, Offensiveness, Social Value

Extract from testimony United States of America
vs. William L. Hamling, et al., San Diego
December 7, 1971

(Questions [Q's] by Larry Butcher, Criminal Department, Department of Justice, Washington, D.C., counsel for the plaintiff, the U. S. Government)

Q. Now, Dr. Larsen, coming back to my inquiry, can you tell the Court and jury what in your opinion the attributes would be, if any, of a photograph that has as its dominant theme an appeal to the prurient interest?...What must we show?

A.   I can tell you what I have learned about that.

Q.   Please do.

A.   And it is reported in the commission chapter on effects...as to what kind of material presented in what fashion evokes various kinds of reaction including arousal, including disgust, including things that could, I think, logically be allied to the notions of prurience and all of its synonyms.

The important thing is that the perception of prurience varies by type of population and by mode of presentation. As a matter of fact, the portrayal of heterosexual intercourse is for the largest proportion of the population the most stimulating, the most arousing; but many people are not, in the jargon of the day, turned on by sexually explicit materials. Some people, for example, are more turned on by leather goods, pictures of leather goods, or by music, even classical music.

I wish I could give you a simple answer, and tell you what prurience is. Our research does not afford that.

Q. In sum, then, and correct me if I have misstated it, but you are saying, are you not, that unless there is some arousal of some shameful, morbid, or lustful feelings on the part of the viewer--absent that arousal, the picture cannot be said to have an appeal to the prurient interest, is that your testimony?

A. I would say that is a clear and understandable definition. I am not competent to judge its legal adequacy, but as a sociologist I would take that kind of response as being an indicator of prurience. We call it an operational definition...If you want to add some other features, tell me what those features are.

Q. I was in hope that you would. You said this is only an indicator. What other elements would you have to see, or what other factual data would have to be placed, before that would persuade you to think that a given picture has as its dominant theme an appeal to the prurient interest?

A. ...If you take an absolutist moral position...then obviously any pictorial presentation of the material under consideration would fall into this category...Most people when presented with that argument in our surveys don't accept...having someone tell them what it is, they tell us...what is prurient for them...it is a highly variable response.

Q. ...Are you saying, with only that material in front of us--we would be unable to say that a given picture is or does or does not have an appeal to the prurient interest?

A. ...You can make your judgment, but I would be unwilling to attribute, knowing what I know from my field of work, any absolute value to any photograph or any symbol, because I have seen it variously received, and to me it is the result that counts...Words and pictures express ideas, some of which are unpopular or even unpleasant...What American society is about is learning to tolerate diversity. It is a tough thing to do these days.

Q. Speaking of tolerance, you spoke of a certain tolerance level, in part when you responded to Mr. Fleishman (Stanley Fleishman, Hollywood, California, attorney for the defendants) in his inquiry as to the contemporary community standards--

A. Yes.

Q. (Continuing)--your testimony, as I recall was that this material is not patently offensive to contemporary community standards because of varying degree of tolerance and the availability of material in the adult bookstores throughout the country, is that correct?

A. I believe there is a greater tolerance. I can give you a simple illustration. In the late 1930s there was a movie called "Gone With the Wind." It was almost bounced because Clark Gable dared to use a four-letter word, "damn."

"Love Story," another movie, has recently appeared and all kinds of people are saying, "We are returning to basic values with this again." If you see that movie you will discover very explicit language and behavior, including pre-marital sexual acts, being portrayed.

This means, if this is a return to old values--and that statement, incidentally, came from the White House--then old values have certainly had some evolution....

Note that I am not advocating that these things be distributed freely or openly. I am advocating that people make their own choices, and I am suggesting today there is a greater tolerance for that...

I am not even saying that we should applaud the new level of tolerance, but I am saying there is a great deal of safety in Americans making their own decisions instead of having others, including the government, make them for them.

Q. Would you look at Color Plate XVII, please? By the way, did you see the movie "Love Story?"

A. Yes.

Q. Did you see any acts depicted in "Love Story" that looked like Plate XVII?

(Note: the caption under the two photographs in Color Plate XVII read: "In the Katzman studies, 1970, for the Commission, see page 180, some 90 photographs were rated on five-point scales for 'obscene' and 'sexually stimulating'...Group activity scenes of the type here illustrated could have been part of the 90. Both these group sex pictures are from the Danish magazine Porno Club No. 3, supposedly this was filmed at a 'live show' night club in Copenhagen. There are many similar clubs.")

A. No, not anything as explicit as this.

Q. Then you weren't really trying to imply to the jury that "Love Story" and this book are equally candid in their depiction.

A.   No. I was responding to your question about changing tolerance levels. We could hardly tolerate the word "damn" in 1939, and in 1969 we have gone a little farther.

Q.   Right.

A.   For good or ill.

Q.   Is it your testimony that we have gone far enough that the populace now tolerates to the extent that they accept this material, or do they just tolerate it, period?

A. Let's take the most extreme of the five kinds of sexual behavior that the national survey asked about: sadomasochistic behavior. Thirty percent of the adults expressed support for the right of adults to witness that if they wanted to, the lowest percentage for any of the forms of sexual behavior tested....

Q. Does that imply that it is acceptable to the --

A. (Interposing) Not at all.

Q. (Continuing)--national community or that they are just merely willing to tolerate it?

A. Toleration is important. It bears on who shall decide. Who shall decide?

Q. Is that your conception of what is at issue here, not whether or not it substantially exceeds the national community standards, but, rather, whether or not the community, 30 percent of them, think that we should let other people decide?

A. That wasn't your question but I will be glad to address that, if you like.

Q. Go right ahead.

A. Okay...If you will examine the Effects Panel report very carefully you will find from the national survey exactly what proportion would (a) Let people see it, but (b) more than that, be aroused by it, or be entertained, or be informed, or be repulsed by it....Now there is another important point that we found from our national study. Most people will tell you that their tolerance for this thing is...more liberal, but they will project intolerance on others...As a matter of fact, they project on others effects that they don't accept for themselves....

The Court: (Honorable Gordon Thompson, Jr., Judge of the U.S. District Court, Southern District of California): Dr. Larsen, you testified here with respect to prurient appeal. When you define prurient appeal, do you define it as its result or as its projection, irrespective of result?

The Witness: Your Honor, I would say it is a transaction between the two, what the communicator is intending and what response is engendered.

The Court: In other words, there must be a response engendered?

The Witness: I would say that would be the position of a behavioral scientist. That is my position.

The Court: Are you testifying when you say with regard to the community standards that the material is not patently offensive because it does not affront community standards relating to the description or representation in sexual matters? Are you basing that on the fact there are available in adult bookstores under restricted conditions similar materials?

The Witness: No, not entirely. Substantial segments of the population scientifically sampled by a national survey, adolescents as well as adults, when confronted with this material, and confronted with the pertinent question, gave answers indicative of tolerance.

The Court: Of tolerance?

The Witness: What was the phrase in the question you asked?

The Court: Whether or not it was patently offensive because it affronts community standards.

The Witness: Was not offensive--was not offensive in the sense that they were asked about 12 different options and five of those were what you might call socially approved, middle categories were neutral, and a number were negative, including being judged offensive.

The point is that answers are distributed across all those options. You can, in fact, find at one and the same time, your Honor, positive, neutral, and negative attributes assigned to a message by the same person. That is the puzzling, curious, thing about the complex stimuli of sex material.

The Court: Then in one part it would offend and in another part it would not, is that what you mean?

The Witness: Yes.

The Court: All right. We are now concerned with the book as a whole and the pictures included within the book. Now when you say the material has redeeming social value, are you basing it on the use you put it to or the use you think it can be put to by others, if any?

The Witness: I think there are elements of both. I mean by value to present information, facts, and realities, on the nature of a critical issue in our society...There is social value in being able to confront the issue with the alternatives that there are and the facts that were generated. I find this useful in the classroom.

Moreover, inferring from what people said in our studies about how they used explicit sexual material, they found it valuable in terms of information, education, enhanced communication, and along other dimensions as well.

The Court: All right. Anything else, gentlemen?

Mr. Fleishman: No, your Honor.

Mr. Butcher: No, your Honor. (Witness Excused.)

***

(**Postscript:** On December 20, 1971, a sentence of four years in prison and fines totaling $87,000 were handed down in U.S. District Court against the publisher of *The Illustrated Presidential Report of the Commission on Obscenity and Pornography*. The publisher, William Hamling, 50, was sentenced on 12 counts involving the mailing of obscene brochures advertising the book. The jury failed to agree whether the book itself was obscene.)

Chapter 15

Are Sex and Violence Identical Twins?

Better Homes and Gardens Creative Group Conference,
Kiawah Island, South Carolina
March 15, 1978

I favor better homes and gardens, and thus I am pleased to accept your invitation to address the editors who march under that proud banner. However, my words will bear more on homes than on gardens.

I suppose you do your work in part because you believe that you have influence. You may even have impact in a realm seemingly remote from your particular mission. Thus, I want to discuss some problems confronting editorial judgment about sex and violence.

Not long ago, the slogans of the Vietnam war period posted conflicting messages about these matters. We were importuned to:

- ♥　　　*"Make love, not war,"* or to
- ♥　　　*"Make love after the war,"* or to
- ♥　　　*"Make love and war."*

Simply translated the choices seemed to be to have sex but not violence, to have sex after the violence is over, or to have both sex and violence. Thus the graffiti of the day posted options and priorities about how to service two vital human impulses.

How is the world of words and pictures about sex and violence related to the real world where these behaviors are manifest? Put simply, what behavior follows from exposure to media sex and violence? Anti-social conduct? Aggression? Crime? Catharsis?

Tougher questions, and presumably greater concern, mount as possible crossover effects are projected. That is, could the portrayal of sex lead to violent behavior, or could the portrayal of violence lead to a sexual response? Additionally, is violent behavior more apt to follow from sexual repression or from sexual arousal. Or, to continue the complications, where are the risks greater, with expression or with repression?

Each query poses a potent puzzle. In the absence of sure knowledge, many believe it not unreasonable for a society to inhibit media treatment of both sex and violence in order to avoid the possibility of disruption, personal deviance or social damage.

What, then, do we know, and what policies would our knowledge-base support? As a first approximation it is clear that large audiences are attracted by the portrayal of sex and violence, but many persons are also repulsed by it. Box office, TV ratings, and print sales go up in proportion to the presentation of both panting passion and powerful punches. That is, sex and violence sell. But, words and pictures about sex and violence also kindle public revulsion, alarm, criticism, and controversy.

This outcome suggests a kind of national bifocal ethics that researchers of media audiences sense when they find that it is not easy to get people to admit that what they watch or read and what they say about it are always the same thing. (Here one is reminded of the famous characterization of voters in certain areas in the United States who vote *dry* but drink *wet*).

Accordingly, the phenomenon invites inspection on many grounds, not the least of which is the challenge thrust on social scientists to come up some understandable answers about the effects of exposure to words and pictures in these realms. Had Winston Churchill been a sociologist, he no doubt would have characterized sex and violence as the soft underbelly of the continent of mass communication. When we attempt to penetrate this continent, the issue of effects quickly broadens into moral, political, legal, familial, social and other public policy concerns.

Ironically, as public concerns broaden, popular conception of cause narrows. Indeed, in the lexicon of mass media critics, including powerful interest groups, *sexandviolence* has become one word. To many, that word symbolizes the cause of a vast array of evil in society. Or, in Churchillian terms, never have so many attributed so much to so compressed a notion.

Certain editorial judgments could be affected if the lumping together of sex and violence is warranted in terms of what we know about the effects of their media presentation. While there is no easy linkage of knowledge to policy, the outcome of serious, scientific inquiry can inform the shaping of policy including self-regulation by the media over messages they transmit. It is essential, therefore, to be critical not only about what our studies do and what they do not tell us, but also to be curious about why they seem to tell us what they do.

And so I am going to turn to something of an intramural battle in social and behavioral science about what studies of words and pictures portraying sex and violence tell us about effects. The drama turns around whether we should expect similar outcomes from exposure to each body of content. Are the findings from the two sensitive domains consistent? If not, why not?

These questions have been at the center of debate for about a decade. The unplanned juxtaposition of two national commissions--one initiated by the President and one mandated by the Congress--yielded results and interpretations that fired the debate. Let me outline the arguments. They throw some light on the general question of media effects and generate considerable heat about possible media controls.

Contradictory Conclusions

History tells us that sex and violence have always lurked around the White House. However, in 1968 they appeared simultaneously as a formal, official, public matter. The response led to two commissions.

Prompted by assassinations, rising violent crime rates, and student protests over the Vietnam war, President Johnson appointed a National Commission on the Causes and Prevention of Violence. The mandate ranged over civil disobedience, crime, assassinations, riots, disorders, and the media portrayal of violence. The latter portion of the Commission's work led to the following conclusion: *The preponderance of the available research evidence strongly suggests that violence in television programs can and does have adverse effects upon audiences--particularly child audiences.*

At about the same time, at the behest of a Congress locked in a legislative deadlock between "anti-smut" and "anti-censorship" concerns, President Johnson also appointed a Commission on Obscenity and Pornography. The majority report of this commission adopted the position that harmful effects of pornography were not supported by the weight of the evidence and concluded: *Empirical*

research designed to clarify the issue has found no reliable evidence
that exposure to sexually explicit materials plays a significant role in
the causation of delinquent or criminal sexual behavior among youth
or adults.

Reactions by Social Scientists

After the publication of the commission reports, scholars were
mobilized to project critical reviews. There were mixed reactions, but
a number of objections were repeatedly voiced. The Pornography
Commission was criticized for precluding experiments on children,
ignoring long-term effects of exposure to sexually explicit materials
(as well as the effects of long-term exposure), using a tone of
advocacy, and ignoring violent content in some sexually explicit
materials. A major criticism of the Violence Commission was that the
measures of aggression used in the studies cited (for example, hitting
Bobo dolls and administering ostensible electric shocks) were not
generalizable beyond the laboratory.

One critic commanded popular attention by declaring the reports
little more than ideological tracts intended to promulgate the liberal
view that *sex is fine, and suppression of its depiction is censorship;*
but violence is bad, and suppression of its depiction is a form of
justifiable regulation.

Aside from specific objections, a more fundamental charge was
leveled against the commissions--fundamental because it was
regarded as *prima facie* evidence that at least one of the two reports
was "wrong."

Though stated in various forms, the criticism reduces to the
assertion that the two reports are blatantly contradictory: exposure to
media violence has harmful effects on viewers, while exposure to
sexually explicit materials has no harmful effects. As one psychologist
phrased it: *The reports indicated that although exposure to media*
violence lead to viewer aggression, exposure to sexually explicit
material seems harmless, possibly reducing deviance.

Examining the Contradiction

Controversy over the apparent contradiction was lively. Several
writers captured the issue in a rhetorical question, "Sex and Violence:
Can Research Have it Both Ways?" The prevailing answer was a firm

"no," and its essence is illustrated in a commentary by a prominent psychologist, Leonard Berkowitz, from the University of Wisconsin.

According to Berkowitz, the disparity between the conclusions and recommendations of the two Commissions was not supported by the empirical evidence. On the contrary, he said, the empirical evidence mustered by the two Commissions was "strikingly similar." Berkowitz then elaborates by noting that "There are close parallels in the actual research results. Both observed aggression, and media sex has a temporary stimulating effect, and in both realms the probability that the observer will take open actions depends in part on his attitude toward the portrayed event. Further, we don't know if the media depiction's of both sex and aggression have any long-term consequences independent of other environmental supports."

Given the similar research results, the Wisconsin psychologist then asserts that the same conclusions and policy statements must be made in regard to public exposure to violent and to sexually explicit materials. "There is some chance that media violence will prompt at least a few viewers to attack others. . . . We can't have it both ways. The same possibility exists in the case of sexual portrayals."

But, this was not the final word, not even among psychologists. A contrary assessment comes from another distinguished psychologist who, having analyzed both reports, thought that research could have it both ways. Clearly, facts do not stand alone. Their meanings falter, move along, or are altered as contrary suppositions produce alternative interpretations. Editors, put your reporters on alert. Maybe there is a story here that would go beyond quick judgments on sex and violence to reveal understandings that might bear on better homes...if not gardens.

Richard Dienstbier, who chairs the Department of Psychology at the University of Nebraska, asserted that there is no contradiction between the two commission reports. He believes that exposure to violent and sexually explicit materials should be expected to have differential effects on viewers. From whence, then, cometh the contradiction?

The Nebraska psychologist suggests that the appearance of a contradiction results from two factors: (1) An assumption that explicit sex and violence are both "evils," coupled with an assumption that "evil causes evil," and (2) the uncritical use by investigators of a simplistic social learning model which assumes that, if exposure to one type of media content (violence) produces particular effects, then exposure to a different form of media content (sex) should produce the same effects.

Dienstbier rejects the first argument as a dubious value judgment, noting that "sexuality is a force underlying some of society's most venerable institutions, including love, marriage, and reproduction. On the other hand,...it is difficult to think of examples of positive uses of violence," which is associated with hate and rejection. Thus different value approaches to sex and aggression seem quite appropriate because these phenomena are embedded in quite different value structures in society. Media sex and violence do not equally promote deviancy, or do equal harm, since normal sexuality and normal aggression are quite different in harm or deviance value potency.

As for the second assumption, the manner in which we learn about these phenomena as we grow up is quite different. Dienstbier notes, therefore, that there is every reason to expect differential impact of exposure to sex and to violence in the media. Looking at cultural factors alone, he argues, sexual behavior and knowledge is suppressed in childhood and expected in to emerge in adulthood as a positive, frequent, important form of human behavior. On the other hand, violent behavior is condoned in childhood (at least in play) and must be almost totally suppressed in adulthood. "Based on the vastly different accounts of prior information, experience, and cultural restrictions, differential impact should be expected from explicit sexuality vs. explicit violence."

Thus, two arresting points suggest that media messages filtered through values and socialization patterns make it unlikely that sex and violence are twin born. Dienstbier then draws from biological mechanisms to clinch his case for differentiation. If our capacity or need for sexuality has a different character than our capacity and need for violence, then this, too, would influence impact. Accordingly, he notes that "sexual and aggressive tendencies are effectively aroused by different classes of stimuli, developed and sustained differently through the various stages, and released through different arousal-release patterns....This too would influence the impact made by exposure to explicit sexuality or media violence."

This is strong stuff. Dienstbier's three ideas point to a possible explanation of the apparent contradiction in the findings on effects from the violence and obscenity commissions.

His first point tells us that these phenomena are embedded in quite different value structures. This has powerful implications for differential impact.

Second, the manner in which we learn about these phenomena as we grow up are quite different. This important idea is clear when we hear it, but not obvious as we live it.

Third, he tells us that to the extent that we differ in biological inheritance, this difference in capacities and needs, too, would influence the differential impact from media exposure to sex and to violence.

Conclusion

So, we have an unresolved issue. While sex and violence may not be twin born, the exact kin relationship is not yet clear. If it can be resolved, ultimately the answer will come from crucial tests of competing models of media effects.

The work here goes on. It merits monitoring by the media, particularly by your form, printed expression, which has unique capacities to question, to probe, and to clarify issues and present them in depth for thoughtful readers.

Almost a decade ago I joined colleagues on the Commission on Obscenity and Pornography in calling for more research in critical areas of effects. Some response has been forthcoming, enough to arrest my attention and to resurrect old concerns.

Efforts have now progressed to the point where no one working in the area seriously disputes the assertion that, under experimental conditions, exposure to erotic stimuli in media communications can facilitate post-exposure aggression. The central dispute is over why this occurs, and under precisely what conditions it occurs.

In my estimation, the research literature on sexual arousal and aggression that has accumulated in the past decade raises serious new questions about how exposure to sexually explicit content may lead to harmful effects. Nevertheless, that evidence is not as yet sufficient to overturn the empirically based effect conclusions of the Commission on Obscenity and Pornography. The contention that sexual arousal facilitates aggression rests almost entirely on small-scale experimental research. This is a story you should follow and translate into calm understanding by concerned advocates of better homes...if not gardens.

It is not easy to convey the idea that it is in the public interest to require diligent replication and refinement of studies before the evidence on sexual arousal and aggression is sufficient to warrant control recommendations.

Should that evidence be forthcoming, it will be ironic, indeed, if it suggests a policy of restricting public access to sexually explicit materials. The guiding philosophy of the Commission on Obscenity and Pornography was that policy recommendations pertaining to the use and distribution of explicit sex materials should be based on the empirically demonstrable effects of exposure to such words and pictures. That philosophy was soundly rejected by the Supreme Court when it ruled in 1973 that negative effects of pornography could be assumed despite scientific evidence to the contrary. The decision apparently delighted critics of the Commission who favored censorship of pornography. Yet those critics may be dismayed by the Court ruling if subsequent evidence supports a conclusion of adverse effects based on empirical, scientific evidence that is no longer deemed legally pertinent.

By denying the relevance of scientific evidence to public policy in this realm, the Court appeased critics of the Commission. It also rendered the private judgment of harm as the criterion for public policy. That is one major reason why obscenity law has not been effective in controlling the growth and spread of explicit materials in contemporary society.

Sociological Organization

The Commission on Obscenity and pornography did have more than one unintended effect.

For me, the experience incubated "Potomac Fever." My appetite for further political combat in the nation's capitol was whetted by all those journeys to meetings in Washington, a rich site for field studies of the participant-observation type.

That made it easier for me to decide to return again later, which I did twice. From 1972-75, I served as Executive Officer of the American Sociological Association; and, from 1980-86, I held social science leadership positions in the National Science Foundation.

I think that my continuing curiosity about matters of communication built a bridge over which I found it easy to cross back and forth between the University of Washington in Seattle and Washington, D.C. There were political pressures and professional pleasures in both places. And organizations always give rise to questions or matters that involve doubt, uncertainty, or difficulty.

But the most rewarding experience was trying to utilize knowledge of mass communications while mastering some principles of persuasion in interpersonal and organizational settings. There were achievements, but also enough failures to ensure a continuing curiosity about the relationship between interpersonal and mediated communication.

The five presentations below deal with organizational views and experience engendered by my commitment to sociology.

The first one, a satirical statement about the flourishing state of opportunities for sociologists in the 1960s, might have kept me out of serious contention for formal participation in the leadership of the central sociological organization in the 1970s, except for one thing:

the establishment, including Talcott Parsons and Robert Merton, responded to the statement with hearty approval. I then went on to confront serious challenges in the national organization of sociologists.

My entry came on a typically hot and humid August day in the nation's capital when I first walked up Connecticut Avenue and turned right on N street to find the red brick ASA building at 1722.

It is a gracious locale, whose serenity is disturbed only by symbols bearing distant memories of discord. John Kennedy was buried from the Cathedral nearby. Franklin Roosevelt and Senator Joseph McCarthy had once worked from offices within the block.

Inside 1722 N Street I found a veritable bee-hive buzzing with records involving membership, finances, publications, the annual meeting, caucuses, committees, and the council agenda. A staff of 14 members worked with exceptional skill to shape solutions to a web of doubts, uncertainties, and difficulties.

Everett Hughes, one of the great past-presidents of the organization, a man with a dogged commitment to principles, offered counsel time and again about the nature of the ASA. He reminded us that he and a few others had resisted the shift in our name from a society to an association. This he said was to emphasize the importance of maintaining our identity as a learned society and to resist pressures to become just another professional or trade association. There was tension over changing organizational identity throughout my term.

I also learned what ultimately becomes apparent to every executive officer: while problems must be addressed they rarely are solved, at least in a permanent sense. We innovate, we muddle through, but mostly we redirect attention to new doubts and uncertainties that tend to compound difficulties. That tactic is not surprising. In a way, it is mandated by the constitution and by-laws of the American Sociological Association.

The constitution reminds us that the ASA is not a federation of departments of sociology or an alliance of affiliated societies. We are, instead, a voluntary association of individual members. And thus bonded, what do we pursue as organizational goals?

Article II, Section 1 of our constitution clearly states that "The objectives of the Association shall be to *stimulate and improve research, instruction, and discussion, and to encourage cooperative relations among persons engaged in the scientific study of society.*"

That's it. That is what were supposed to be about.

Strict constructionists would note that many things undertaken by the ASA are not mentioned as objectives. For example, there is not explicit reference to selling insurance or to composing resolutions and writing letters to political leaders, foreign and domestic, reprimanding them for their endless faults, unless of course such acts are interpreted as encouraging cooperative relations among persons engaged in the scientific study of society.

Article III, Section 4 of the by-laws adds that the Executive Officer, among other duties and obligations, "... shall *formulate plans* for the accomplishment of the Association's objectives, and. . . .shall be responsible for *coordinating the public relations* activities of the Association."

Clearly, then, the Executive Officer has authority to address problems. But, he or she also has the capacity, and perhaps the necessity, to create problems, or at least to post images and manage perceptions about them. That, of course, is what I enjoyed trying to do.

Given the current evolution of sociological organization, some readers, particularly sociologists with long memories, may have trouble in distinguishing the conventional or formal recounting of facts from the sometimes whimsical satirical mode of communication in this section. Either way, the intent was serious.

I really did care about the state of our organization. In fact, I still do.

Chapter 16

The Year Sociology Stood Still
37th Annual Meeing, Pacific Sociological Association, Vancouver, B. C.
April 9, 1966

I suppose I should commence with some serious comments before I present my prepared remarks.

Certainly I share with this distinguished panel a concern for the future of sociology. While the problems I am about to discuss are not matters peculiar to sociology either as a discipline or as a profession, they are nonetheless amenable to sociological knowledge and worthy of collective deliberation by sociologists. We, too, are part of academia and must share concerns lest universities lose their faculties.

Since we are honored by the presence of President Wilbert Moore of the American Sociological Association, I would like to cast some observations in a context that draws inspiration from his theme at the forthcoming Miami meetings, namely, "Forecasting the Future."

To do this, I ask you now to leap five years ahead in your sociological imagination to the 1971 meeting of the Pacific Sociological Association, which, given our current expansionist vitality, will either be held in Honolulu or Omaha.

Leaving aside territoriality, let us begin by assuming that current trends in the profession will continue to move in the direction they are now headed. What, then, will be the state of sociology just five years from now?

My answer to that vexing question is that later generations will come to refer to 1971 as The Year That Sociology Stood Still.

Let me describe that fateful posture.

A Frozen State

Imagine that it is 1971. More precisely, as universities use the calendar, it is 1970-71. And while departments of sociology in these universities are crowded to the corridors with students and faculty, the production of new sociological knowledge has come to a complete standstill. The wheels that grind out research are locked in a frozen state. Punch cards remain unpunched. Computers are silent. Secretaries are sullen as mimeograph machines sit untouched. The flow of manuscripts to journals has run dry. Not a single paper has been submitted to session organizers of the annual professional meetings. Impromptu panel discussions have come to dominate the programs. No new books or monographs are being written. Publishers scurry to reprint material from earlier decades all in soft covers and projected by a hard-sell campaign calling it a classic in the field. The National Science Foundation (NSF), the National Institute of Health (NIH), the Russell Sage Foundation (RSF), and the recently created National Institute for Balanced Behavioral-Life-Ecological Studies (NIBBLES), report a huge surplus of funds as sociologists cease their search for grants and awards.

How could this solid state come into being? What brought impotence to the institutes and paralysis to this proud profession? What are the underlying factors, the intervening variables, the overriding considerations?

Caught in the Personnel Ploy

A hint of the source of the difficulty can be gained by a glance at the content of the *American Sociological Review* for that historic year At this point a disclaimer should be posted. The new editor of the journal is a Professor of Sociology from the University of Mississippi. This fact has nothing to do with the pattern of content under question. However, his appointment was greeted by many as a significant stroke in breaking the stranglehold that the Eastern establishment, extending all the way from Harvard to Berkeley, had held over the ASA publications for many years.

What, then, characterized the content of the journal? Absent were the reports of studies and experiments. Mute was the call for further research. Significantly, not a chi-square was in sight. Also missing were the annual resurrections of Durkheim, Simmel, Weber, and

Patrick Geddes. Indeed not only had the shoulders of giants disappeared but so too had all other parts of their anatomy.

However, publication of the journal had not ceased. A content analysis shows that the 1970-71 *ASR* (whose cover, incidentally, had just been changed to a bright magnolia pink) contained page after page reporting departmental staff changes, column after column noting the makeup of departmental recruiting subcommittees, and section after section announcing attractive positions still available in the respective departments for persons at all levels.

So desperate was the manpower situation that status-scented appeals were directed to students who were only thinking about majoring in sociology. They were urged to accept federally financed traineeships as assistants to Acting-Assistant Professors. Later some eager departments had these notices reproduced as leaflets and they were dropped from friendly hands into high school lunch rooms.

There were also elaborate announcements of opportunities for new Ph.D.'s, with or without dissertation completed, imploring them to accept positions that offered limited teaching responsibilities, open salaries, air-conditioned offices with two windows, an unlimited campus parking privileges at a special rate. Some departments began adding exotic new inducements. Each new staff member received a guarantee that he could spend every other year in Palo Alto or in one of the overseas annexes of his university such as at Baden-Baden in Europe or at the African counterpart in Addis Ababa.

It was also noteworthy that 62 prominent sociology professors were reported as having departed from their departments that year to become deans, 14 others had joined foundations, 181 became corporation vice-presidents in charge of public affairs, and one joined the Peace Corps. Finally, during that academic year it was reported that 78.4 percent of all departments were looking for a new chairman.

The implication from this content analysis of the leading sociological journal is clear: sociologists were active, very active, but sociology was caught in the paralysis of the personnel ploy. Thus sociology stood still as sociologists were enmeshed in the activity of preparing or reading vitas, writing or reading letters of recommendation, making or receiving urgent telephone calls, visiting or hosting the visits of prospective colleagues, and bargaining while negotiating with deans and provosts. All of this meant endless hours of interviewing individuals, conniving in cliques, searching in sub-committees, fault finding in faculty meetings, and unwinding with wives over the intellectual promise, the personality traits, and the peculiar backgrounds of students who needed to be placed, colleagues who needed to be retained, and prospects who needed to be lured into one of the over 200 up-and-coming departments in the country.

Adaptations

These intense patters of interaction did lead to strain and some new forms of neuroses, but by and large the professorial corps readily adapted to the pressing communicative demands. Indeed, new diplomatic skills emerged as each professor built up the image of his own department for others while simultaneously secretly surveying or cleverly manipulating his own opportunities in distant pastures that either appeared greener or could produce more of the green stuff at home.

Viewed historically, the first clear signs of the gathering difficulty were visible as early as 1966. You all remember how mad the marketplace was becoming and how mirthful the game of academic musical chairs seemed to appear. Every department had at least six openings (not counting the chairmanship), and there weren't nearly enough Ph.D.'s, with or without dissertation completed, to fill the need. That was the year when status began to be measured not by the number of publications that a person could offer, but by the number of offers that a person could muster. While it was then not yet quite polite to openly flaunt these offers, they soon became visible to colleagues by the number of long-distance telephone calls received or by the frequency of airline trips out of town.

In many departments, particularly during the Fall term, it is estimated that fully one-third of the faculty was up in the air at one time. "Buy now, pay later," referred not only to airline tickets but also to the rationale underlying recruitment policies. Gradually the worth of a sociologist became based more on someone's perception of future prospects than on the record of past performance. Thus the phrase "publish or perish" lost it peril, and the phrase "circulate or suffocate" came to supplant it.

There were anxieties about these developments as early as 1966, but no organized reactions from universities or professional associations were apparent. For a time, this appeared to be a triumph over organization as individual professors reaped rapid profit in both money and rank. True, it was embarrassing for some to gain rank through the back door to the Dean's office. But for many there was the compensating thrill of financial escalation induced by the threat to accept an offer at another institution.

Other Factors

More recently, students of the history of sociological knowledge have identified factors that may have contributed to grinding the discipline to an intellectual halt. The contention is that in the late 1960s sociologists were so obsessed with the organizational structure of their profession that little energy remained either for scholarship or for collective deliberation to unlock the vice-like grip of personnel demands. Thus, the intellectual life of sociology was being strangled not only by manpower pressures and the subtle intrusion of the mores of the marketplace, but also by the delusion that preoccupation with constitutions and bylaws had relevance for research and scholarship.

Such neo-functionalist doctrine would seem to call for further specification of fact. You all remember the appearance of the so-called "Faris Committee Report" back in 1966. You will recall that after long labors this committee came up with a 14-point program, the first on the scene, I believe, since Woodrow Wilson's time. These 14 points called for revision of the constitution and bylaws of the American Sociological Association including changes in the structure of the Committee on Committees. This latter proposal had a particularly difficult history and went through the hands of several subcommittees before the whole Committee reached consensus on what to recommend about the Committee on Committees. Incidentally, none of the 14 points offered had any direct bearing on the personnel problems then sharply emerging on the operational level of sociological activity.

I'm sure that you will also remember the heroic efforts of the then President, Wilbert Moore, who, along with other members of a "Truth Squad" form the Washington office, visited each meeting of a regional society to discuss the report. Despite these efforts, great controversy broke out and persisted for several years. The major bone of contention was over representation from the regional societies to the Council of the ASA. Later this point faded from consideration because so many sociologists were changing institutional affiliations so frequently that by 1968 all of them belonged to at least four regional bodies and none of them felt a real identification with any.

But bitter arguments persisted. By 1969 the controversy had heated to the point where several delegations threatened to walk out of the annual American Sociological Association meeting, then being held in Las Vegas, to attempt to establish a competing body to be called the Federal Sociological Association. This effort aborted, however, when cooler heads prevailed and full attention was turned to theme of the meeting which was "The Uses of Game Theory in Sociology."

By 1971, all the compromises had been accommodated and the structure of the American Sociological Association had stabilized. By then, however, it was abundantly apparent that the other problem was with us and drastic steps were needed to get sociological scholarship moving again. Fortunately the reorganization of the ASA left the office of the President with enough power to appoint a special committee to prepare a special report on how this would be accomplished.

Outlook

This brings us just about up to date. As you know, here in 1971 the President of the ASA has chosen this committee with great care so that it would not constitute a kind of mindless Greek chorus for its chairman, Professor Wilbert Moore.

Professor Moore brings a rich foundation of experience to the task of heading this new committee. He is a son of the West who conquered the East. Not only is he a former President of the Association, but he also has a clear memory of what sociological scholarship and research were all about.

We now await the "Moore Committee Report." Rumors are circulating that it will recommend that the Association break the personnel paralysis and unleash the creative talent by establishing a Commissioner on Personnel (COP) who will be empowered to act in much the same fashion as do the commissioners of professional football and baseball.

This, of course, would require the organization of sociology departments into leagues with departmental chairmen reclassified as "managers." With this structure, recruiting practices would change drastically. New Ph.D.'s, with or without dissertations completed, would be drafted in accord with principles giving the department at the bottom of the league standings at the end of each season the first choice in the draft.

Further comment at this time on the forthcoming report would merely add conjecture to rumor. It is a fact, however, that some midwestern professors have already written letters in opposition to any proposals. Furthermore, the "Moore Committee Report" has already been roundly denounced for whatever it might contain by the Society for the Study of Social Problems.

For the rest of us, let me conclude by counseling patience. Here in 1971, let every sociologist emulate the current state of his discipline so that we, too, stand still, at least until the "Moore Committee Report" appears. When that document is made public, I am confident that we will find it to be the truly joint product of an extremely able, conscientious, and hard-working group of colleagues drawn from some of the best teams across the country.

Conclusion

It matters not who wins the game, but how the game was lost.

Chapter 17

How Far from Providence?

37th Annual Meeting, Southern Sociological Society, Atlanta , Georgia
April 19, 1974

Where shall we discover our past?

The American Sociological Association is currently negotiating with a leading library to establish an archives where publications, correspondence, records, and ledgers will be deposited.

If, in the distant future, some heroic historian comes across our archival materials, what might such a scholar find that bears on the theme of this meeting, "The Use of Social Research in Shaping the Future of Society"?

The initial exposure could tantalize. Our birth certificate might startle historians. In the first annual meeting of the American Sociological Society held in Providence, Rhode Island in December, 1906, Lester F. Ward concluded his presidential address by proclaiming: "In other words, sociology, established as a pure science, is now entering upon its applied stage, which is the great practical object for which it exists."

Thus, sixty-eight years ago, sociologists were prodded to move briskly from the development of basic knowledge to the stage of practical application. How effective was this prod? Whatever the full record reveals, one senses that sociologists today remain in an uncertain posture with respect to both promise and performance in this realm.

The style of doing sociology undergoes constant revision. More and more sociologists are trained. They tend to huddle together in ever more complex professional organizations.

What do these organizations have to do with priorities given to research, to allocation of opportunities, to the nature of the problems investigated, to the quality of effort, to rewards for achievement, and to the utilization's of results?

In short, does the growth of professional societies help or hinder the research process, whether pure or applied? The desire to explore such matters suggests that we will continue to haunted by Lester Ward. And so I ask, how far are we from Providence?

Pride and Problems from Growth

Since Providence, sociology has flourished as an organized enterprise. Professional societies prosper on international, national, regional, and state levels. Consider the following facts:

The International Sociological Association is twenty-five years old. At its first World Congress in 1950, 120 sociologists were in attendance; at its most recent meeting in 1970, over 4,000 persons participated.

At its founding in 1906, the American Sociological Society included a total of 115 members (14 of these, or 12 percent, were women). In 1974, the ASA has 14,047 members (3,505 of these, or 25 percent, are women). The ASA membership currently includes 1,683 persons from 79 countries outside the United States.

The Soviet Union has the second largest national sociological organization with a current membership reported at about 2,000 persons.

There are seven regional sociological associations in the United States including the Southern, the Southwestern, the Pacific, the Midwest, the North Central, the District of Columbia, and the Eastern societies. Several of these now have memberships over 1,000 persons.

There are 25 state sociological associations in the United States. Michigan is the oldest (1935) and Oklahoma the newest (1973). Seven of these organizations have more than 100 members.

Membership growth is more than numbers. At every regional or national meeting one can sense feelings of pride when officers announce that "this is the largest convention ever held by this organization." I heard such expressions this year at the annual meeting of three regional sociological societies: the Pacific (their 45th), the Midwest (their 38th), and the Southern (their 37th).

The growth in regional gatherings makes them appear more like a national meeting of just a few years ago. In fact, that is exactly what has happened. The number of sessions and participants at each regional meeting this year exceeded the scope of the ASA program just ten years ago.

And the annual meeting of the American Sociological Association has burgeoned into a vast supermarket of ideas and activities. In 1964, when the ASA met in Montreal, 329 sociologists participated in 72 sessions. Now, ten years later, when once again we will return to Montreal, over 1,000 persons will participate in 140 sessions. In this sense, we have come a long way from Providence where, in addition to the Presidential address, only six papers were read.

Growth yields pride. It also confers other consequences. Most organizations began as simple primary groups to share learned or scientific interests. The central idea was to encourage research by promoting communication and cooperative relations among scholars. Growth brought greater diversity and a declining consensus about organizational goals.

Our sister association of American psychologists, which has grown from 4,000 to 32,000 in 25 years, is today concerned about its growth. They report that "With increase in size comes an increase in the power of subgroups that may wish to use the organization as a whole to further their own preferred ends. While size can mean visibility, and political and social salience, the accompanying diversity may mean that on certain issues major actions of the Association as a whole can only be compromises that satisfy few, if any, of the subgroups with differing goals."

They go on to note that size also tends to increase the power of those in positions of authority and thus the potential to misuse that power. Moreover, they observe that size also means increased costs, as efforts that once were made voluntarily are turned over to paid staff. ("Structure and Function of the APA," *American Psychologist*, 27, January, 1972, p. 2.)

It is encouraging to note that psychologists use standard sociological elements for their assessment. Little wonder, then, that their analysis stirs affinity as we ponder the future of the organizational fate of sociology.

In my two years as Executive Officer of the ASA, more and more members press us to emulate our colleagues in psychology. They are impressed by the fact that the APA has a membership more than double our size and an office staff about ten times as large as that of the ASA. But, there are other models. The economists run their association on a college campus with a very small staff, and the

American Physical Society, with a membership of 28,000, has a staff of only seven persons.

Every disciplinary association performs two central functions that are tied to the research enterprise. They organize an annual meeting and they publish professional journals. This is a symbiotic linkage.

The meeting incubates ideas that are later formalized in publications.

The ramification of growth and size, and the discovery that research is or should be relevant, pressures disciplinary associations to expand functions. The question becomes, will this diffuse whatever vitality they traditionally have had to sustain a commitment by the membership to research?

There is no question that disciplinary associations are increasingly subject to demands that add up to new notions of professionalism. Some would emphasize activities that would make us a prestige association, or a qualifying association, or an occupational association, or even a trade association, not to mention the outcome of obvious political or recreational pressures.

Before discussing the balancing of these forces, let me elaborate on how associations have been linked to the research enterprise. To simplify matters, the focus will be on the American Sociological Association.

The ASA as a Research Hatchery

In some ways, the ASA is like a chicken-house wherein birds of a feather flock together only to engage in combat to try to establish that they are different from one another.

Traditionally, the sociological pecking-order is largely established by research performance and by the perception of the products of that activity. The structure has primarily been geared to encourage, recognize, and reward research. Until recently, at least, most of our mechanisms and resources have been directed toward promoting and displaying the research activities of members. Less attention has been given to the problems of teaching, the application of knowledge, the training of sociologists for non-academic roles, and other professional concerns.

Entry to journals is highly competitive and highly prized. One only has to go to an annual meeting to observe how privileges are attached to the high rank achieved through the research enterprise.

Observing sociologists at their annual convention suggests striking similarities to what may be noted in observing a flock of chickens. Chickens that rank high in the peck-order gain first chance at the food trough, the dusting areas, the roost, and the nest boxes. The low members of the hierarchy may find themselves driven out ruthlessly from the pen, especially during the earlier phases of peck-order formation. Much of the time, they keep out of the way of their superiors in secluded places. They have a cowed, submissive appearance--the head usually lowered, the body feathers ruffled and unpreened. By contrast, the high-ranking birds strut proudly.

The high-ranking birds also feed regularly during the day and crowd together on the roosts for warmth at night. The low-ranking birds have to feed at twilight or early in the morning while their superiors are roosting.

But a chicken's memory is short. Birds that have been separated for two weeks or more will fight the battle for dominance all over again when they are brought together. Further, it has been observed that when flocks of chickens are mixed, there is severe disruption, sometimes causing some birds to stop laying.

From such observations, one is tempted to ask, what happens as the sociological flock grows larger, more varied, and the birds get mixed more frequently?

For the ASA, I think, it means an adjustment in priorities and a re-allocation of resources so that research is no longer the primary organizational focus. A wide range of new professional concerns is gaining attention. A new pattern is in process, and the full consequences are not yet in view.

Some old members debate departure as they ponder dues payments. Some additional members, with a new mix of characteristics, are being attracted to the flock.

One consequence for the top of the old pecking-order is suggested by a final observation about chickens. It has been noted that while pecking results in seniority rights, a bird that spends a short time daily with each of several flocks has different ranks in the different flocks. An implication is that a new source of status inconsistency may soon be at hand.

Sorting Out Priorities

What, then, is going on at the ASA? Consideration is being given or action is being taken to construct mechanisms to recruit disadvantaged sectors of the population, to promote equity in employment opportunities, to advance the importance of teaching, to certify competence, to monitor and interpret matters of public policy, to intercede in some political processes, to enforce codes of ethics, to protect the freedom of research and teaching, to adjudicate grievances, to validate credentials in a competitive market place, and to provide a variety of personal and social services. We are also being asked to endorse various political prescriptions, to provide hospitality for foreign guests, to arrange child-care at the annual meetings, to offer insurance programs for members, and to muster official representation at educational conferences, inaugurals, and dedicatory ceremonies. This is only a partial listing.

Some of these activities bear on the research enterprise as they affect the selection and training of sociologists, the nature of the problems that might be addressed, and the conditions under which research might proceed. Indeed, many pressures in Washington are exerted for us to become more active in the political process that affects research budgets, key appointments, problem priorities, rules governing research procedures, and the utilization of research to address national needs.

For the ASA to service this rising tide of interests will require either greater total resources or a redirection of present resources from conventional modes of research facilitation. Traditionally, as I have noted, the ASA serves as a clearing-house for information about research. Thus, we collect and impart information about research opportunities; we identify gatekeepers who affect access to research funds; we stage meetings where research is reported, discussed, and refined; we screen research reports for publication; we allocate awards for meritorious achievement in research; and, occasionally, we instigate inquiry by providing funds for preliminary investigations of theoretical and methodological problems of interest to the discipline.

Currently, the elected policy-makers of the ASA spend a great deal of time trying to sort out priorities as they attempt to balance continuing interests in facilitating research along established lines with the growing needs posted by the elaboration of professional concerns. If their proposed solutions are not always clear or consistent, it is probably because there is not a clear grasp of problems, or that the state of the discipline is in such flux that no consensus can be reached about the core of our organizational mission. Often the result is an ad hoc patchwork arrangement of committees to which resources are allocated, not in terms of a rational ordering of priorities but in response to quasi-political pressures from small groups of active constituents.

Among members, and within each governing unit, the debate on organizational direction has at least as many dimensions as the debate on the future of the discipline itself. While the fate of the discipline rests on a broader base than that provided by organizations like the ASA, the use of social research in shaping the future of society will hinge, I believe, on the nature and vitality of our organizational efforts.

In response, I hear strong voices asking, why don't we return to a direct, straightforward concern with fostering the growth of the knowledge base of our discipline? Others inquire, do we any longer have a choice between being a scientific-learned society or a broader based professional association?

Frankly, I don't know the answer. I am beginning to learn about the arena in which resolution, if any, will be reached. Let me conclude by trying to sketch why I believe that stress cannot be reduced by tipping in one direction at the expense of the other.

Conclusion

Lester Ward's pronouncement was premature. Particularly so if he intended to proclaim that sociologists are equipped to enter the applied stage with the professionalism that is required.

The agony of organization now being experienced may be what is required to bring us back to Providence. As I see it, the fundamental issue for sociological organizations as they link to the research enterprise is not the pull of discipline versus profession; rather it emanates from misunderstandings about professionalism.

The development and dissemination of knowledge has consequences. One cannot be successful in fostering the growth of knowledge without confronting the question, knowledge for what? Thus, as we succeed in our mission as scientific researchers, we stimulate the possibilities for successful application and also the need to gain more ready access to research support. This, in turn, breeds the necessity for professionalization that can reinforce social legitimacy.

While sociologists have long been part of the academic profession, only in recent years have they evidenced serious interest in their own professionalism. Many occupations make the struggle for professional identification; few make the grade. We will persist if for no other reason than we have discovered that identification as a professional has become a way to redefine failure as success.

Our appetite for a distinctive professional status has been whetted by a number of historical events, none, perhaps, more important than the call for our expertise during the Great Depression, World War II, and the more recent attempts to engineer the Great Society. In each instance, sociologists were called to duty because someone thought our knowledge and our research skills might be useful in solving problems.

Whatever else transpired, the experience was exhilarating. Members of Congress, and other policy makers, began to be able to pronounce the word "sociology" and even sensed that this was something different from "socialism" and "social work." Thus, the two basic characteristics of a true profession came clearly into view. Self-interest and selfless service merged. The prolonged specialized training of sociologists in a body of abstract knowledge was collectively joined to a strong social service motivation and opportunity.

Sociology began to be sought out as a profession. But elements continue to surface that may yet corrupt the prodding of a Lester Ward. Pressures mount to distort the classical meaning of professional. As a parting shot, I leave you with two challenging examples:

♦ Professionalism generally means a high level of autonomy in research. But who among us has not made accommodations in order to receive research support primarily to enhance personal prestige or the image of the institution in which we work?

♦ Professionalism generally means a high degree of colleagueship wherein persons join organizations as an obligation to the profession and as an opportunity to exchange ideas in a mutual aid framework. But, who among us does not hold membership in the ASA, or in regional organizations, merely to manipulate the system for self-serving, careerist ends?

As we proceed to disentangle such knots, we may discover how far we are from Providence.

Chapter 18

Counsel to Council on Planning
American Sociological Association, Washington, D. C.
March 17, 1975

It is not difficult to sense frustration in this Council.

You exhaust yourselves with talk over details routinely put before you. You would like to consider issues beyond those that affect day-to-day governance. You feel pressed to make decisions without reference to priorities, long-term consequences, or general principles linked to basic goals.

You are tired of trees and would like to catch a glimpse of the forest.

My task today is to respond by outlining a possible way for you to engage long-term planning. The full argument is presented in a memorandum. If this general idea is adopted, other memoranda on implementation will follow.

Questions, Assumptions, Dispositions

Five years from now, in 1980, we will celebrate ASA's 75th anniversary. What will be the shape of our organization at that time? What ought we to be doing that we are not doing today? What are we doing today that should be terminated by then? What changes, if any, are required in our governing structure to maintain desired activities or to pursue new goals? To what extent can or should Council initiate change, and how would it organize any broader participation in the process?

Before you invest further energy, you might want to pause to see how much agreement there is about two assumptions:

    ◆   Worrying about the ASA is worthwhile because the manner in which American sociologists are organized affects the development, dissemination, and utilization of sociological knowledge; and

    ◆   Planning now can (will) shape the future of the ASA in directions that are intended and that are deemed desirable.

Agreement here may be more apparent than real. The itch to plan is real, but the scratch can be costly; moreover, intent and effort are sometimes diverted by deeper dispositions.

Before we start, maybe we ought to sort out our dispositions, perhaps by matching them against the words of three past presidents, one from outside and two from inside our organization:

    ◆   Harry Truman--"I don't know why it is when you've got a good thing, you've got to monkey around changing it."

    ◆   Wilbert Moore--"The utility of utopias is simple. In the degree that utopias are taken seriously, they determine the course of present action and become, in a restricted sense, self-fulfilling. . .The future is the cause of the present in substantial degree."

    ◆   Everett Hughes--"Whatever solutions are arrived at will be compromises. They will be better compromises if no one has any illusions about settling the problem once and for all; if it is kept in mind that the conflict lies deep in many occupations, and that all solutions to it are tentative, based on limited time predictions about the effects of various actions."

From whatever presidential position Council members may start, the prospect of final agreement will probably be enhanced if you enter the planning process by reviewing basic facts about money and membership. Those facts, including charts and figures, are in the memorandum before you, along with provocative questions about trends.

With that background, the more general question becomes how to get mobilized to treat the issues identified, to locate additional ones, and to move on with the planning process?

A New Division of Labor

Council is the governing body of the Association and has ultimate authority for all ASA's actions. In the mid 1960s, the ASA constitution was revised and the size of the Council was reduced from 32 to 18 voting members. The intent was to enable Council to have full discussion around important decisions. It hasn't quite worked that way. You do have full discussions, but the issues aren't always of the order desired. We need a social invention, one that would create a dual agenda for each of the quarterly Council meetings whereby time would be devoted not only to conventional decision-making but also to the planning process.

While the entire Council must continue to deliberate and enact policies, I think it is not feasible for body as a whole to generate the required materials for planning. Some division of labor is required based on a continuing structure for the assignment of responsibilities. What structure and what responsibilities?

The structure should, I think, afford the automatic assignment of Council members to a limited set of small task groups in such a way that there would be movement of members through each of the set of responsibilities as she or he serves out the three year term of office. Furthermore, each task group should have representatives who are in their first, second, and third year of office.

In selecting the responsibilities for each task group, the assignments are bound to have overlapping concerns. However, they should also have some special focus that would both encompass the general objectives of the organization and allow every activity, issue, program, etc., new or old, to have a primary base for planning analysis.

The Constitution specifies that our objectives shall be "to stimulate and improve research, instruction, and discussion and to encourage cooperative relations among persons engaged in the scientific study of society." Research, instruction, and discussion are formidable challenges. But for planning purposes, I would prefer that the general objectives of the ASA be re-phrased to read, "The objectives of the Association shall be to stimulate and improve the development, dissemination, and utilization of sociological knowledge. . ."

This thrust would elevate our instrumental role. It would not be sufficient therefore merely to direct planning toward the survival of the ASA, the satisfaction of interest groups, or the maintenance of certain membership mix unless these elements, in turn, contributed to a more general set of objectives centering on knowledge development, dissemination, and utilization.

I propose, therefore, that Council organize itself into three task groups for planning.

♦   Task Group I would be concerned with the role of the ASA in the development of sociological knowledge (research support, peer review, training and standards, data banks, etc.).

♦   Task Group II would focus on the role of the ASA in the dissemination of sociological knowledge (instruction, publications, mass media, meetings, the public understanding of sociology, linkages to other organizations, etc.).

♦   Task Group III would be concerned with the role of the ASA in the utilization of sociological knowledge (public policy, legislation, advisory panels, social impact analysis, evaluation, career options, client relationships, etc.).

Formation around these three themes is not intended to draw rigid boundaries so that one and only one group would initiate and address a given issue, program, or proposal. Nearly everything we do, publications, for example, could undergo planning analysis from each perspective. Furthermore, each group could be expected to consider both the professional and the scientific aspects of ASA involvement with items they address.

Implementation

How do we get this machinery started? Some details are in your memorandum. Each cycle starts at the first session of Council each year at the annual meeting. Members could be assigned to one of the three planning groups according to positions, years on Council, and an alphabetical listing of the at-large members by the year of term in office.

Following our quarterly meeting schedule, each Task Group could meet for one-half day at the annual meeting to set plans for the year's work. At the December and March meetings of Council, another half-day each time could be devoted to interim reports from each panel. The year's work could then culminate in a two-day June meeting of Council where each panel would present a position paper with recommendations for immediate action, recommendations affecting committee assignments and budget planning for the coming year, and a posting of problems that remain for the next cycle of planning by another set of Council planners who would be rotated onto one of the three panels at the next annual meeting. An Executive Office staff person could be assigned to each panel for the entire year to provide information, support, and to facilitate the exchange of working papers.

Many issues that the task groups could generate or confront would not, and perhaps should not, yield recommendations for immediate action. It is, after all, a planning effort geared to 1980 and beyond. Alternatives could be presented to the membership in various ways before policy and administrative decisions were reached. For example, position papers could be ventilated in Council sponsored panels at the annual meeting followed by summaries of contending views in *Footnotes*.

The success of a planning venture would not be immediately apparent; nor, given the time frame and the cumulative intent of the effort, will it be easy for a given Council to ascertain. Ultimately, I believe, success will hinge on the evolution of orderly and effective procedures that will permit Council to act as a deliberative body where options will be developed, analyzed, and tested in communications with the membership before commitments to action are made.

In this manner, Council would exhibit intellectual and professional leadership, and decision-making would be instructed not only by the wishes but by the informed consent of the membership. With some such scheme for systematic long-range planning, the tempo of participation will quicken and we will merit survival because we will have turned our best talents to stimulating and improving the development, dissemination, and utilization of sociological knowledge.

Chapter 19

The Year the Annual Meeting Stood Still
Executive Officer Retirement Party
70th Annual Meeting, American Sociological Association,
Hilton Hotel, San Francisco
August 28, 1975

I meet with the elite for the last time tonight. Here's my parting shot.

Leap ahead six years. Imagine that the year was 1981. Make one more leap. Assume that present trends continue. What then?

Kansas City had been selected as the site, largely because the Council had determined by a ten to eight vote that it was about equal distance from everywhere. After several preference polls of the membership, the dates had finally been set for the first two weeks starting July 4th.

A hard-working and harmonious program committee had labored long to organize this 76th annual gathering of sociologists. While the total ASA membership had not increased markedly in over a decade, more and more sociologists, members and non-members, individuals and organized sub-groups, sought access to the program.

Individual participation was highly prized, perhaps only second to commanding facilities for round-the-clock expression of special-interest concerns. The 1981 program committee responded enthusiastically to each and every request for participation and accommodations. Thus the birth of the first two-week annual meeting in ASA history.

When the preliminary program was issued, the scale of participation became apparent. A total of 4,989 persons were to be involved in 982 sessions. This included twelve grand plenaries and thirty-two plenary panels, organized by Joyce Ward Montgomery, a great, great, granddaughter of the first ASA President, Lester Ward. The theme, of course, was "Whither Sociology?"

The size of the meeting had also been nourished by the continuous growth in the number of sections, a trend started in the mid-1970s. There were now forty-one sections with the most recent inclusion of the Section on Non-Critical Sociology and the Section on Extra-terrestrial Sociology.

With this number, it became necessary to round up every round table in Kansas City in order to stage, in four giant ballrooms, a continuous flow of workshops and informal sessions for the presentation of preliminary findings from pilot studies.

Apart from expansion, features of the program remained remarkably similar to those of earlier years.

To be sure, hard-cover books had long-since disappeared to be supplanted by microfiche readers and computer printouts in the publisher's exhibit halls. And there were now five, instead of the traditional two, business meetings which provided an ample flow of resolutions to insure the overhaul of the constitution each year.

There was also a significant increase in the number of prizes and awards offered annually by the ASA to supplement the recognition traditionally accorded via the Sorokin, Stouffer, and DuBois-Johnson-Frazier awards. For example, prominent among the new prizes was the annual Dennis Wrong--Charles Wright Ethics Award.

Despite continuities, a number of forces coalesced in 1981 to bring the functioning of the meeting to a near frozen state. Prime among these was the continuation in stagflation that had plagued the American economy since 1975. The country had not yet recovered from the failure of the second Ford administration (Reagan had replaced Rockefeller as Vice-President) to halt inflation or to reduce unemployment. University budgets sagged while prices soared. As a consequence, sociologists, except for those actually scheduled for participation in the program, were unable to attend the Kansas City meeting.

The result was predictable. Of the 4,898 persons on the program, 4,896 registered for the meeting (at the last minute, Amitai Etzioni and Si Goode canceled their joint Didactic Seminar on "Toward a

Codification of Federal Support of Unfunded Policy Research").

The only other persons in attendance at the meeting were Henry Quellmalz, the loyal and dedicated printer of the ASA journals; twenty-seven ASA staff members, including an Executive Specialist for Group Flights; and, six members of the 1981 Program Committee.

1981, then, was the year that the Annual Meeting stood still. Two new records were set simultaneously. Total registration was at a new high, but actual attendance at the 982 sessions was at a new low. In fact, for the vast majority of sessions, the only persons in attendance were the persons making presentations in that part of the program.

This proved embarrassing. It also provoked a great deal of talk about starting a new section on small groups.

The ASA Council moved with all deliberate speed to respond to this curious state of communication. The problem was immediately pumped into the Council's well-established long-range planning mechanism. The results were startling.

Armed with innovative Council policies, the 1982 Program Committee set to work to revamp and revitalize the Annual Meeting. Advanced technology came to the rescue. The six members of the 1982 program committee, loaded with the latest audio-visual technology, visited every region of the country and recorded the presentation of papers, didactic seminars, workshops, roundtable discussions, plenary panels, and even the presidential address for 1982. Everyone who wanted to participate in the program was welcome and was recorded. Another new record in participation was set. Coupons were attached to the preliminary program. Members could now simply request recordings of whatever sessions they desired.

Thus, 1982 marked a new beginning. It was the first Cassette Convention in ASA history.

Expenses were cut to the bone. Travel was eliminated. Time and place decisions were obviated. Child care was obliterated. Resolutions were adumbrated. Symbolic interaction was simulated. Ideas were communicated.

Through the whir of cassettes, the annual meeting no longer stood still

Chapter 20

Mid-Life Crisis Control

86th Annual Meeting, American Sociological Association, Cincinnati, Ohio
August 25, 1991

I have been directed to reflect on problems of the middle years for the ASA executive office.

This task is not unlike that confronted by historians who attempt to account for the development of the Middle Kingdom of ancient China, which doubtless you will recall was designated by the Chou Dynasty as the center of the habitable world some 2400 years ago.

That was the approximate description of Washington, D.C. offered by Jack and Matilda Riley when they finally induced me to flee the western provinces to become Executive Officer of the ASA.

By accepting the call in 1972, I actually became the middle member of that corps of seven executive officers that have served the ASA since it was established in Washington, DC. That is, three persons served before me (Gresh Sykes, Ed Volkhart, Jay Demerath) and three persons completed terms after me (Hans Mauksch, Russ Dynes, Bill D'Antonio). Keep in mind that there would be no need for Executive Officers if there were no problems. And, indeed, there might even be fewer problems if there were no executive officers.

The Middle Years

There is a defensible rationale for designating the first decade of ASA's existence in Washington, DC as the historical referent to the middle years. The period 1964-1974 was a unique time of test for sociology.

As fate would have it, the test would come from the grit of growth, not from the depression of decline. However, even though advance was unexcelled, edgy questions emerged immediately. Could we survive as a needle in the haystack of organized Washington? Was the membership willing to sustain a professional staff in a full-time organization? Would sociologists tax themselves to maintain a federal presence?

The move to the nation's capital was a bold stroke. Risks were involved. Success was by no means assured. The sister disciplines of psychology, anthropology, political science, history, and geography came to set up house in Washington, but economics held on to the older model by maintaining their scholarly headquarters on a campus under part-time leadership (Perhaps this was because they had such a strong representation in Washington anyhow).

The move to Washington in the early 1960s must have been driven by a vision that sociology was particularly relevant for the times. The thrust was that we could go beyond development and dissemination to a more directed utilization of knowledge.

The social and political context, including the civil rights movement and the social engineering efforts of the Johnson administration, certainly reinforced an activist proclivity. New opportunities blossomed for sociologists to do evaluative research, to serve on commissions, and to offer expert counsel.

Was this a golden era? Perhaps. By several indicators it was at least a high-water mark for our discipline.

For example, the total doctoral output in sociology accelerated from 162 in 1960 to its historic highs around 700 annually in the mid-1970s.

Furthermore, the total federal funding earmarked specifically for sociological research reached its historic peak rising from $6 million in 1962 to $119 million in 1972.

The latter figure has not been eclipsed since. Moreover, in terms of sociology's share of the total federal investment in social science research, this was a startling four-fold gain from 10 to 39 percent in one decade.

There may be irony in the fact that sociology reached its peak of prominence during the Nixon administration when over the three years from 1971 to 1973 it captured more than a third of federal social science research funds. Under the later administrations of Ford, Carter, Reagan, and Bush, it wavered around a 12 to 15 percent share (dropping to low point of $52 million in 1982) and never exceeding a 20 percent share again in the years up through 1990.

The critical factor in building this pinnacle for sociology was the emphatic commitment of the federal government to applied research, coupled to the perception that this was what sociology was all about.

In the past forty years of federal funding, it was only during the first Nixon administration that more than eighty percent of the research dollars for sociology were allocated for applied research, reaching the apex of 88 percent in 1973. This compares to the low of 46 percent under the Bush administration in 1990.

As it turned out, the dynamic externalities of the middle period made it a propitious time for the ASA to try plant organizational roots in Washington.

But, even these roots required special nourishment to accommodate growth, to professionalize service, and to respond to the growing pluralistic disposition of the membership.

The challenge is reflected in a few numbers that merit note in a comparative form. First, what happened to membership?

Membership

The eighty-five year history of the ASA has been marked by periods of both slow and rapid growth, periods of decline, and periods of relative stability in membership size.

In its first year, 1906, the society had 115 members and fourteen years later the 1,000 mark was reached for the first time. Another quarter century elapsed before we reached 2,000. It then only took three years more before we numbered 3,000, and another three years to reached 4,000.

By the time of our 50th anniversary in 1957, the ASA was 5,000 persons strong. Nine years later, membership had doubled to 10,000. After that, about a thousand members were added each year until the peak of 14,827 was reached in 1971, the all-time apogee for the ASA.

Membership stabilized over 14,000 at end of the middle period. Since that time, membership declined to a low of 11,223 in 1984, followed by a resurgence to 12,992 members today, almost precisely the size we were in 1968.

While total membership reached a high during the middle period, it was not a feature without problems. Each annual report made that clear. For example, in 1974 we noted that 25 percent of the 4,182 faculty persons listed in the *ASA Guide to Graduate Departments* were not members of the association.

A solicitation yielded 100 new members from this category and a flock of letters explaining, usually in cost-benefit terms, the reasons for declining the invitation. Why, these people asked, should we join the ASA when we can read the journals in the library?

Our counter argument, not often persuasive, was to point out that while dues constituted about one-third of ASA income and publications constitute about one-half of expenditures, dues nonetheless help made it possible to put journals in the library and support the organization that creates other major channels of communication for scientific and professional purposes.

In 1974, policies also were being shaped to elicit greater membership diversity. Appeals were directed to sociologists in non-academic settings and to teachers in institutions without graduate programs. How far and in what ways would this modify our traditional "learned society" model of organization? I encouraged council to contemplate this because "Ancient but muted issues like accreditation, certification, and licensing could...rise to the surface along with other pressures to expand professional and political services."

Money

Membership growth in the middle period also meant a marked increase in revenue for the ASA. Thus, between November 1964 and June 1974, annual revenue quadrupled ($219,282 to $864,925). In only one year, 1971, was there a deficit. Over the same period, the equity of the association increased more than sevenfold (from $33,396 to $246,482).

One major investment, problematic as it was at the time that Jay Demerath engineered it, will ultimately yield significant returns. The 1990 audit suggests that the value of the property at 1722 N Street is now set at $1.4 million. That's up about ten-fold from the initial investment made in 1971.

Solutions Reveal Problems

Organizational direction was at the core of difficulties that agitated the middle years. The most eloquent expression of its fundamental dimensions was penned by Milton Yinger in his final report as

Secretary of ASA in 1974.

Yinger deftly penetrated into fixed fissures of thought that threatened the viability of the ASA. Since World War II the ASA had evolved from a homogeneous to a more rambunctious and diverse organization. Now there are splits that could immobilize the ASA. "Antiestablishmentarianism", a fear of orthodoxy, of bureaucracy, of premature closing of debate, stands at one pole. This view holds that we should not set standards, because standards imply orthodoxy. On the other side, according to Yinger, are deep-seated assumptions that a science of society, culture, and human behavior is possible, that human beings are part of nature, that the empirical and logical methds of science are applicable to their study.

Moreover, voices mount to foster teaching practices instead of merely encouraging the publication of research. Other voices call for an activist stance on social policy. Yinger, having blended the perplexities of research, teaching and policy, concluded on a note of uncertainty.

Uncertainties from the move to Washington, and the press to manage and sustain growth, most likely prompted Yinger's farewell formulation. The record also reveals an on-going accommodation to his concerns. Some were directed toward research, others toward teaching, and some toward policy matters. For example, in my second annual report, the following acts were said to have constituted a "season of successful starts."

♦ The ASA received funding of $99,760 for the first of a proposed three year project entitled "A Program of Assessment, Articulation, and Experimentation in Undergraduate Teaching of Sociology in the United States" (Hans Mauksch's leadership).

♦ We selected the first 20 ASA Fellows to be fully funded for graduate training in Ph.D departments under the Minority Fellowship Program. This number of fellowships was double the number initially planned with the 1974 grant from NIMH of $131,364 because, under the effective guidance of Acting Program Director, Cheryl Leggon, an additional $75,000 was received from NIE.

♦ We joined with other social science associations to sponsor a year-long study of problems concerning confidentiality in social science research (funded by the Russell Sage Foundation).

♦ We launched a new effort to move the discipline forward by awarding small grants totaling $8,500 to eight sets of sociologist concerned with theoretical and methodological issues. A total of 41 persons are involved in the interchanges taking place.

♦ We made arrangements with the Library of Congress to establish an ASA archives.

♦ We received $2,000 from a private foundation to support travel to World Congress by the Research Committee on Sex Roles. The ASA was also awarded $10,000 to support the Congress and, in particular, travel by junior scholars from developing countries.

♦ We implemented a system of "open nominations" for all elective officers of the ASA.

♦ We changed policies so that authors of articles in ASA journals will share equally with the copyright holder, the ASA, all royalties received from reprint rights.

♦ We approved plans for a new Section on the Sociology of World Conflicts.

♦ We created three new committees: Environmental Sociology; Rights of Non-Academic Sociologists; and Non-sexist Terminology in Publications.

Other efforts to enhance symbolism or to advance solutions to issues churned around extending membership, gaining money, and broadening representation in governance. Some items even drifted into current history where, honed by improvements, they have become part of our institutional character. At their inception, many involved complex negotiations. Few were adopted without tension between the interests of researchers, teachers, and policy makers. The record is laced with examples, including:

♦ The founding of *Footnotes* and the return of *The American Sociologist* to a quarterly journal to deal in a scholarly manner with professional developments.

♦ The conversion of caucuses to standing ASA committees to open formal channels for the concerns of minorities and women.

♦ The shift of annual membership dues to a graduated income scale.

♦ The disappearing publisher's parties were transformed into DAN, the Departmental Alumni Night.

♦ To strengthen representative governance, Council meetings were moved up to a quarterly basis.

♦ To enhance the prestige of the Rose Monographs, the series was transferred from in-house publishing to the Cambridge University Press.

But enough of details. The ASA survived the middle-period. More important, under the skilled leadership of Hans Mauksch, Russ Dynes, and Bill D'Antonio the organization marched briskly into the contemporary era.

Political Instrumentation

Unmentioned problems must await other forums. One in particular will merit special attention: the evolution of COSSA, the Consortium of Social Science Associations.

I attended more than thirty meetings of COSSA during its early years before it became the most significant political instrument in Washington for sociology and for all of social science. The genesis of COSSA in the middle period is interesting. It stemmed from two factors: isolation of position and status deprivation.

In the beginning, COSSA meant that the executive officers of sociology, psychology, anthropology, political science, history, geography, statistics, and the law associations, huddled together for comfort, mutual aid and support.

The exchange of ideas was helpful for the respective associations, but, so too was commiseration for the common trials of office. For more than 300 days a year executive officers occupy a somewhat lonely professional position. Besieged by written complaints and requests starting, "Why doesn't your organization do something about..." it isn't until the annual meeting or the periodic meetings of governing councils that they gain personal feedback.

But there was something more critical than that.

During the middle period, the disciplinary associations were particularly estranged from the prestigious national centers of science, including the National Science Foundation and the National Research Council. Even more to the point, these associations felt that they were not taking seriously by the likes of their own Social Science Research Council. Accordingly, the disciplinary associations felt left out of any serious fight against ignorance about the scientific merit of the social sciences. The executive officers worried a lot about those strained relations as they met in the informal meetings of COSSA.

Then came a profound threat to all of social and behavioral science in 1980. COSSA was reborn, with political muscle. Unified action brought credibility and brilliantly enhanced our capacity to survive, and possibly thrive, in Washington.

Our man of the hour knows this. Bill D'Antonio contributed significantly to the effort. He focused on the transformation of COSSA in his recent farewell report. Clearly, sociology has given, and has also gained, political strength and intellectual vitality from a unity of effort with the other social and behavioral sciences.

Thus, a new day has dawned. Social science is now armed better than ever to fight the mother of all doubts, uncertainties, and difficulties on the federal scene.

This was a vision barely discerned in that long-ago when the ASA boldly ventured into its Middle Kingdom in search of the center of the habitable world.

Social Science

Ten years can shake any world, including most specifically the personal one. It positively did for me in organizational activity and in intellectual outlook.

By the 1970s, after considerable indoctrination and some isolation, I acted, often energetically, as if sociology was either at the center of the intellectual universe, or, given its broad scope, perhaps even the whole of it. A correction was overdue.

It came in the 1980s as fate brought me to other organizational activities where I was immediately challenged to curb residual parochial impulses stemming from a commitment to a single discipline (including trying to gain a budget advantage for sociology at the expense of psychology, economics, political science or anthropology). From being identified as a sociologist, I began a transformation of commitment through gaining an understanding, and partaking in a political defense, of all social and behavioral science.

Visions of that broader universe are on display in the seven selections that follow.

Actually, the first item on "Mapping Human Relations" from 1952 indicates that I had a long-standing, if not finely tuned, disposition to become a missionary for social science. It wasn't until the 1980s, however, that I was given the fullest opportunity to exercise that inclination through a call to serve at the National Science Foundation.

The NSF was not only a site for missionary work, it was also a remarkable place for intense exposure to the exciting intellectual ferment in every field.

I became a student again, with brilliant instruction available as I observed researchers gather in peer review meetings to sift out the relative merits of proposals for research.

The integrity of the review process was impressive. The method was approved or disapproved. Innovations from within disciplines and linkages between fields sparked forth from keen, competitive, communication.

As never before, I came to appreciate the quality of the specialized work by separate disciplines. I was impressed by technical and substantive advances in economics, linguistics, political science, geography, anthropology, etc.

Even more exciting, was the discovery of common concerns. Cross-disciplinary work infused methodological advances and the development of time-series data bases, with results that clearly delineated and advanced knowledge and understanding.

The prospects for intellectual gain from common lines of inquiry were compelling. In the pursuit of scarce research resources, disciplines discovered each other. Their follow-on reaction would determine whether knowledge gains would enhance the perception of social science.

From its start in 1950, the Foundation was the site of unrelenting trials over the legitimacy of social science as science. Gains were gradually made, but were never totally secure. After the presidential election of 1980, the ideology of the new administration led to policies that threatened the very existence of programs in the social and behavioral sciences.

The response was historically unique. It included a unified defense of the merits of social science mustered across the boundaries of all science to result in a rescue that maintained opportunities for the social and behavioral sciences. Perilous acts were performed in this fascinating theater for the politics of science. Some views on the ongoing drama are presented in the six scripts that follow the dispositional curtain-raiser.

(A five decade chronicle of social science at NSF, by the present author, can be found in *Milestones and Millstones*, New Brunswick, N.J.: Transaction Publishers, 1992)

Chapter 21

Mapping Human Relations

Grand View College Homecoming , Des Moines, Iowa

May 3, 1952

Nostalgia rules this night. Time and again our attention has turned back to 1942 and to 1927 as we honor the graduates from ten and twenty-five years ago.

Currents of humor and gales of glory from that golden past have washed around us, enough so that I must avoid drowning you with additional memories. For 1927 that will be easy. All I know about that year is that Calvin Coolidge was in the White House and that he issued a proclamation against sin. This act, I am told, provoked immediate agitation campus wide protest, led by the seminarians, moved the students to hang the President in effigy.

So much for the roaring twenties.

It is more difficult to refrain from amplifying moments from the early 1940s. Here I must avoid drawing from material that I used as Pegasus editor for the disclosures of faculty foibles and student shenanigans. The record reveals every pun, innuendo, joke, spoof, lampoon, and parody known to the world of buffoonery. I suspect that there are more than a few persons present who will applaud being spared a resurrection of the overripe barbs from that period.

There was also a serious side to the life of the class of 1942. Like our elders from 1927, we, too, engaged in protest. Up until December 7, 1941, there was strong opposition to possible involvement in the European war. Isolationists outnumbered interventionists in the Midwest heartland. Some of us joined a march on the state capital to underscore the plea for peace. "America-Firsters" cheered. The

American Legion jeered. Eggs were thrown along with epithets. All of that ended with the attack on Pearl Harbor. Shortly thereafter most of the class of 1942 marched off to World War II.

Those of us here tonight are the fortunate survivors. We can now congregate to tell tall stories about hardships, heroic feats, and novel benefits. Among the latter, none is more significant than the G.I. Bill. Without it, it is unlikely that I would have been asked to speak here tonight, and certainly not on the matter I have chosen to address. With the G.I. Bill, I went on to graduate training and gained the impulse to talk about education in a world of change.

Persistence of Change

I confess that such a topic is not exactly standard after-banquet fare. Nor are my motives particularly exalted. Several of my first professors are in the audience tonight. Ten years ago they strove mightily to impart learning. I now feel the urge to try to impress them with some exhibition of maturation, itself a form of change.

I am particularly haunted by a course in philosophy. Professor Ammentorp had us visit the thoughts of the ancient Greeks. Heraclitus, in particular, cast a long shadow. By observing that one cannot step into the same river twice, he understood that no two things are exactly alike, but also that no one thing is ever twice the same. Yes, the river flows and the one who steps into it also changes.

In recent years, rivers seem to be rising, currents are faster, eddies more turbulent, and streams overflow more frequently. Viewed in this manner, change challenges contemporary thoughtways.

In the pursuit of higher education, I have become something of a "salesman for science" as applied to the social realm. Now there is a river I hadn't imagined that I would step into when I started college here over a decade ago. And since we are all old friends, I shall try to be mindful of the late hour lest the length and the tone of this argument be the death of a salesman's audience.

Forces of change can threaten traditional beliefs, general rules, and ancient creeds. But these forces can also prod productive inquiry and prompt exciting lines of investigation.

It is the latter that concerns me tonight on this return to the college where I first began to explore generalizations, chiefly those stemming from humanistic and religious concerns. Perhaps that background accounts for the missionary impulses about to be revealed.

No challenge is greater today than that of coping with problems of social behavior. Implicit is the need to learn how to change the ways in which human beings relate to each other. Given Heraclitus, is this at all possible?

In the realm of human relations, the word change often evokes emotions. It can threaten. It yields visions of protesting students, wild-eyed radicals, or bomb throwing revolutionaries.

But change is also denoted by more moderate terms such as education, training, or therapy. Most of us are probably more disposed to have others "educate" us than to have them "change" us. But, I would ask, how well is modern education equipped to prompt the basic changes required to right whatever is deemed wrong in our world today?

History recites a long-standing argument over what education properly attempts to modify. Should educators simply impart knowledge, or is it warranted to strive to bring about fundamental shifts in attitudes and values and thus to try to instill new and presumably better ways of life?

Gifted people express diverse views about this mission. However, such contestants as Robert Hutchins and John Dewey agree that education today suffers from the lack of a unifying principle.

Controversy arises over what that unifying principle ought to be. Some say it will be found through the classics, and they prescribe a curriculum involving one-hundred great books. Others believe that it can be found in science.

Unity of Science

The latter orientation now fascinates me. And since there is widespread misunderstanding about the nature of science, I will attempt to clarify concepts and explore a few implications that flow from a commitment to this thoughtway.

We live in a day of penicillin, plastics, and pens that write under water. The bountiful technological products of scientific effort, whatever their value, do not constitute the primary case for an assertion that we live in an age of science. If science is cast only in these terms, we would have to look elsewhere for a unifying principle in education.

Science is not gadgets, nor is it merely a subject matter like chemistry or physics.

Science is a method of asking clear and answerable questions so that we may discover the conditions under which events occur. This orientation requires the assembly of verifiable observations, an accurate account of findings, and the arrangement of data so that valid conclusions can be drawn.

Social science, a relative newcomer to this realm, is largely driven by this conception today. Inquiry is prompted by curiosities and concerns. Some have practical interest, others address longer-range theoretical claims.

To cite examples from just one department in one university, my colleagues are currently concerned about the conditions under which racial tension and race riots occur, under which the mass media have an impact on attitudes and behavior, under which birth rates and other population changes affect foreign policy, under which leadership can facilitate or hinder consensus building in organizations, and under which values are altered or sustained.

Technical methodologies vary for each curiosity, but the commitment to the tenets of the scientific method is universal. What of the product?

Let me state a belief, one that is supported by a growing body of evidence. It was after chemists and biologists had made considerable headway in developing basic knowledge in their realms that pharmacists and physicians produced and applied the wonders of synthetic chemistry, the vaccines, vitamins, and antibiotics to control disease and promote health. I believe that scientific effort in the social realm will develop knowledge with a similar high utility.

The need is apparent in the crush of war, crime, mental disease, race antagonisms, labor-management disputes, marital maladjustment, and so forth. But, the ultimate outcome will, I believe, depend in great part on how each succeeding generation of students comprehends and extends the assumptions and practices of science.

Implications for Change

If educators take this orientation seriously, how might this affect the content of education?

It will not necessarily mean more physics and chemistry. Nor will it mean more current-events classes, and similar developments which have passed for social science. Nor would it mean a de-emphasis of those subjects to which persons have looked for solace and spiritual satisfaction throughout the ages.

One change seems certain. It will require alteration in the methods of teaching the nature and use of symbols, particularly language. I don't mean old-fashioned grammar. The essential point is to utilize a system of language which corresponds more closely to the world as it is.

In a basic way, this is important for human survival. The unique survival mechanism of human beings is not, as among oysters, a hard shell and extreme fecundity; not, as among wolves, ferocity and sharp teeth; not, as among giraffes, long necks and flatness of feet. The unique survival mechanism for human beings is the ability to organize social cooperation and to accumulate knowledge over generations through the use of symbols, particularly language.

The infant science of semantics, where human behavior is viewed in terms of the use and misuse of symbols, will play a larger role in a science-oriented curriculum.

One of the things this outlook would do is to disabuse students of the common all-or-none way of looking at the world. This is the habit that oversimplifies matters of human relations with dualistic designations of true or false, right or wrong, good or bad, just or unjust, communism or capitalism, heredity or environment. Reality requires the specification of degrees that lie between the polarities that readily capture public attention.

In addition, we must get across the simple idea that words are not the things they stand for. Words may be thought of as maps, and with certain characteristics they have reliable utility.

Consider, for example, the ordinary automobile road map. With it we can plan and carry out journeys over territory we have never covered, and estimate the time and difficulty involved in getting there. We can also see before we start a trip that if we take certain routes we shall never arrive where we want to go.

Short sentences like "Shake well before using" and "Do not open before Christmas" may be regarded as simple word-maps designed to guide behavior. Humans have also developed more abstract and comprehensive word-maps to guide larger realms of human conduct. The Constitution, the Communist Manifesto, the Apostles Creed, and the Theory of Relativity are of this type.

Commitment to the scientific orientation sensitizes us to three general points about mapping.

First, a word-map will be useful when it corresponds to the

territory it supposedly represents.

Second, maps never represent everything about the territory.

And finally, even the best maps are likely to become obsolete sooner or later because the things they represent change or our interest in them changes.

In general, however, all problem solving requires some kind accurate map-making. If we wish to bake a cake, we have to know about the characteristics of the flour and other ingredients we intend to use; if we wish to build a bridge, we have to know about the properties of steel and concrete, the strength of the current and the width of river to be bridged; if we seek an effective government, there must be accurate assessment of traditions, needs, resources, and modes for responsive participation.

Whether we successfully bake a cake, build the bridge, or govern a nation depends in great degree on how well the territory of concern has been mapped. Scientists are map makers; social scientists aspire to make accurate maps of human relationships.

Conclusion

Educators working with such an orientation would not be concerned primarily either with depriving students of their beliefs or of inculcating new ones. Rather, they would be interested in communicating to students a method by which they may test for themselves the validity and adequacy of their own route to aspiration and action.

In the social realm, that work can be guided by an assessment of the probable costs and consequences of programs proposed for amelioration. It is the function of social science to make that assessment. Science is not a substitute for ideals, it is the most effective instrument yet devised to seek their attainment. The function and power of ideals in human affairs is not being questioned by the scientific orientation. But science can help us to distinguish between ideals and illusions.

Intuition, understanding, and insight are not methods that compete with science. They are the goals at which all methods aim. The precise techniques of the scientific orientation are merely the more refined tools by which we acquire insight and understanding. If we hope to achieve some measure of control over social problems, similar to that gained by science in the physical and biological realm, then, I believe, society must develop new talents and apply resources to social research on a scale such as that has been applied in the sister realms.

Accordingly, when I return to this college for the 25th reunion of the class of 1942, I hope to see facilities for instruction and research in social science comparable to that now extended to physics and chemistry.

One final testy observation. Whether education will help us map our human relations depends ultimately on the validity of what we teach. Much of what we now teach about human relations is worse than useless, because it is heavily weighted with error, prejudice, and speculation from bygone generations. Unless knowledge is constantly tested and replenished through scientific research, education may be an obstacle rather than an aid to social progress.

Mapping human relations is an exciting scientific challenge. When pursued via the orientation that I have advocated, it is, above all else, a technique of agreement that systematically seeks to reach across cultural divisions of race, religion, and social standing in order to extend human cooperation.

Every graduate of this college from 1927 and 1942 is endowed with a special appreciation of that possibility. I hope that these remarks on mapping human relations will refresh and renew our affinity to that condition.

Chapter 22

Turtles and the National Science Board
227th Meeting of the National Science Board, Woods Hole , Massachusetts
June 18, 1981

Let me be blunt. The National Science Board has a turtle problem.

If you can be relieved of this enigma then the uncertainty and political embarrassment that social science has visited upon this distinguished body for the past thirty years will be exorcised.

What is the turtle problem? Its essence came to William James of Harvard after he delivered a stirring public address on the "Nature of the Universe."

Following his lecture, a little old lady approached to express appreciation but also to register dissent. "It was a good talk," she said, "but you got it all wrong." Intrigued, the professor asked the fateful question, "What do you mean?"

"Well," said the lady, "the world is not as you describe it. You see, professor, the earth rests on the back of a turtle."

"Ah," replied William James, "and what holds that turtle up?"

"Another turtle, of course," came the answer.

"Well," said James pressing on, "what, then, does that turtle rest on?"

"Now, professor, I have got you" came the twinkling reply. "You see, from there on it is turtles all the way down."

And so it has been at NSF.

The perception of social science has never crawled off the back of the original turtle.

My intent is to move you away from that error, compounded as it has become over the years, by sketching some elementary facts about social science at NSF.

If this moves you to a more thorough examination of the record, then I am confident that pride in achievement will overcome uncertainty and shield you from political embarrassment. So much for intent.

Special Plea

At every level of behavior--from self to society, from interpersonal to institutional--the human landscape today is marked by unmet challenges and unsolved problems. New and deeper understandings about ourselves and our social actions are required to allow full expression of individual initiative, to increase productivity, and to enhance the quality of life.

Having read the justifications for recent NSF budget requests, I assume that you would not quarrel with these general goals.

What, then, is social science all about? In broad, general terms, it seeks to advance and organize knowledge about the forms, processes, and consequences of human interaction whether at the interpersonal, group, organizational, or societal level.

Every person gains experience and has responsibilities at these levels and, by and large, acts and copes through common sense trial and error. Nevertheless, living in a family or working in an organization does not automatically make one a social scientist, any more than swimming in the sea makes one an oceanographer or being an animal breeder makes one a geneticist.

More specific questions follow. What are the social and behavioral sciences? What do they do? What part of the science world are they? Why should public funds finance their research?

Specific answers to these questions are provided in a memorandum that I have included in the agenda book for this meeting. To supplement that understanding, I want to add a few more general points about social science and about our programs at NSF.

I know that this is special pleading. But never before has the state of social science been under such siege at NSF. My hope is to use this privilege of appearing before you to generate a clearer estimate of the worth of social science, real and potential, that will move you to a strong defense of its place in the National Science Foundation.

Countering Skepticism

Stephen Jay Gould, whom I'm sure you all know as a distinguished Harvard paleontologist, recently observed that "Science is the most dialectical of human endeavors. Embedded in culture, it possesses unparalleled power to alter the very systems that nurture it."

The excitement of scientific discovery is rooted in this claim. So, too, is an implication of value uncertainty. New knowledge always contains threat as well as promise. As this body is astutely aware, the alteration power of physics, chemistry, and biology is demonstrated regularly through engineering feats that are widely sensed and usually, but not always, valued. Not so for economics, sociology, or political science. The impact of the social sciences is more subtle, less readily acknowledged, and more often challenged in terms of worth.

There are many reasons for skepticism about social science as science--some profound, some erroneous and misguided. At the base of several arguments is the idea that while the nature of physical, chemical, and biological phenomena allow for regularities and thus for predictability, the nature of human nature is individualistic, volatile, changeable by virtue of observation, and, therefore, not really a matter to be understood in scientific terms--terms that require repetition, regularities, patterns.

This position implies that atoms are more real than attitudes, or that microbes and molecules are more stable and observable than, say, migration, monogamy, or monetary systems.

Can one really be scientific about how people influence one another, how economies function, how organizations grow and decay, how rules and laws emerge and affect our lives, or why it is that there is not war of all against all? The answer would have to be "no" if such phenomena were, in fact, not patterned.

But patterns do exist. They emerge not to create a social science but to sustain and extend all that is human.

In political, economic, cultural, and social matters, a wide range of behaviors is possible. The challenge is to discover which acts really occur, with what frequency, and under what conditions.

In social science, as in physical and biological research realms, it is exciting to discover the source of patterns, how they emerge, what forms they take, the linkages between them, how the patterns break, and how they change.

Human social behavior does not yield meekly to probes that seek understanding through scientific research. But, over time and with increasingly sophisticated sets of observational and analytic tools, the substance of social science is maturing, even as its conceptions are changing.

How much money the federal government should expend for social science research depends, in part, on the value placed on the information, discoveries, and explanations that such research yields. Here the record becomes important. What achievements can be identified from past investments? Clearly, the case for social science does not rely merely on findings that yield startling results.

Social science involves the painstaking process of discovery and explanation that builds knowledge incrementally as findings are tested and understandings are revised. Knowledge of this sorts is not divisible into private and public realms; it is a common good that requires public investments.

Ultimately, costs must be measured against the gains in understanding and also against the risks in not proceeding with disciplined inquiry to discover just how social phenomena work and why social actions do not always work out as intended.

Each program in the Division of Social and Economic Science at NSF supports research that will add significantly to the fund of knowledge. Let me briefly underscore a few lines of inquiry that have gained support from our programs in social science.

Economics

Economics tries to explain decisions about the allocation of scarce resources.

The research that we support includes studies of decision making under uncertainty and the resulting behavior of the economic system; the formation of expectations regarding future states of the economy and their impact on public policy interventions; and tool-building activities in the mathematical formulation of economic theory and the analysis of economic data.

Such lines of inquiry have laid the groundwork for a new generation of macro econometric models, which can be estimated and validated more rigorously than earlier models to generate more accurate forecasts of economic activity.

For many years theorists have been striving for a better understanding of how the real world departs from the assumptions of the perfectly competitive model. Diverse research now embraces both perfect and imperfect competition. This opens new understandings of the way businesses operate, how workers search for and perform their jobs, and how government agencies are organized to achieve economic objectives.

Recent work on decentralized choice suggests that the next decade could see radical change in modes of governmental and individual decision-making. This is possible from work building on a significant advance in social and economic theories that occurred a generation ago with the development of life cycle models of decisions.

In these models, individuals consider not only their present state but also their expectations about the future. Data inadequacies at first slowed empirical research in this area, but reliable social and economic data are now becoming available to track individual and family decisions over long periods of time. That follows from the NSF supported Panel Study of Family Income Dynamics.

We also support methodological research to enable the analysis of the incredible detail and complexity of observations from panel studies that cannot be managed by current estimation methods. This new capability opens up important findings on such matters on how wealth is transmitted from one generation to another and how important demographic changes take place.

Geography and Regional Science

The primary objective of research in human geography is to advance understanding of the criteria, processes, and problems involved in the location decisions of people, firms, and institutions that produce the spatial organization of society and economic activity.

Traditionally, research has concentrated on the study of land use; the location of settlements, cultural groups, and economic activity; resource management; man-environment relationships; the migration of people; the movement of commodities; and the spatial diffusion of information.

Recent geographic research has focused on location theory, regional economic development and stagnation (including urban regions), population redistribution, and the spatial analysis of social pathologies and public policy. Many services, such as those provided by ambulances and fire-fighting equipment, are useful to the extent that they can respond quickly to calls. Clinics, hospital emergency rooms, schools and colleges, the farmer's grain elevator, and the urban shopping center also need to be optimally located for the efficient use of time and energy.

Today, computer programs and mathematical methods of analysis are used to identify ideal locations. These approaches, developed by geographers and other social scientists with NSF support during the past ten years, include the use of mathematical theorems, special algorithms tested in a variety of conditions, computer graphics enabling visual presentation of demand data and of alternative planning schemes, and new modes of spatial analysis. As a result, decision makers in the public and private sectors can evaluate locations for different activities and decide which best meets defined criteria.

Important scientific questions remain concerning spatial-choice processes and the spatial organization of society. Geographic models and conclusions must be tested against comparative data from other countries to improve the worth of theoretical conclusions.

Political Science

During the last twenty years, marked change has occurred in the ways that political scientists conduct their research. Often referred to as the "behavioral revolution," this method views politics as an outcome of human interaction processes and decisions rather than merely as a product of legal statements and formal rules. The result is an advance in the scientific understanding of basic political processes. Rigorous modes of explanation and analysis offer a contrast to conventional descriptive and literary approaches.

Important work in political science continues to be conducted at the intersection of disciplines. Thus we support (a) studies of public opinion, electoral behavior, and elite decision making which draw upon theories of cognitive processes or economic rationality; (b) studies of domestic and international political economy integrating macro-economic and political processes; and (c) research on political development and social change informed by recent theoretical and methodological advances in sociology and anthropology.

The NSF program encourages the development and empirical testing of deductive theories and formal models. However, the most important new direction will be increased support for the construction and enrichment of political data bases, including our long-standing investment in the National Election Study.

Law and Social Science

In less than two decades, scholars in this growing field have converged from across the social and behavioral disciplines to advance generic knowledge about the properties of law and law-like systems of rules, human behavior as it relates to law, and the role of law in normative ordering.

Significantly, departing from formalistic, doctrinal analysis of official rules, laws, and regulatory forms, current research considers law as a dynamic institution that is as amenable to study as are the economic, political, and cultural systems of society. From this vantage, law is no longer treated as a constant or dependent variable in the environment, but instead is conceptualized as a fundamental feature of social life whose processes, patterns, and regularities are susceptible to rigorous research.

The six most active areas of study being supported by NSF include: (1) dispute resolution strategies, processes, and mechanisms; (2) social and economic consequences of variations in law; (3) determinants of legal decision making; (4) legal development and the linkages to social, economic, and technological change; (5) the relationship between state laws and various customary and indigenous systems in society; and (6) deterrence processes and the conditions that engender legal compliance.

Important work is also being pursued through longitudinal and comparative studies addressed to such issues as (a) in what ways size of social units and specialization within the legal system is an independent determinant of system change; (b) how legal systems accommodate technological innovation; (c) the effects of different legal arrangements on the definition and stability of social relations, such as the transmission of wealth; and (d) the relationship between urbanization and price fluctuation and the use of law.

Organizational Research

Sociological focus has long been directed to large-scale organizations that occupy a crucial place in modern societies and to the processes of status and income attainment, which play an important role in the careers and well-being of individuals and families.

In the 1960s, significant progress was made in analyzing organizational growth, change, and decay. Advances were also made in understanding how labor market outcomes for individuals were affected by training, education, race, and other personal characteristics. Limitations in theory, methods and data made it difficult to link labor force and organizational variables and to formalize knowledge about this interaction.

One important research development supported by the National Science Foundation in the 1970s brought these two streams of research together. Studies of status attainment and social mobility began to consider how labor-market opportunities were affected by the social context and by employers' demands for labor. Analyses of organizations began to consider how management decisions affected the flow of personnel through the organizations.

One line of analysis disaggregated the national labor market and described regional labor markets, industrial and occupational sectors, and even specific firms and organizations.

Such inquiries documented labor-market segmentation. The segments were internally organized by rules for entry and promotion. Such rules affect the opportunities for individual advancement. The size and rate of growth of employing organizations, and the composition of the labor force, helped to explain differentials in the distribution of income and other job rewards.

The theoretical and methodological basis for much of the recent research on the links between the internal operations of organizations and job opportunities was presented by Harrison White in his *Chains of Opportunity* (1970). He conceptualized the process of labor mobility as based on chains of vacancies. Whether vacancies that occur in an organizational hierarchy are filled internally or from the outside and the rate at which they occur have significant consequences for turnover, worker productivity, and worker motivation.

This research represents a fundamental re-conceptualization of labor markets and attainment processes. Its contributions to understanding institutionalized sources of opportunity, organizational change, and effective use of labor are substantial.

Robert Coles' research on Japan's labor force shows that with limited entry points, permanent employment, and few vacancies at any level, the costs of turnover to employer and employee are reduced. At the same time, motivation and efficiency remains high due to seniority rules and a system of deferred rewards. Productivity is high in part because there is little resistance to technological change.

U.S. firms, in contrast, have a more flexible labor supply characterized by high voluntary quit rates. There is also considerable resistance to technological change in the labor force.

Shelby Stewman's study of internal labor markets gauges the consequences of change in organizational size, age of workers, seniority distributions, and salary schedules. Using mathematical models of vacancy chains and labor mobility in firms, he demonstrates that a decrease in system size does not result in lower costs, even when holding salary schedules constant. The major factor here is an increase in the average salary of staff caused by seniority-related increases. Similarly, a policy of lateral recruitment, rather than internal promotion, results in significant additions to labor costs. It also affects worker motivation and firm productivity.

These studies make it possible to assess, with increased precision, the impact of organizational characteristics and management decisions on employment opportunities and on the costs and benefits of different labor policies.

One of the current thrusts of social science at NSF is continued support of research bringing sociological theory and methods to labor-force analysis. This will require additional research on sampling techniques and methods of analyzing job networks as well as application of increment-decrement models in demography to the labor force. Structural characteristics must be integrated with individual attributes to understand the complex relationships between labor supply and how the organization of demands affects employers and workers.

History and Philosophy of Science

From its earliest days, NSF has supported research into the historical and philosophical foundations of science itself. These studies illuminate the nature of science as a source of knowledge and explain the various modes in the development of scientific disciplines. Currently, emphasis continues on studies of science development along with exploration of the logic, language, and mode of inference in scientific discovery and research. Attention is being directed toward differences and similarities in the role of evidence, modes of explanation, and nature of proof between natural and social science.

Emerging thrusts include studies of science-technology interaction and historical investigations of the nature and processes of technological innovation. Considerable investment has been made in support of the scientific editions of the Einstein and Edison papers.

The period of the 1960s support was extended for the development of Thomas Kuhn's *Structure of Scientific Revolutions*. The book captured large audiences both inside and outside the scientific community with its thesis that scientific theories are culturally relative pictures of the world, not absolute objective explanations.

Subsequently, historians and philosophers stepped up their analysis of the view that science is a strict, logico-deductive system that builds on prior work in a constant march toward "truth." Philosophers showed that this system simply would not work as a description of scientific explanation. Historians showed that the dominant system of logical analysis did not coincide with historical fact. Furthermore, they documented how many non-rational or even irrational factors affected the growth of science.

Research in the 1970s began a reconstruction of such basic ideas as the relation of theory and observation, the problem of inference, the nature of scientific explanation, and the interpretation of probability in statistical science.

Studies supported by NSF of the most recent "revolution" in science--that of plate tectonics in geology--support the evolutionary mode even when a Kuhnian revolution seems to have occurred.

Plate tectonics successfully predicts new phenomena and appears to overthrow the accepted "steady state" theory. By careful analysis, however, historians and philosophers have found not so much a revolution but a shift in dominance. Plate tectonics is not a new conception. Earlier version of it had been competing with the "steady state" theory for over half a century.

Various theoretical explanations developed over this period. During most of this century, the steady state theory held the allegiance of most geologists. With the discoveries from ocean drilling expeditions, however, the allegiance of the majority of geologists shifted to the plate tectonics theory. Can a process of competition over a fifty-year period be called a revolution. Not likely, at least not in the Kuhnian sense.

Other projects supported by NSF have shown that what occurred in plate theory change was not the same as what occurred in another great revolution in our time--that of recombinant DNA. In this case we have no major theory shift but a change in technique that has revolutionized the conduct of biology as much or more than any recent theory change.

Historians and philosophers of science are also directing inquiry to the great debate in systematics about the mode of operation of evolution--whether it occurs in increments or great leaps.

Similarly, NSF has supported research to follow events in weak interaction in high-energy physics and in neutrino observations of the sun to see if and how "theory change" occurs in these disciplines.

Historians also carefully study the great "revolutions" of the past-- the Newtonian, Darwinian, and Einsteinian revolutions--to gain greater insight into those events.

There are multiple paths to theory change, and the forces operating to bring about these changes are much more complex than was assumed in the 1960s. It is on this central issue that we offer support for research in the history and philosophy of science.

Measurement Methods and Data Resources

Perhaps the most visible and widely applauded investment made by social science at NSF has been its support for the development and utilization of various national data bases.

The big three are the National Election Studies, the General Social Survey, and the Panel Study of Family Income Dynamics.

But there are others also such as the U. S. Manufacturing Establishments Data Base, the U.S. Quality of Life Survey Series, the National Time Allocation Data Series, the 1940/1950 Censuses Public Use Sample Files, and the Industrial Change and Occupational Mobility International Data Archive.

The extended use of large bodies of stored social data, in conjunction with modern data processing technology and sophisticated methods of statistical analysis, has become the hallmark of contemporary social science research.

The maintenance of key data series and the facilities which make them accessible has been the special responsibility of the Measurement Methods and Data Resources Program, but this responsibility is increasingly being shared by all programs in the Division of Social and Economic Science.

Building on this experience, exciting new initiatives are now under way to support three interdisciplinary areas of opportunity: (1) Maximizing the scientific yield of the vast amounts of data collected annually for administrative purposes by the federal statistical system; (2) Improving survey research--the predominant method for collecting social data--by borrowing form the corpus of knowledge and techniques recently developed in cognitive science, linguistics, and artificial intelligence; and (3) applying newly formulated principles of knowledge management to social science data structures.

The growing availability of large data sets, with more and more users interacting with them, requires a return to the foundations of data storage and analysis if these vast masses of numbers are not to outdistance our ability to ascertain the underlying meanings. The search for the deeper meanings in data now represents a critical new thrust in social and economic science.

Conclusion

My written statement to you closes with eight answers to the question "Why does the National Science Foundation fund research in the social and behavioral sciences?"

I will not repeat those justifications, except to note that when they are coupled to what I have tried to sketch for you today about current lines of inquiry, I trust that your appraisal of social science will never again rest on the back of turtles.

Chapter 23

Innovation and Productivity
House Committee on Science and Technology, Washington, D.C.
September 10, 1981

Mr. Chairman and Members of the Subcommittee:

I am pleased to describe research on human factors affecting innovation and productivity and to comment on the role of the National Science Foundation. You have my full statement. I will merely emphasize a few points from it.

The Bearing of Social Science

For social and behavioral scientists, the theme of these hearings represents a welcome innovation. It implies that the issue is not only technical or engineering but also behavioral and organizational, and that it is the linkage among these elements that needs to be better understood if we are to improve the productive capacities of our society.

Currently, there are at least twelve research support programs in three of NSF's directorates that are vitally concerned with human factors at both the organizational and personal levels. These programs support efforts to learn more about elements and conditions that enhance or inhibit productivity and innovation; to better understand the consequences, intended and unintended, of the introduction of the new socio-technical designs; and to seek out alternative means of assessing benefits, risks, and costs of innovation in the world of work.

Serious technical challenges face social science investigators as they pursue knowledge in this realm. How do we know that innovative structures move us toward specified goals? Clearly, we will not know unless we proceed with the construction of relevant and essential measures for empirical inquiry.

Six months ago, the general import of that effort was emphasized before this Subcommittee by Kenneth Prewitt, President of the Social Science Research Council, when he noted that: "Social science itself will be the source of social innovations. Previous examples include econometric forecasting, demographic projections, input-output matrices, standardized testing, man-machine system design, operant conditioning. Presently, scholars are working on management strategies for complex organizations, on risk analysis, and on optimal sampling design--all areas in which innovations will be forthcoming."

To provide some specific instances of gain from effort, I would now like to sketch elements of a few NSF-supported studies where human factors, innovation, and productivity connect.

Research on Innovation

First, here are some brief notes on a work under way on innovation:

♦ Robert Yin of the Rand Corporation has investigated how innovations are stabilized or routinized in an organization. The long-term survival of an innovation is unlikely unless it is incorporated into organizational rules and manuals, budget cycles, and unless it survives equipment turnover, etc. Thus, innovation, is not a simple yes-no decision, but a complex longitudinal process that demands continuous organizational adjustments.

♦ Martha Hollis at the University of California, Irvine has looked at the process of adoption in a variety of municipalities considering the implementation of Fiscal Impact Budgeting Systems using computer models to forecast growth in local economies. The models are more likely to be permanently adopted when local governments are characterized by relative certainty over the course of urban growth and development.

♦ Richard Kolodny and Bertrand Horowitz of the University of Maryland have studied how firm-level decision making concerning R&D is affected by changes in Federal policy. They found that increases in government-mandated reporting requirements tended to suppress the level of R&D actually performed in small firms which, in turn, slows the pace of technological development.

♦   A Northwestern University interdisciplinary team of engineers and social scientists, is examining innovation required to integrate sets of neighborhood-scale technologies to meet basic needs for food, water, waste management, shelter, and energy in older urban neighborhoods.

Research on Productivity

Now let me turn to some research with an emphasis on productivity.

♦   At the National Bureau of Economic Research, Zvi Griliches is doing a major study on the relationships between technological change and long-term productivity growth. The work builds a detailed data-set for a large number of firms on R&D expenditures, patents, sales, employment, assets, and market value. These data will advance knowledge about productivity, private and social returns to R&D, and the usefulness of patents as a measure of innovation.

♦   Studies by Frank Stafford at the University of Michigan of what people actually do when they are at work suggest that part of the recent decline in the rate of productivity increase may result from nothing more than a measurement error in labor hours. Comparisons of time actually spent at the work place in the mid-1970s with similar data for the mid-1960s indicates that actual hours have declined, relative to conventional reports of hours worked, at the rate of approximately one percent per year.

♦   Research by Paul David and Moses Abramovitz, Stanford University, finds that the pace and the character of technological and organizational innovation has changed historically from the nineteenth to the twentieth century and this change has altered the relative productivity's of various agents of production. The improvement in the productivity of investments in education, research, and health in the twentieth century relative to investments in more factories or machinery is shown to have major implications for social and economic organization in America.

♦   Michael Brill of Buffalo is studying how the office environment affects job satisfaction and productivity. The findings will have implications for the design of a physical structure to create balanced conditions to facilitate both privacy and communication. How much should an organization spend for a particular administrative service?

♦   Research by Charles Kriebel of Carnegie Mellon University tests an operational theory in an industrial organization to provide evidence on productivity improvement through various models of resource allocation.

♦   Michael Shuster of Syracuse University is comparing firms with and without union-management cooperation plans to see the effects on productivity, employment, and grievances. The study also examines how the level of technology in a firm affects success of a union-management cooperation plan.

♦   Research by Sandra Kirmeyer of Cornell University focuses on the effects of workload on stress experienced by service workers. The proportion of the work force employed in service occupations is expanding as the population increases and life expectancy lengthens. How hospital emergency room workers, and other personnel, respond to productivity demands bears on the quality of services provided in both the public and private sectors of the economy.

♦   Albert Bruno and Tyzoon Tyebjee of the University of Santa Clara find that venture capitalists perceive the limited availability of opportunities to be more of a constraint on investment than the availability of capital. They suggest how both economic and non-economic factors (such as decision making practices), can remedy market imperfections.

♦   Jerome Corsi at the University of Denver has completed an experiment in New Mexico to indicate that telephone teleconferencing in two state agencies, the Department of Human Services, and the Department of Employment Security, increased agency productivity and significantly reduced costs.

Challenging Research Issues

Mr. Chairman, this brief account of research supported by Foundation programs, limited as the sample is and diverse as the empirical efforts are, suggests how improved ways are emerging to analyze the consequences of different organizational designs; new tools are being devised to determine the optimum level of investment in R&D; and national data resources are being developed to give better estimates of the linkages among human factors, technological change, and economic growth.

However, what are some of the things that we need to know more about? Among the important research issues are the following:

♦ Acceptance of technological change to improve productive efficiency is often hampered by failure to consider fully social and interpersonal elements in the workplace. More sophisticated research is needed on attitudes, morale, satisfaction, employee-employer interactions, and conflict resolution under conditions bearing on the adoption of innovations.

♦ With major innovations come opportunities where some will gain and others will lose. This can affect the value of fixed capital, the skill of workers, and the markets of firms. We do not know enough about the differential consequences of major innovations, particularly of their impact on communities and regions. How do inter-regional shifts in resource availability, industrial bases, and population affect political power, economic advantages, and social cohesion? Research is needed on the impacts and discontinuities of growth and change to prepare the way for possible further innovations.

♦ That social institutions and complex organizations have a role in stimulating or impeding technological change is clearly apparent. Understanding the particular effects of strategies of regulation and deregulation, or of organizational size, complexity and bureaucratic procedures, however, remains an important research challenge. Work in this area is needed to overcome the uncertainty, confusion, and hesitation associated with developing and adopting novel technologies.

One final note on future research needs and directions involves an earlier connection between the Foundation and this Committee.

In the 1979 *National Science Foundation Authorization Report*, your Committee encouraged the Foundation to develop a research program on comparative risk analysis, an area bound to become increasingly important with the growth of technological innovation.

The Foundation responded by establishing a Technology Assessment and Risk Analysis Group in August 1989. It supports research on the adequacy of data for estimating the risks associated with technological innovation; how issues of equity and distribution are considered in deciding whether or not to proceed with innovation; and how decision makers make choices under conditions of imperfect and incomplete information.

Conclusion

That final phrase suggests an appropriate point to turn from my presentation to your questions. I do so by posting two conclusions that I draw from our experience:

♦   First, a major part of the uncertainty about the future of economic growth of the U.S. is due to our inadequate understanding of the processes that determine the rate of investment, private and public, in knowledge production, the productivity of such investments, and how such knowledge gets utilized in the process of technological change.

Knowledge has the properties of a public good but it is also produced privately. We need better measures and more usable models to encourage and reflect the involvement of both sectors in its production and use; and finally,

♦   Technology policies should not be divorced from economic and social policies and the research on human factors that under girds our understanding of their interaction.

Chapter 24

High Above Cayuga's Waters
Cornell University, Ithaca, New York
November 24, 1981

I am pleased to visit Cornell University where one immediately senses an intensity of activity and a clarity of purpose.

That you have selected this extraordinary site, high above Cayuga's waters, for this celebration, and, as I understand it, for the future headquarters of the Cornell Institute for Social and Economic Research (CISER), clearly indicates that you know what you are doing.

That contrasts with our condition in Washington this past week. Some of you have asked, "What is it like when the government closes down?" One good question deserves another, so let me recall what Dorothy Parker said when she was notified that President Calvin Coolidge had died. "How can you tell?" she asked.

But life does goes on. Today, I would like to briefly address three quite different questions:

♦ Is federal support for social science research dead?

♦ If not, why not? and

♦ Why is CISER important not only for Cornell, but for the advancement of social science generally?

Death Threat

First, let me assure you that the news or the rumors of our death are premature. Yes, in budget terms we were probably scheduled for extinction. Certainly we face a severe reduction in federal support for social science research. For example, the proposed budget for the

Division of Social and Economic Science at NSF would have us drop to about $10 million in 1982 from about $33 million a year or so ago.

This is a serious matter for the advancement of social science, and possibly for some of your work at Cornell. But before I tell you a bit about efforts to turn this decision around, let me note another troublesome fact, one that kindles visions of a self-fulfilling prophecy.

Proposals from social scientists for research support have dropped dramatically in the past few months--to a point where if the budget process doesn't kill us, the decline in proposals might. This is because administrators and budget-makers use it as justification for cuts already made and as rationalization for more of the same.

But, a decline in proposals also provides unique opportunities for diligent researchers. I would say that is a pretty good time right now to go shopping for the funds you need to support your best quality projects. Federal support for fundamental research in social science is not dead. Nor are the efforts to advance the understanding of the merits of our case with the government, with other scientists, and with the public. If things are to get better for social science, the linkages to each of these sectors must be strengthened even beyond ways that have been forged in the political fires of the past few months.

Nineteen eighty-one may be remembered as the year that social scientists paused from their ancient wars with each other (as when psychologists, economists, anthropologists, political scientists, and sociologists go to the same Dean each convinced that they have the best case for the same slice of pie) to engage an external threat that became defined as a larger enemy.

It wasn't just that David Stockman's budget cuts were deep and damaging to every discipline. It was also that the manner in which they were proposed impeached the worth and integrity of social science as a science.

Social Scientists as Citizens

The response was remarkable and historically unique. Social scientists, individually and collectively, activated their citizen roles. Letters poured into Congress. Visits were made, strong testimony was delivered, and fresh explanations of worth were offered.

Furthermore, the most prestigious national science bodies--the National Academy of Science, the American Association for the Advancement of Science, and the National Science Board--came to the defense of the social sciences. The Social Science Research Council and the Assembly of Behavioral and Social Sciences exercised strong leadership. The Consortium of Social Science Association (COSSA) taxed themselves to hire a full-time and very effective legislative representative. No lobbying, of course, but keen efforts to inform and to educate.

It is probably true that never before have so many good things been said in the halls of Congress about social science. Even the representatives themselves challenged old stereotypes and adorned the record with new understandings. Some positive votes resulted. Ultimately these may even yield favorable budget revisions.

However, it is prudent to remember that to be re-discovered is to run new risks of being found out. To cope will require more than the building of networks to flex political muscle. Even if we manage to convince the White House that without social science there could not be a National Indicator System, such as that they are now utilizing to regularly brief the President on social, economic, demographic and political trends, we would still have the fundamental problem of advancing social science as science. That is why new organizations like CISER are so critical for our future.

Give Substance to Social Science

Social science, I believe, must seize this moment of history to create new capacity to strengthen its scientific integrity. That is the only sure route to sustaining a perception of utility in the political arena.

The magnitude of our knowledge needs requires the innovative, multidisciplinary approach that you are making. That's the inner reality. The external fact is that, as times get tougher, there is more of a disposition to allocate resources in these terms. Politicians sense this. Academic administrators do, too. So it is time for social scientists to augment specialized, disciplinary studies with genuine, solid, multidisciplinary, interdisciplinary, and cross-disciplinary work. In other words, let's give tough, operational meaning to the concept of social science. CISER can do this. And that is why I think we should all be excited about what you are doing here at Cornell.

CISER is important. It can foster relations between specialists. It can stimulate intellectual risk-taking beyond conventional boundaries. It can initiate longitudinal and comparative data bases. It can monitor and explain changes and trends by coordinating basic work in methodology. It can legitimate and reward work outside narrow disciplinary units. It can exploit external resources in ways that individuals cannot match.

CISER will, of course, do many mundane things. It will facilitate the research of professors and students by aiding with a number of technical tasks that involve records, forms, computers, etc. Efficiency will be served. Communication of results will be enhanced. Political scientists, sociologists, anthropologists, psychologists, economists, geographers, demographers, statisticians, will start talking to each other on a regular basis. My God, what a revolution! You may even find new ways of doing research that lessens dependence on Washington funding.

Out of this, social science at Cornell will gain a collective image, an emergent identity to build on the already significant contributions by individual Cornell scholars.

A positive collective image for social science is not a trivial matter. But it will have lasting significance only if it is based on an organizational structure that advances premium quality research and regularly yields sound, tested, ideas. I congratulate this university for drawing its resources together to meet this challenge.

Chapter 25

Pain from Knowledge Gain in Social Science

79th Annual Meeting, American Sociological Association
San Antonio, Texas
August 29, 1984

I once thought I knew something about the uses and control of knowledge.

From 1968 to 1970, I served on the notorious Commission on Obscenity and Pornography. The model was simple: do good, empirical research; generate plausible explanations; post the probable costs and consequences of alternative courses of action. All of these would naturally lead to rational decision-making and effective public policy.

Well, it didn't then--and it rarely does now. How come?

Why don't we make better use of science? Is it a matter of ignorance, incompetence, perversity, or greed? Or is it because ambiguity marks both scientific findings and policy values? Or, because it is not easy to couple probabilistic scientific information to decisions that require discrete choices among alternatives? Or, is it that we really do not have much of a cumulative knowledge base?

Let me dodge these harsh questions and step back from knowledge application to the arena where resources are allocated for knowledge production.

I am going to comment on features that continue to affect the knowledge structure of social science. The whole story of the uses and control of social science knowledge cannot be captured from one site, but the case at hand is not a trivial one.

Progress for Whom?

For four years I have had the privilege of working in the National Science Foundation (NSF). Since its founding in 1950, it is the only federal agency charged by statute "to promote the progress of science" and "to initiate and support basic scientific research." Thus, NSF is an important actor in the knowledge game.

The evolution of social science in that game has been traced by sociologists such as George Lundberg, Harry Alpert, James Zuiches, and Thomas Gieryn. Their accounts merit more attention than time now permits. They provide vital ingredients for a definitive history of the unfolding, if not the undoing, of American social science. This is not a flip remark. The current shape and direction of our history is problematic. Many, myself included, have been too optimistic about the progress of social science.

From the perspective of its evolution at NSF, American social science research has a precarious support base, has made very little progress in legitimating its scientific status, and confronts a serious collective, intellectual challenge bearing on the uses and control of knowledge. There have been gains, but some are illusory, and others have been offset by losses. That is the core of my claim.

The first social scientist in a leadership role at NSF was a sociologist, the late Harry Alpert. Through skillful maneuvering, he gained a foothold for social science in the early 1950s. Following Alpert, other sociologists filled whatever leadership positions were made available at NSF: in the 1960s, Henry Riecken; in the 1970s, Herbert Costner; and in the 1980s, Otto Larsen. Yes, sociologists have had a hand in the fate of social science at NSF.

What has that fate been?

The good news is that social science has survived, even through a recent period in which budgetary extinction was a real possibility. The realistic news is that social science today is held in the same disesteem that marked its beginning.

Fundamentally, there has been no change in the way in which social science is understood by the dominant figures from physics, engineering, chemistry, and mathematics.

The rhetoric from those in control, with notable exceptions particularly from the leadership in biology, remains caustic and constant. It is not just that social sciences are deemed "soft." Rather, it is a genuine skepticism about whether they are sciences at all.

Politics and Budgets

There is another concern. While social science is small in terms of expenditures, it looms large in political trouble-making capacity that could jeopardize support for all of NSF. Fear is aroused by social science with each budget cycle.

More than psychological states are involved. Actions flow from such conceptions and are translated into controls that limit the presentation of the social-science-knowledge self. In critical decision processes, such knowledge as our research produces is not fully under our control. A good place to observe this is in the annual iterations of the budget process.

Every year Congress receives NSF's claim for support. A complicated process precedes and follows the presentation. Each program's plea for dollars is accompanied by exemplars of sound research investments. No matter what the dollars, social science receives special attention. Its case material is carefully monitored and edited by the highest officials.

The boundaries for reporting are very little different from the limits on funding that Alpert described in a 1958. In a report to the National Science Board, Alpert asserted that NSF had demonstrated success in defining its social science program to omit sex, religion, race and politics. These fields, he asserted, were more appropriately supported by private foundations or by governmental agencies with applied social science missions. He concluded, "It would be the intention of the NSF not to support research in sensitive, controversial fields no matter how significant such research may be."

While these taboos are no longer operative in the funding of research, political prudence still dictates that findings from such social science inquiries, and others such as those on poverty and unemployment, be carefully controlled. It is assumed that such control has beneficial effects.

An examination of the social science presentation in every budget book from 1956 through 1985, with a comparison of dollars requested to those finally allocated, leaves doubt in my mind on this point. In only six years during this period was the number of dollars received equal to or in excess of those requested.

The evolution of the size of the "opening bid" for social sciences seems to denote "progress." It started at $55,258 in 1956, increased regularly for thirteen years to $18.7 million in 1958, then fluctuated until reaching a peak in 1982 of $65.1. Later that year, when Reagan replaced Carter, the bid was reduced to $21.1 million. By 1985, it had crawled back up to $42.8 million, approximately the amount sought seven years earlier in 1978.

The growth in the budget request for social science seems impressive; however, at no point did it ever gain significantly as a proportion of the total research funds requested by NSF.

From the beginning, this opening bid has hovered around 2 to 4 percent of that total. This index of institutional aspiration for social science can be contrasted with the fact that social and behavioral scientists have consistently constituted from 25 to 30 percent of the total number of Ph.D.'s. in all the sciences and engineering fields in the United States.

The evolution of statements supporting the budget bid is also instructive. Emphases were variously placed on arguments for basic research, dwindling alternative resources, research opportunities, problem solving potentials, and accounts of significant contributions. These denoted organizational changes and also seemed to reflect the political flavor of the passing decades.

Prior to 1960, there was no textual reference to social science in the budget book. There were line items on "Socio-Physical Sciences" and "Anthropology and Related Sciences" until 1958, and then under "Social Sciences Research" in 1959. For the first decade, NSF's approach was exploratory. The mandate made support permissive but not mandatory. Funds were allocated where there was an "effective integration and partnership between natural and social science."

This policy of convergence yielded support for basic research in areas described in other NSF documents as "mathematical social science," "economic engineering," "human ecology," "statistical design," "functional archaeology," and "experimental and quantitative social psychology."

Organizational Identity

Invisibility via convergence in the 1950s gave way to the emergence of a distinct social science identity in the 1960s. Organizationally, social science was transformed from being listed under "Other Sciences," to becoming a "Program," then an "Office," and finally in 1969 a full-fledged "Division," equal in organizational standing to all other research fields in NSF. This was the high-water mark in organizational status for social science at NSF.

An editorial in *Science* on December 16, 1960, heralded the event and proclaimed that all scientists would be pleased both with the symbolic value of the new status and with the promise of increased support. However, the editorial emphasized, support for social science will be for basic research that meets high standards of conceptual and methodological rigor, not for "applied craftsmanship in social affairs."

Social science had at last come out of NSF's closet. Its first budget statement of 1960 reaffirmed a concentration "on fundamental research on human behavior," and made reference to efforts that would follow-up a congressional mandate to investigate the social and economic consequences of science.

With each succeeding year, commitments to basic research, methodological improvement, measurement issues, and the development of more formal empirically relevant theory were made.

The format permitted expanded expression. Confident, integrated essays on achievements appeared. Programs grew in number and took on disciplinary titles. The number of grants awarded and their average size grew from 114 at $20,527 in 1960 to 426 at $34,400 in 1968. That year also culminated in a significant symbolic triumph: the act of 1950 was amended to include social science in the legislative mandate for the first time. After eighteen years, social science had gained full legal status in the foundation.

As NSF social science moved into the seventies, a new direction was signaled. The budget statements began to reflect pressures for knowledge to appear relevant. The 1970 claim was that "Special emphasis will be given to supporting research projects directly underlying or relevant to current social problems." The 1971 appeal referred to "the use of new knowledge in practical situations." The 1972 statement opened with these words, "The growing seriousness of the Nation's social problems and the recognition that the Social Sciences can contribute to their solution have given new impetus to research in the Social Sciences."

All of this coincided with the establishment of the Research Applied to National Needs Program (RANN) in 1971 which contained a substantial social science component. In its six-and-a-half year life to 1977, RANN allocated $468.3 million. Each year its budget for applied social science research was more than that expended for basic research in the Division of Social Science.

Later in the decade, behavioral and social science were separated into two divisions. It is not yet clear how this organizational revision altered what appeared to be the steady growth of a unified activity to a secure scientific status.

From 1970-75, obligations for basic social science research almost doubled (from $14.2 to $27.1 million). A plateau was approached-- insured in part by the growing impact of inflation and by the onset of severe political scrutiny from those such as Senator Proxmire and Representative Ashbrook in the late 1970s.

The budget cuts of 1981-82 underscored a process under way. This can be seen by noting that in constant (1972) dollars, the obligations for social science research at NSF never again exceeded the 1976 level in any of the years through 1984.

For the nine-year period, 1976-84, the decline for social science in current dollars was 4.6 percent and in constant dollars it was 44.5 percent. While support for social science was going downhill for a decade, increased support for all other areas of science at NSF was accelerating. For example, in that same time period, support for biology increased 120.3 percent in current dollars and 28.1 percent in constant dollars.

Political and Scientific Mobilization

These hard facts support my thesis. In the sixteen years since the legal certification of social science, that symbolic gain has not been translated into secure scientific legitimation. Nor has it meant consistent or even minimally appropriate levels of financial support. Nor has it brought about institutionalized representation at the highest policy and managerial levels. Assumption about the uses of social science knowledge has, in a variety of ways, led to the effective control of opportunities to extend that knowledge.

True, in very recent times, shocked by the trauma of 1981 and 1982, we have gained some insulation from the shifting and often bitter political winds that blow through the corridors of Washington. This is largely the product of a remarkable effort to mobilize the research community into a national political-educational force.

We owe a lot to the Consortium of Social Science Associations (COSSA); the Federation of Behavioral, Psychological and Cognitive Sciences; and the Association for the Advancement of Psychology. Their efforts demonstrate how the social and behavioral sciences, despite splendidly varied theoretical interests and methodological approaches, can curtail old competitive habits and make common cause to effectively explain and defend their scientific interests in legislative halls, and in the court of public opinion.

This will not be enough. New collective efforts, such as those under way at the National Academy of Science, are required. There, a distinguished committee has launched an innovative inquiry to project a ten-year outlook emphasizing exciting scientific frontiers, leading research questions, unsolved but tractable knowledge problems, and new resources needed over the next decade for significant progress in social and behavioral science.

The question becomes: having demonstrated political unity, can social and behavioral scientists now muster intellectual unity to advance knowledge through a forceful specification of ripe research opportunities?

If the answer is yes, there is a good probability of gaining substantial new resources for social and behavioral science at NSF. If the answer is no, there is evidence both from the political decision-making arena and the high-science policy scene that our march to scientific credibility will continue to creep along and only grudgingly be nourished by resources they control.

We may not like that pressure. However, consider the value to social science of a challenge to draw from all of our intellectual resources. Much of the phenomena we seek to explain probably will not surrender to the probes of a single discipline. It is time to reach across old boundaries. Multidisciplinary efforts could propel us forward so that our knowledge might, in fact, become powerful enough to actually warrant concern about control.

Conclusion

Many roads can lead to knowledge gains in social science. But we should not overstate our capacity to produce knowledge. Nor should we promise too much about the ultimate use of our effort. Missteps lend credibility to the severe judgment recently passed by Paul Johnson in his 1983 book, *Modern Times: The World from the Twenties to the Eighties:*

Johnson gloats over the growing disesteem for social science. In his view, we deserve the judgment because "*Economics, sociology, psychology...scarcely sciences at all...had constructed a juggernaut of social engineering, which had crushed beneath it so much wealth and so many lives."* Johnson finds tragedy in that *social science* fell into disfavor only in the 1970s. As a result, the *"effects of the social science fallacy"* will be felt until the year 2000. But, Johnson expresses hope. He anticipates that the influence of social science *"will steadily diminish and never again, perhaps, will humanity put so much trust in this modern metaphysic"*.

I do not subscribe to this estimate of worth. However, I do take such perceptions, and similar ones at NSF noted earlier, as real data.

How can we hasten the day when trust displaces disesteem? The answer has to be by doing better science. Beyond that, more effective ways must be forged to confront the scientific and political leadership with the actual record of research achievement.

If checked, that record at NSF is impressive. Truly significant knowledge gains have emerged from investments in econometrics, cognition, social indicators, decision theory, measurement methods, and organizational change., to mention but a few of the vital areas being supported. Rarely, however, do achievements modify stereotyped conceptions of social science as "soft" or as merely being some form of ideological advocacy.

A new challenge has been posted. It places the burden on us to make hard choices and to justify investment in ways more specific than in the past. The competition for scarce resources is real.We must construct a coherent set of priorities for advancing knowledge. That is a serius intellectual challenge. It merits a vigorous, creative, and consensual response.

I hope that each of us will not only monitor that effort, but will also participate in it with colleagues from all across the pluralistic enterprise of social and behavioral science.

Chapter 26

An Overview of the Underdog

Advisory Committee for Biological, Behavioral, and Social Science
National Science Foundation, Washington, D.C.
February 4, 1985

In the next few minutes I must say something about the history of the social and behavioral sciences at the National Science Foundation. That history spans about 35 years that reach into five decades. The time constraint suggests a *Reader's Digest* version of history. Or, even worse, the product has to be like the content of a magazine that came out in the 1950s called *Quick*, a publication that presented summaries of articles from the *Reader's Digest* for people who were really in a hurry.

Next year when I retire from NSF, I plan to attempt a full and systematic account of this topic. There are rich materials to be mined. A great mix of personalities, organizations, disciplines, ideas, perceptions, and political processes, not to mention chance factors, have shaped the appearance and evolution of these programs at NSF.

In turn, and this is the important lesson from history: the social and behavioral sciences at NSF, however buffeted or however nourished, are a prime force in affecting the scope, strength, and the validity of knowledge produced by these sciences everywhere.

That is a powerful claim. It is also the warrant for being even a little bit curious about the hard-ball history of the so-called "soft-sciences" at NSF.

Certain landmarks stand out. Let me note a few.

1950 was the year that the federal government created NSF, a science agency dedicated to the support of basic research. Social science was not mandated for inclusion, but was to be tolerated for a limited role under strict controls. It could earn its way to legitimacy through linkage to the needs and norms of physical science.

1958 was the year that the separate identity of social science began to emerge. A Program in social science was authorized. About 100 research proposals came into NSF requesting about $4 million; 49 grants were made, allocating $725,000 to social scientists.

1960 was the year that the Director and the Board awarded social science equal organizational standing to all other areas of science. A Division of Social Science was created in the one general research directorate. That year, about $3.4 million was allocated to support about 130 grants in social science. Included on the Advisory Board to the new division were Leonard Cottrell, President of the Russell Sage Foundation; John Gardner, President of the Carnegie Foundation; Pendleton Herring, President of the Social Science Research Council; and, Dael Wolfle, Executive Director of the American Association for the Advancement of Science.

1968 was the year that the Congress rewrote the legislative mandate and explicitly included social science in the revised statutory authority of NSF. It also added applied research to the general authority of the foundation.

1975 was the year of the birth of behavioral science at NSF. Social and behavioral science became separate divisions in the directorate that this committee now advises.

Current Programs

The press recently carried a picture of the Director of NSF wearing a T-shirt with a message that reminded us of our general mission, "At NSF we accept proposals."

There are five programs in behavioral science and nine programs in social and economic science that currently do that. If one general statement could encompass the variation in all this disciplinary effort, I would say that the goal of each program is to support scientific inquiry that leads to the cumulative development of empirically verified generalizations about the conditions under which events occur and about how these phenomena are organized and interrelated.

To achieve such aims requires money. And I don't need to remind you that there has been a lot less of it lately. In fact, the total budgets for the 14 programs in social and behavioral science for the past five years have moved from $52.5 million in 1980, to $43.7 million in 1981, to $32.6 million in 1982, to 35.9 million in 1983, and to an estimated 41.2 million in 1984.

A few more details from the peak year. In 1980, the 14 programs received and processed 2,062 research proposals. Only 33 percent of these were funded. This compares with success ratios of 64 percent in physics, 39 percent in chemistry, and 37 percent in biology. Furthermore, the social and behavioral sciences were only able to allot 21 percent of the dollars requested while physics granted 54 percent, chemistry 32 percent, and biology 32 percent.

Clearly, equity is a problem. There are also pressures from rising client populations. In 1980, there were 17,195 new Ph.D.'s. granted in all of science; 34 percent came from the social and behavioral sciences. Overall, we constitute about 30 percent of the approximate 350,000 Ph.D. science and engineering work force in the United States.

We also recognize that while everyone seeks greater support, NSF must make choices. The political excitement around social and behavioral science brought the National Science Board in June, 1981, and the Director in September, 1981, to specify general priorities for social and behavioral science.

Both emphasized a balanced tripartite approach to meet critical research needs in (1) the maintenance and development of key national data bases; (2) the improvement and development of research methodologies and techniques; and (3) support for investigator-initiated projects intended to strengthen the foundations of understanding behavioral and social phenomena.

As we allocate funds to meet these interests, our program decisions continue to be guided by:

♦ The probability of achieving significant scientific advances.

♦ The "ripeness" of the field, and the availability of requisite personnel.

♦ The likelihood of use of the results or interests in them beyond the interests of the researcher or the area being studied.

♦ The opportunity costs for apportioning funds to X relative to Y.

♦ The availability of alternative sources of support.

And let me underscore that even with modest dollar resources, the social and behavioral programs loom large in qualitative terms, and they have an efficient multiplier effect.

The latter is gained by adhering to the highest standards, by locating the best and most creative talent, and by emphasizing innovative and basic work.

It should also be noted that NSF programs can and do serve both specialized disciplinary needs and generalized social science interests. Thus, for example, in 1981 the sociology program awarded 62 grants amounting to $2.9 million, but that same year, sociologists went elsewhere in NSF to receive $5.3 million in 46 grants from 13 different programs.

Excitement

The social and behavioral sciences at NSF respond to pluralistic interests ranging from the way the human brain receives and processes external stimuli to the causes of conflict between nations.

There is intellectual excitement in every effort. Let me cite a few general instances.

◆   The anthropology program is excited about its crucial role in advancing understanding of how the human species has developed. All of the major fossils recovered in the past 20 years resulted from NSF supported research.

◆   The cognitive science program is excited about important advances in understanding how knowledge is represented, stored, and retrieved, and how learning modifies these processes.

◆   The joint efforts of psychologists, linguists, and biologists may soon be fused with the concerns of survey researchers in new efforts to reduce non-sampling errors that plagues the $4 billion a year polling industry in the United States.

◆   The economics program and the measurement methods and data resources program are excited about current findings and the future potential of the longitudinal panel study of family income dynamics. Cumulative panel data will permit an evaluation of the effectiveness of how supply-side incentives influence savings behavior.

This 16-year old annual survey of 5,000 families (with their offspring now bringing it up to 7,000 families) has already guided important corrections in our understanding of the scope of poverty and the extent of welfare dependency. The longitudinal data show that, while poverty is clearly passed on from one generation to the next, there is no persuasive evidence that welfare dependency is passed on.

Apparently we do not have, as cross-sectional studies suggest, a poor and dependent underclass of something like 10 percent of the population. Over the decade of the 1970s, the longitudinal studies show that less than one percent were dependent on welfare during every year (and a similar percent of different persons were poor at that time).

While researchers get excited about counter-intuitive findings, political figures may not. One unnamed President of the United States once made that clear by asserting: "I can't make a damn thing out of this tax problem. I listen to one side and they seem right, and then-- God!--I talk to the other side and they seem just as right, and here I am where I started. I know that somewhere there is a book that will give me the truth, but, hell, I couldn't read the book. I know that somewhere there is an economist who knows the truth, but I don't know where to find him and haven't the sense to know him and trust him when I find him. God! What a job!"

We can worry about how difficult it is for that job to integrate knowledge and policy. But it will never be relieved by letting up on our efforts to pursue the basic understandings required.

In my overview social and behavioral science at NSF, I get excited about the possibility of a genuine referent to social science, something that transcends the specialization of the several disciplines.

There are important convergent developments including, for example, advances in ways in which we elicit and collect data, including computer assisted interviewing and standardization of official data.

In tough-minded ways, NSF contributes to the pursuit of this and other exciting vistas which you can draw out from the most important actors present--the Program Officers in social and behavioral science.

Chapter 27

Terrible Parable on Politics of Science
Consortium of Social Science Associations, Washington, D.C.
February 10, 1986

I am pleased to come to this reception to say farewell to the mighty warriors who defend social and behavioral science.

I return to the university strengthened by your efforts that have made it legitimate for professors to participate in the political process. You have helped us to discover that if we redirect internal conflict toward external forces we gain some control over choices otherwise made for us.

The Uses of Adversity

In parting, perhaps we should now acknowledge that some good may have come from the hard times visited upon us during the early stages of the Reagan administration.

The budget wars and the politics of science have brought our disparate disciplinary forces together. Formerly, we fought only each other for scarce resources. We have learned that there must be a collective justification for public support. This has produced new inventories of achievements. COSSA has orchestrated many occasions for the display of multidisciplinary intellectual wares.

This suggests that there is a chance that economists, psychologists, sociologists, anthropologists, historians, statisticians, and political scientists might discover even higher scientific vistas than the common political ground that we now collectively defend.

The uses of adversity would be sweet, indeed, if social and behavioral scientists would now forge a coherent set of research priorities that command respect and support because they clearly specified exciting possibilities for fundamental knowledge gain.

With apologies to those who may have heard my terrible parable in other forums, let me conclude by reciting how these parting shots first occurred to me. The setting was the National Zoo.

Another Government Commission

I first went to the zoo with a team of social scientists newly appointed to the National Commission on Zoos. Having served on similar bodies, I was interested to see how the state of the art had evolved.

The social scientists were charged with evaluating practices and recommending policies. Data were required. Gaps were to be closed. The first thing on the agenda was to undertake a study of the effects of looking at caged animals. This required the cooperation of the chief zoo-keeper.

The zoo keeper was approached. He said he'd consider the matter. But, first, as a true professional, he wanted to consult his colleagues. So, possibly because he was a Republican appointee, he turned to the elephant cage which housed three very wise, old elephants of the *Loxodonta Africana* species. Curiously, these pachyderms also happened to be blind.

After consulting his blind elephants, the zoo keeper offered his cooperation--contingent, however, on a set of reciprocal observations. Accordingly, an agreement was reached whereby a social scientist, selected at random, would lie down and each blind elephant would reach out, feel the social scientist, and report what he had found.

The first elephant put his five-toed foot down on the social scientist's head. A strange, echoing hollow-sound resulted. From his observation, the elephant reported that while social scientists used their heads to count, classify, and correlate, their concepts were fuzzy and jargon-laden and therefore the exercise was fruitless. If they didn't know what they were doing, why do it with such labored precision?

The second elephant flapped his prehensile trunk around the social scientist's mid-section. There was a dull slurp and swish. This elephant concluded that social scientists didn't seem to have the stomach for tackling really difficult problems and were unable to digest theoretical alternatives, so why should they be fed another opportunity to influence zoo policies.

The third elephant pressed his ivory tusks against the social scientist's leg. There was a resounding crunch and crack. This elephant allowed that while his colleagues might be right, he felt obliged to make a more pointed conclusion. Social scientists, he asserted, are merely model builders and are unwilling or unable to do the empirical leg-work necessary for serious research.

Moral of Story

Now, I suppose, the moral of this story is that no matter where or how you touch, you will find a vulnerable spot in social science.

Or, if elephants press on, sooner or later social scientists might find new intellectual strength to address obvious areas of weakness.

To which some social scientists might respond, "If the elephants were not so well fed, they wouldn't be heavy enough to do the damage they do."

Clearly, funds should be reallocated for more research. Thank you COSSA for understanding that.

Chapter 28

The Future of Social Science Through a Rear-View Mirror

70th Anniversary, Social Science Research Council, New York City
June 4, 1993

I am pleased to give an informal talk on this special occasion. You can tell it is informal because I have written it all out.

Fifteen years ago, the last time I was at an SSRC dinner, it was my privilege to introduce Ken Prewitt as our newly appointed President.

On this 70th anniversary, we note yet another presidential landmark. Thus, I applaud the announcement that David Featherman will continue to lead this organization up to its diamond anniversary five years from now.

The vitality of leadership from past and present SSRC Presidents became apparent to me in the great Battle of the Potomac during the decade of the 80s. Sir Ken of Chicago and Sir David of Madison rode bravely into Washington to help slay dragons that menaced our treasury and threatened the integrity of social and behavioral science.

Now, across the moats of New York, their lances continue to pierce ignorance both at home and abroad. Once again, I salute their dedicated efforts.

Thematic Quest

To prepare for this talk, I had to probe for an appropriate theme. The first thought was to celebrate this 70th anniversary by going back to 1923 to examine the founding of this Council. A full historical review was soon aborted. Let me explain why.

As you know, the move to create the SSRC was initiated by the American Political Science Association's Committee on Research headed by Charles E. Merriam. A preliminary meeting was held February 24, 1923 to consider the organization. A second meeting, May 17, 1923, also in Chicago, attended by eight representatives from sociology, economics, statistics and political science, completed the formal organization of the Council.

The critical stimulus was a request from the National Research Council for help in a study of human migration. This was an historic moment. Never before had the NRC sought advice from social science. It would not be the last time that demography would open the door for such opportunities. In pursuit of this story, I made a startling discovery.

At the very moment of the founding of the SSRC, another meeting of eight men took place across town at the Edgewater Beach Hotel. Present were financiers who controlled more wealth than there was in the United States Treasury. Newspapers printed their success stories. They were portrayed as role models for American young people. No mention was made of the social scientists simultaneously in session at the university.

But, turn the clock ahead. What was the fate of what today would be called the financegate eight? The record reveals that within 25 years:

◆ The president of the largest independent steel company, Charles Schwab, was bankrupt and lived on borrowed money for five years before his death.

◆ The president of the greatest utility company, Samuel Insull, died a fugitive from justice and penniless in a foreign land.

◆ The greatest wheat speculator, Arthur Cutten, died abroad, insolvent.

◆ The president of the New York Stock Exchange, Richard Whitney, had been released from Sing Sing penitentiary.

◆ The member of the President's Cabinet, Albert Fall, was pardoned from prison so he could die at home.

◆ The greatest "bear" on Wall Street, Jesse Livermore, died a suicide.

◆ The President of the Bank of International Settlements, Leon Frazer, died a suicide.

◆ The head of the world's greatest monopoly, Ivar Krueger, died a suicide.

As for the fate of the founders of the SSRC, I lost interest in pursuing it. Those details must be left to more daring and more competent historical hands. Instead, let me skip ahead about sixty years to events that I experienced first hand. My claim will be modest. Unlike today's financiers from Merrill-Lynch, we do not have to be bullish, but merely buoyant, about the future.

Rediscovering the Rear View Mirror

To be buoyant can refer to the tendency to float. But it can also denote a disposition to invigorate, or an inclination to be cheerful.

The Social Science Research Council is not a floater. For seventy years it has been dedicated to invigoration, even when the odds did not favor being cheerful about it.

The case I want to make recounts ideas from four persons, three of whom you know as vital members of this Council. Before revealing their insights, let me tell you how I recaptured the words of Berk, Berra, Williams and Featherman. This requires a brief excursion into the territory of retirement.

Here I have made another discovery. Senior citizens tend to view life through a rear-view mirror. There is security in looking backwards when the prospect of going forward is uncertain. However, not all retired social scientists look back in the same way. Some embrace while others abandon their professional past.

For example, Cyril Smith, an eminent British social scientist who once headed the British Social Science Research Council recently wrote to me: "Now that I have finally accepted retirement, life seems to be falling into some kind of pattern: winters in London and summers in France. . .As I mentioned when I last wrote, I have renounced my vocation, sociology and social science. I am now trying my best to understand the Victorian mind...as expressed in and about the lesser arts...which means John Ruskin, the pre-Raphaelites, William Morris and the Arts and Crafts Movement."

In a few weeks I will travel to the south of France to accost my old friend in his lair. I hope to learn what advance Cyril has made in understanding the Victorian mind. I thought we had exhausted that topic in the British journal *Minerva* when we compared how Reagan and Thatcher had treated social science in the 1980s. If not that, at least our joint effort underscored Churchill's claim that the United States and Britain are two countries separated only by a common language.

Like Cyril Smith, I also retired seven years ago. My adjustment,
involves two pleasurable Victorian-like activities: (1) observing how
five grandchildren cope with this world, and (2) sorting through
personal archives to see what records of mischief I managed to
collect.

Now the trick for tonight is to draw data from these sources to
illuminate the future of social science. Perhaps it's all for naught.
Fundamentally it may depend on whether we follow Lord Byron who
said, "The best prophet of the future is the past," or Edmund Burke
who countered, "You can never plan the future by the past."

Whatever the outcome, let me tell you how I proceeded. In a box
in the basement labeled "Talks, Speeches, and Sermons," I found old
transcripts, notes and tapes going back over 40 years. The symptoms
were unmistakable. The disease, I believe, is called "logorrhea." I had
gone far beyond the classroom to infect other sectors of society with
oral outbursts.

Nonetheless, inspired by the notion that my grandchildren might
someday be curious about their evangelistic grandfather, I set about
organizing a manuscript called *Voicing Social Concern*. Evidence
from research was present, but footnotes and tables were absent.
There were also signs of a natural disposition to let tongue-in-cheek
exposition produce the jeopardy of foot-in-mouth disclosure.

Ultimately, I selected 33 scripts. These had been voiced to
librarians, natural scientists, newspaper publishers, members of
congress, magazine editors and a variety of student and faculty
audiences.

The central theme throughout was the promise of social science as
science. I was obviously mimicking my mentor, George Lundberg,
who once described his missionary efforts as resembling those of John
the Baptist crying in the wilderness about greater things to come.

A good number of my talks were voiced in the wilderness of the
nation's capital where, during the six years starting in 1980, my major
role at NSF was to explain, defend, and promote social and behavioral
science.

Given the enormous need for innovative argument, I proceeded to
beg, borrow, and steal ideas. Especially useful were accounts of
achievement. But also important were lists of aspirations and
admonitions.

Borrowing Buoyant Messages

Among the best of the involuntary donors were Berk, Berra, Williams and Featherman. To blend their thoughts into the fabric of argument was to gain confidence that a buoyant message might penetrate a murky environment. Let me characterize that atmosphere.

The history of social science at NSF is in large part a continuous recycling of confused attributions about basic versus applied science. In *Milestones and Millstones* I documented how our quest for scientific legitimacy turned on that axis for nearly five decades.

The dominant perception was that social science was a political burden, possibly useful as a handmaiden to basic science, and one that might be accommodated as an applied endeavor even if this did not qualify as real science.

That bitter bite came from sullen members of the National Science Board, surly agents from the OMB, and the usual skeptics on Capitol Hill. That trio was a prime target for edification. The first problem was to gain their attention.

Richard Berk, a tough-minded sociologist from the University of California who served on this Council from 1985 to 1991, provided artful argument to counter the notion that quantitative methods, the tools of real science, were beyond the reach of the so-called "soft" sciences.

Several times, my presentations were peppered with material from the September, 1981 draft of Berk's provocative paper, "Training and Retooling in Quantitative Methods for Applied Sociological Research." The title alone captured attention. The content yielded consternation, and, ultimately, some persuasion.

Berk's focus resonated with the reigning paradigm at NSF. There was particular curiosity about his predictions for the year 2000. He identified six thrusts under way:

♦   *Computational power will no longer be a significant obstacle for quantitative research because of advances in numerical analysis, more efficient algorithms, and development of friendly computers responsive to simple English commands.*

♦   *Significant advances in ways in which we elicit and collect data, including computer assisted interviewing and standardization of official data.*

♦   *Powerful advances in classification, clustering, and scaling techniques.*

♦   *Cross-fertilization of research designs across the social sciences, including embedding randomized experiments within sample surveys and vice versa, and integration of probability sampling, randomized experiments and quasi-experimental procedures into one general data collection model.*

♦ *An influx of methods from operations research, including concern for optimization.*

♦ *A general statistical model for causal analysis put together from measurement processes producing the observed data, including error estimates; stochastic terms not limited to normal distributions; components of sampling; a model that will allow for multiple equations, reciprocal causation, complicated lag structures and non-linear functional forms.*

Certainly, that sounded like science. It was helpful in many ways.

In early 1982 when I was using Berk's ideas, personal computers had not yet arrived at NSF, but a letter about their merits did come from my 12-year old grandson. Berk's thoughts on training the next generation came to the fore as I pondered this letter from Seattle:

Dear Grandpa Otto: March 19, 1982

Right now at school I'm in a class called computer core...Our assignments are making programs to figure out the average test score of some students, printing the numbers from 1 to 50 going horizontally across the screen, or writing a program for a flow chart...

I have always been fascinated with these complex machines. After using them, and going to the computer fair at the U of W, I want to have one, so I have been saving money from my paper route to get an ATARI 800 personal computer.

This model is bigger and better than the ATARI 400. Here are some of the reasons: the 400 doesn't come with Basic (which is needed to operate the computer)THE 800 DOES. The 400 doesn't come with an adapter jack to hook up to your TV. THE 800 DOES. The 400 has finger-indented keys on its key board. THE 800 HAS A KEY BOARD LIKE TYPEWRITERS AND OTHER COMPUTERS.

The 400 has 8K of memory (which is not very much--it can only have 8000 numbers and/or letters in its memory). THE 800 COMES WITH 16K OF MEMORY, AND YOU CAN BUY MORE MEMORY, 16K of it for only $100. On the 400 to boost the memory you have to buy it and put it in the shop and pay them for putting it in!

The reason I'm writing this letter to you is I want to get the ATARI 800 as soon as possible, so I would like to know if you could loan me $500, then I could get it around Mother's Day. The ATARI'S cost is $752.49. Right now I have $82.49. That leaves $170 which I can get with $85 for two months.

The way I would pay you back is by monthly payments of $50 for ten months. I can't stress how much I would appreciate getting this loan. One of my friends who lives in Laurelhurst has one and it is so fun to use I can't believe it. I would like to talk to you about it some time.

LOVE, YOUR GRANDSON,   Daniel Nyholm Larsen

I was moved by this letter. However, there was a problem.

It wasn't the $500, particularly after I discovered why his father could not make the loan. The problem was that I had to deal with all those crumpled, musty, one-dollar bills collected on his paper route each month. But, we signed a contract and Dan got his computer.

I sent a copy of Dan's letter to the President of Atari, Inc. in Sunnyvale, CA. to suggest that if all 12-year old boys in America knew the difference between the 800 and the 400 models, I am sure he wouldn't object.

A week later I received a warm acknowledgment. The Chairman of the Board said he was sending some software to Seattle and concluded that, "You certainly have a very smart grandson."

After the big box arrived, I received one more letter from Dan. The message was brief and pointed: "Did you send a letter to the President of Atari? If so, would you send me a copy because a friend of mine wants his grandfather to write him a letter."   I had to reject that request.

Ten years later, Dan graduated the University of California after a five year program in Computer Science. Today he is a fired-up computer research specialist as an employee of the Scripps Oceanographic Institute

Every time he visits Seattle on holidays, he updates my equipment, sometimes on temporary loans that I make from him. He also throws in a lot of free software.

Thanks Atari, and thanks to Dick Berk for prolonging buoyancy.

Now, having come to a fork in the road--let me take it. This is by way of turning to the contributions of the great folk philosopher, Yogi Berra.

There were a number of occasions during my NSF period, particularly during the latter stages, when I was asked to summarize issues that resounded from science politics to affect the status of social science. Here, thanks to Yogi Berra, I was able to concoct a concise estimate that invariably yielded a buoyant response.

That disquisition is now pertinent in another way. Or, maybe, as Yogi would say, it's *deja vu* all over again.

Our second grandson, Andrew, who is five, shows some athletic propensity. In economic terms, a career in baseball would certainly be buoyant. However, when he finds his copy of the manuscript, I want him to see that there is a ready alternative. Social science and baseball share fundamental proclivities.

Let me explain.

Critics constantly hover over social science inside the Washington beltway. They never hesitate to advise on how we ought to conduct social and behavioral science at NSF. The message usually comes down to four points.

Repeatedly, we are told to be more empirical, less defensive about our status, more modest in our claims, and always quantitative in our work.

In the 1980s, we were assured that these approaches would please the Director, who was usually a physicist or an engineer, would calm the National Science Board, which also included biologists and chemists, would comfort OMB whose personnel were never far from the White House, and would soothe Congressional committees, whose members could not understand social science but were devoted to Yogi Berra.

Accordingly, based on my experience in both baseball and social science, I usually summed up the situation as follows:

♦   On being empirical, Yogi Berra used to say, *"You can observe a lot just by watching."*

♦   On being less defensive, Yogi said, *"If the people don't want to come out to the park, nobody is going to stop 'em."*

♦   On being more modest about our claims, he said *"We made too many wrong mistakes."*

♦   And finally, on emphasizing the quantitative, it was either Yogi or Casey Stengel who said, *"Ninety percent of this game is half-mental."*

Yogi's wit helped make serious points bearing on both the political and the scientific streams of communication that flow at NSF.

Arguments must be made to gain funds before they can be allocated. Claims must be made about expected achievements, but modesty sometimes helps foster a favorable political climate. Defensiveness is readily prompted, particularly when excited by the prospect of "Golden Fleece Awards" or by the novelty of proposals that might have appeal to congressional constituents. Let me illustrate with the following letter that arrived on my desk from Teresa L. Moreland of Route 1, Box 82, Kingsville, Missouri in June, 1981.

Dear Sir:

I am interested in applying for a government grant to study the ecological implication of the growth in the American Quarter Horse population. My concern, and the subject of my study, is that there are now more than 1,300,000 of these horses listed in the breed's current registry. These animals deposit on the average 3 piles of manure apiece on the ground daily--more if they are nervous about something.

The piles weigh on the average 2.5 pounds apiece. This is 9,750,000 pounds of horseshit per day being deposited on the United States of America by one breed of horse alone!   68,250,000 pounds per week!   273,000,000 pounds per month!   This virtual avalanche...has to be affecting the earth's crust, not to mention atmospheric temperature.

I have read of various government grants given for things far less urgent than the study of this situation and I am hopeful that you can put through my request for a grant right away, before we wake up one morning to find...our highways and parking lots buried, our railroad tracks and airport runways covered, our missile silos inoperable, transportation destroyed, defense systems gummed up--you see the possibilities.

I hope you will respond promptly with a check for at least $50,000 so I can start my research into this critical situation.

Sincerely,

Teresa L. Moreland

Despite its obvious appeal to the supporters of research that applies to national needs, I hasten to note that this proposal was rejected--and not merely because there was a shortage of peers to conduct the review.

But not all innovative ideas are rejected. And, over the years, both conventional and unconventional projects yielded a substantial record of knowledge gains from empirical effort. This achievement was not widely appreciated. I tried to remedy that. One major remedial education project cost NSF, and the taxpayers, nearly a million dollars. Some critics sensed that we had funded a Quarter Horse Study. They were wrong.

I do not apologize for prompting huge expenditures to support the Committee on Basic Research in the Behavioral and Social Sciences of the National Research Council. That committee produced three volumes each recording notable discoveries and achievements in social and behavioral science.

Whatever the scientific impact of this prodigious effort, I can assure you that its political importance was critical.

In the short run, it helped keep us in the game. In the longer run it was not unrelated to the ultimate gain made at NSF in 1991 with the establishment of a separate directorate for Social, Behavioral and Economic Sciences, now ably sparked by the leadership of another SSRC stalwart, Cora Marrett.

Let me cite another rich source of ideas. Somewhere in the early 1980s, I think it was at a conference up the Hudson at the Harriman estate, Robin Williams, a member of this Council from 1956 to 1961, gave one of his insightful overviews of the state of understanding from social science.

All present were moved by his forthright estimates. A few wondered if he hadn't carried a commitment to modest claims a bit too far. But, like Yogi, Robin wanted to be sure that we did not make too many wrong mistakes.

I, of course, immediately adopted his seven point summary to provoke other audiences. The language was not that of formal research, but his seven points reflected inquiry that struck out against oversimplified assumptions about the social order. Thus, the Williams Manifesto proclaimed:

♦   *There are no panaceas. Nothing works well for everything, nor very well for very long for anything.*

♦   *All solutions cost something. All attempts to alter undesired conditions require...energy, resources, devotion, and sacrifice.*

♦   *All major social concerns involve multiple values, beliefs, and interests. Many of these are incompatible. Hence, attempted solutions always involve trade-off. Not all values or interests can be maximized at once. Someone almost always "gets hurt."*

♦   *Social systems are complex open systems, with multiple non-linear feedback loops. They behave in rapidly changing, non-obvious ways. They are full of surprises--they are diabolically counter-intuitive.*

♦   *You cannot satisfy all of the people any of the time or any of the people all of the time.*

♦   *We cannot get out of our collective troubles by the rational and prudent pursuit of self-interest alone--for that is just how the Tragedy of the Commons develops. Adam Smith's beneficent invisible hand often turns out to be an unwelcome indiscernible fist.*

♦   *Many consequences of large-scale collective action cannot be foreseen in detail. Intervention will continue to yield unique features not fully anticipated. Miscalculations will abound; some conflicts will not be resolved. Constant monitoring is imperative.*

Robin spoke forcefully. I used his words to underscore that we need to know more than we now know about what we do know and what we don't know.

There are encouraging signs. Old ideologies are crumbling. There is a surge in sensitivity to knowledge needs around fundamental issues. Prime among them is the necessity to come to terms with ecological imperatives that lock us in global interdependence.

This quickly translates into a realization that if undesired collective outcomes are to be minimized, decision-making must involve wider participation and greater accountability by those whose interests are at stake.

So, esteemed colleagues, we social scientists still have work to do.

No clearer vision of the task has been cast than that presented by David Featherman in his most recent annual report to this organization. I need not repeat the details here. Let me merely underscore, and applaud, his three core assumptions and his agenda for six fundamental functions.

David must be right. His views reflect lessons from the flow of history at NSF. The budget wars and the politics of science brought our disparate disciplinary forces together. We learned that there must be collective justification for public support. This produced new inventories of achievements, and now, new challenges for developing and applying fundamental knowledge.

Thus, as you say David, the future of social science will be driven:

♦   by interdisciplinary effort

♦   by research priorities engaging mission-oriented basic research, and

♦   by a cross-cultural and international emphasis.

There are thorns among these themes. But there will also be roses as the social science community mobilizes to implement David's six functions to shape our future. I am, of course, referring to his call:

♦   to broaden the training for the next generation

♦   to extend geocultural knowledge

♦   to expand the range of inter-regional analysis

♦   to explore transnational phenomena

♦   to organize mission-oriented basic research, and

♦   to develop vital social science infrastructures.

Therein lies the future of social science.

Conclusion

Let me now conclude.

Tonight, in the search for the future of social science, I have dispatched:

- ♦   eight financiers
- ♦   six Berkian predictions
- ♦   two letters from Dan
- ♦   four home runs from Yogi
- ♦   seven points from Robin, and
- ♦   three assumptions and six functions from David Featherman.

In the required quantitative terms, that ought to be enough to keep the 90 percent of this game that is half-mental moving robustly toward a very buoyant future.

The Ultramultiversity

Faculty and students are locked in a state of interdependence.

Sometimes, however, their distinctive roles, obligations and opportunities can be considered separately. That is the case for the two talks recorded in this section.

Twenty-three years separate the occasions. First, through satire, I try to expose faculty follies to fellow sociologists and, second, through preachment, I attempt to encourage graduating sociology majors to continue the pursuit of knowledge. The fundamental intent in both cases was to urge that rational detachment be joined to compassionate involvement for effectiveness in dealing with societal concerns.

University life moves in waves, some vigorous, others quiescent. In 1969, as in the years immediately before and after, campus after campus was marked by protests, strikes, sit-ins and other disturbances provoked by anti-war sentiments, racial tensions, and aspirations for social justice. This was a remarkable period of free and volatile expression emanating principally from student quarters. In this context, I chose to examine misdirected role commitments in order to provoke fellow faculty sociologists to move toward relevance and involvement.

Echoes of the late 1960s were very distant for the graduating students of 1992. They might have heard about social turbulence from parents, or in history courses, but their campus life was more apt to be guided by concerns over politically correct ideas. Accordingly, I felt compelled to attempt, in a more conventional way, to delineate a path for involvement consistent with core guidance from sociology.

Voicing Social Concern thus makes two attempts to achieve both effective and successful communication. Perhaps peculiarly, but certainly respectfully, my debt to a university life is hereby acknowledged.

Chapter 29

Professorial Gamesmanship
40th Annual Meeting, Pacific Sociological Association
Olympic Hotel, Seattle, Washington
April 25, 1969

The state of sociology has been assessed by Presidents of this association time and again over our 40 year history. Each time we have managed to rise phoenix-like from the ashes of the analysis.

At our first meeting in 1930, President Emory Bogardus reflected on "The Tools of Sociology." At our meeting last year, President Jack Gibbs discussed "The Issue in Sociology." With such fundamentals cared for, I feel at liberty to seek a salient concern elsewhere.

Tonight I want to focus on the complexities tapped in the term "Ultramultiversity"--a natural extension of what Clark Kerr, in an earlier and more pastoral day, characterized as an aggregation of schools, departments, centers, and institutes held together only by the plumbing.

Today we are more apt to be enmeshed, if not bound together, by computer tapes, by the engulfing flames of student protest, or by the encircling forces of police on campus.

Indeed, the current unrest gives direction to my talk. Student activists tell us that our universities are linked to everything they dislike about modern society, including suppressive regulations, indifference to moral and esthetic values, complicity with a self-serving external establishment, and preoccupation's which exclude overall purpose or meaning to life.

These indictments sting.

All the more because, traditionally, professors hold that universities are guardians of individual freedom and evidence of the liberating belief that disinterested investigation leads to the solution of problems. Far from collaborating with vested interests, we know that professors believe they are among the most significant critics of society.

Ingrained in both student and faculty attitudes is a self-righteousness that does not foster a climate conducive either for learning or for action. If radical dissenters are self-satisfied about moral commitments, we professors may be smug about our detachment from vital human concerns.

On the assumption, then, that we are role making in our detachment more than role taking by real involvement, it is important to examine our professorial role-sets. By so doing, we may find time to participate in the change that sweeps about us in ways that will permit us to help shape these revolutionary forces.

Let us, therefore, consider our behavior as researchers, as authors, and as expert consultants.

Approach

To give this effort a semblance of theoretical respectability, I will draw inspiration, as well as take words, from a former colleague, Dr. James B. Taylor of the Menninger Foundation, who in a moment of blinding brilliance prepared an unpublished paper entitled, "Towards an Incipient Microtheory of Sociological One-Upmanship in the Consultative Conference Setting."

In short, I shall be guided by gamesmanship theories.

Taylor asserts that the general theory of gamesmanship entered sociology through the extensive writings of Erving Goffman. You will recall that Goffman implores us to develop a "sociology of occasions," one where a psychology is necessarily involved, but one stripped and cramped to suit the sociological study of conversations, track meets, banquets, jury trials, and street loitering.

This is an impressive inventory. But it falls short of calling for a sociology of sociological occasions.

Without this, we are left with sparse knowledge of our own transactions. This is a self-gap of alarming proportions.

Why, you may ask, is this the propitious moment for striking out for an inward look at ourselves? Taylor provides a gamesman's answer: At a time when investigations of larger social processes are increasingly inhibited by political, ethical, and legal complications, we cannot but be grateful for a field of study which requires no contact at all with the larger society. The possibilities here are truly unlimited, since we can study not only the sociology of sociology, but also the sociology of students of sociology, and hence, in infinite progression, proceed to the study of the students of the students...of sociology.

Definitions

The brilliant English scholar, Professor Stephen Potter, was the first to give an empirical account of gamesmanship and to reflect on how to achieve a "state of one-upness." His key observation was that it is the ordinary, simple everyday things of life, wherein each one of us can, by ploy or gambit, most naturally gain the advantage.

However, Potter oversimplifies in responding to the question, "What does lifemanship mean?" Here he relies on one of the unpublished notebooks of Rilke from which he takes as his answer the unpublished phrase, "...if you're not one up (Blitzleisch) you're...one down (Rotzleisch)." Despite its possible linkage to Max Weber, this definition simply won't do.

What, for us, are the essential sociological features of "lifemanship" and "one-upmanship"? As employed in our professorial role-set, these adaptive mechanisms refer to any technique for self-presentation which enhances the status of self relative to the status of others.

What, then, is a ploy? Whereas in game theory the concrete occasion is called a play, in gamesmanship it is called a ploy. A ploy is a discernible event-sequence which serves as a subunit in a lifemanship episode, as judged either by self or by other members of the role-set.

The Research Role

To devote first attention to our research role is itself a ploy. It is one that we all have learned to exercise. It counters the incessant demands of students for conferences. It is used against department chairman in confrontations over teaching loads. It deflects demands to paint the porch or to take children to their ballet recital. Commitment to research permits refuge in a backlog of undigested journal articles, unanalyzed computer readouts, and overdue reports.

To ploy effectively in the research role, it has become necessary to expand our repertoire of gambits. As George Sarton, the great historian of science, once said, Science is progressive...; art is...eternal. This mode of citation itself is a ploy of the Type-II Order, one that is especially in vogue in certain sociology departments on the East Coast. Some cynics refer to it as the "Pompous Ploy." It is more discreetly termed the "Learned Hedge."

The possibilities for the practice of gamesmanship are multiplying today with the growing need for work to appear relevant. Accordingly, a large number of relevance ploys have surfaced. Key phrases such as "power structure," "population explosion," "identity crises," "generation gap," "non-negotiable demands," "middle-class morality," "violence," and "pornography" signal the use of a relevance ploy on substantive matters.

With methodological concerns, such vintage phrases as "panel studies" and "focused interviews" have been joined by exotic developments in "ethnomethodology," "path analysis," and "labeling theory" to connote an impending state of one-upness.

Early in every research effort, funds must be secured. The summit of fundmanship is revealed in a series of interviews in Science with Dr. Grant Swinger, Director of the Breakthrough Institute and Chairman of the Board of the Center for the Absorption of Federal Funds.

Already they are on the verge of funding breakthroughs for a project on how to construct a Transcontinental Linear Accelerator that would commence in Berkeley and terminate in Cambridge and thus pass through at least 12 states garnering the support of 24 senators and 100 congressman.

Also relevant was their response to President Johnson's challenge "to teach an animal to speak in this decade." Preliminary exploration into "Which animal?" and "What should the animal be taught to say?" revealed a task that called for an interdisciplinary approach, and for locating the effort in a new administrative structure to be called the National Animal Speech Agency, or NASA.

Let me add that Dr. Swinger's organization has managed to resolve the ancient conflict between teaching and research. Basically, they do neither. They confer, they comment on each other's past papers, and they travel a good deal. Sociologists will recognize these acts as ploys of the Type-I Order.

Reference to travel reminds us to look at the occupation of the researcher in two categories: the mobile and the stationary professor.

The typing of professors by time in location is by now an advanced art. While some resist the lure of distant ivy, others have become adept in manipulating calls from other campuses. This flow sharpens the exchange of ploys between the locals and the cosmopolitans, or, as they allude to each other, between the academic barnacles and the academic butterflies.

The academic barnacle is the object of considerable administrative ambivalence. On the one hand, administrators need not be concerned about mass desertions while they entice butterflies toward their nets with exotic nectars; on the other hand, administrators frequently find that numerous academic barnacles impede the progress of their otherwise sleek vessels. Barnacles frustrate administrative scraping because their shells are composed of tradition, seniority, and contacts in high places. Faced with such formidable defenses, administrators can only rely upon the processes of attrition.

Butterflies twit barnacles by remarking on their lack of motion toward course innovations, new colleagues, and particularly, new locations.

On the other hand, we do not know whether movement by butterflies contributes more than the stability of barnacles to rising student unrest and to the surge of student participation in departmental affairs.

It is, however, important to recognize that both barnacles and butterflies must, of necessity, do research. Each will acknowledge that something good can be said about the other in this regard. If nothing else, they tend to use each other's work as good examples of bad research. This, of course, is the old familiar Up-the-Down-Pecking-Order ploy.

However, it is by research style, more than by the mobility of researchers, the selection of problems, or the application of techniques, that sociologists display the subtleties of lifesmanship in research.

The sophisticated style that I am talking about seeps into sociology in many ways. One has but to recall the salty letters-to-the-editor by a George Lundberg, the witty columns of a Read Bain, the bite in the book reviews of an Ellsworth Faris, or the Élan of a Robert Merton as he beckons us *On the Shoulders of Giants.* But lest we overlook some worthy practitioners, let us reactivate the "Learned Hedge" and turn to the field of biochemistry to find its essence.

Consider the research styles of two eminent scientists, Otto Warburg and Albert Szent-Gyorgi. In a recent book, each was given an opportunity to reminisce on their life's work. Warburg could come with only one page of personal revelation, and that mostly a mere listing of dates and places. He summarized his approach to scientific problems by saying that solutions usually have to be forced by carrying out innumerable experiments without much critical hesitation. Warburg characteristically gave his piece the stark title, "Experiments with Biochemistry."

In sharp contrast, Szent-Gyorgyi called his account, "Lost in the Twentieth Century." He said, I make the wildest theories, connecting up the test tube reaction with the broadest philosophical ideas, but spend most of my time in a laboratory, playing with living matter, keeping my eyes open, observing and pursuing the smallest detail.

Thus, where one researcher forces, another one plays; but, and this is important, they both produce.

This suggests, I propose, that there is no necessary relationship between temperament and success in a chosen line of work. The contrast in style apparently doesn't explain much; but it does permit us to emphasize that a penalty on productivity need not be the price we pay for play.

To be sure, there may be other costs. Many of the sober sided colleagues of Szent-Gyorgyi found it hard to live with the witty Hungarian. When he discovered ascorbic acid, he proposed to name it "ignose"--ose for sugar, and ign for "I don't know." When a prim colleague objected, Szent-Gyorgi countered, "How about Godnose?" He finally had to settle for "hexuronic acid."

So much for researchmanship. Now let us turn to a related facet of our professorial role-set, the matter of authoring articles and books.

The Author Role

Professors must put research to print. The pressure to publish is real. The skill to do so is variable. For some, it is an onerous task; for others, ink runs in their veins.

Only occasionally do we find an institution that minimizes the pressure for continuous publication. Take, for example, a report in the Library Journal on Browser College. Browser College builds strength on its greatest weakness: a lackluster faculty. To offset the dearth of renowned professors in residence, the college treats all famous authors in their library as Browser savants.

To build strength through weakness, Browser transfigures the debased cliche, "Publish or Perish," into "Publish and Cherish." William Shakespeare might have perished had he never published, but he did publish and therefore persists as the greatest teacher of the English-speaking world, and he is a member of the Browser faculty. Jesus neither published nor perished, but His trusted disciples served as willing and faithful reporters. His teachings are therefore available to great and small, enshrined in The New Testament, also available in the Browser library.

As sociologists seek immortality through print, they confront a tempting array of upmanship opportunities. Indeed, one doesn't have to be an author to gain some of the advantages of the role. One merely has to have a contract with a lean and hungry publisher to be able to list, as forthcoming, a new item on the Vita, to draw some advance royalties, or to get special invitations designating the secret hotel room where the publisher's libations will be dispensed.

But consider the makeup of the manuscript itself. The standard opening ploy in many journal articles calls attention, through copious footnotes, to how the literature abounds with studies that have neglected what this article will now take up. After initial skirmishing with procedures, a full statement of positive findings appears, only to followed by circumlocutions masking a network of hesitations, reservations, and downright doubts about the validity and reliability of the whole enterprise.

For experimental studies, these doubts can be codified under a series of principles which have come to be known as Finagle's Laws:

♦ First Law: If anything can go wrong with an experiment, it will.

♦ Second Law: No matter what the result, it can easily be explained.

♦ Third Law: No matter what the result, there is always someone to misinterpret it.

These laws are supplemented by Finagle's Rules as follows:

♦ Rule One: Experiments must be replicated; they should all fail in the same way.

♦ Rule Two: Data are always useful. They indicate that you have been working.

♦ Rule Three: Do not believe in miracles. Just rely on them.

Content analysis produces yet another insight. A systematic check of 73 leading sociology journals, from the date of their first publication to the present, indicates that not once did any of the 308,493 articles published ever conclude with a statement reading The data of this study clearly show that no further research on this topic is suggested, required, or warranted. Surely the absence of such a conclusion opens new ground for the aspiring gamesman.

This is not to imply that sociologists lack humility. Indeed, we pioneered the use of the Humble Hedge. This is a gambit whereby we qualify meaning into nothingness while seeking to be objective. The general strategy follows this simple rule: always convey doubts about your statements. Use hedge verbs such as indicate, suggest, appear to be, may, and might. Depend upon these nouns: speculation, conjecture, and construct.

Hedges can be classified as first, second, and third order, or single, double, and triple-barreled. The quadribarreled hedge is clumsy, and should be avoided. Take the following statement for example: Speculation about etiologic factors might possibly suggest that previous investigators may have been wrong. The sentence could be reduced to a third-order hedge with only a slight loss of ambiguity.

But, happily, almost any publication leads to the researcher being defined as an "expert." Let us now consider some key features of this role.

The Expert Role

As publications gain visibility, the service of the sociologist as a specialist in pantology is sought. A minor publication can lead to a local consultant ship with the Pollution Control Board. A major publication, one that achieves the status by becoming a reprint in the Bobbs-Merrill series, merits service as a "Visiting Scientist" for the ASA, or even a call to a commission in Washington.

One call escalates into others. A conference-seminar-colloquia-symposia-review panel circuit merges as colleagues informally build networks of mutual support.

So interlaced have privileges become among professors, government bureaucrats, and foundation executives, that one almost feels the urge to warn, in classic presidential style, of a new peril not unlike that posed by the military-industrial complex.

However, I want only to deal with a special assemblage of the articulate: that small, scholarly conference, typically convened for a few days off-campus in some grove at Santa Barbara, the Catskills, Palo Alto, or Aspen for the purpose of forging a breakthrough.

Such a conference challenges the one-upsman. Clear role-expectations are lacking. Since the sessions are held in out-of-the-way places, interaction is intense. There is no physical escape. Moreover, participants must validate their expertise in a context of considerable ambiguity.

Topics are general, but participants are specialists. Each expert feels compelled to contribute, there is a frantic search for hooks on which to hang ideas.

Ultramultiversity professors come to such a conference with advantages. Faithful service on committees affords good training in tactics appropriate for the ad hoc advancement of knowledge. Service on such committees also forms a physical posture that can tolerate the torment of being seated for many hours in a leatherette chair.

Any topic will do for a conference, but something with the flavor of international development is ideal. Occasionally, someone will launch a conference on ethnomethodology or sociolinguistics. Meetings of this sort are likely to be held in a YMCA or on a campus in some midwestern site.

The small, scholarly conference has latent functions. The coordinator may wish to expand the contact of his home institution with the wider world of scholarship. Or, more colloquially, "He's looking for another job." The latent function that is most likely to be manifest is that the coordinator is using up the last funds of a grant before it terminates.

To organize such a conference requires skill. The coordinator first communicates with high status professionals. Typically, he finds that some have died since their last publication, others are on sabbatical, while still others are busy at other conferences. As a last resort, the coordinator may have to invite an Assistant Professor from Browser College.

As the conference gets under way, the gates to gamesmanship are thrown open. Two illustrations will suffice. First, the Heart-of-the-Matter ploy. This is signaled by a statement like, "I think we really have to deal with one truly basic issue here." When the sociologist uses this ploy, he reduces his anxiety about why he is there, and he introduces his own work, which can then be expounded at length. This ploy is especially useful when the work in question is, at best, tangential to the topic.

As variants, the following phrases can be used: "Of course you may be right, but isn't that an a-theoretical approach? Or, "You seem to be taking a reductionist position." Since these barbs impinge on affective states, they are essentially unanswerable. But one-upmanship is not successful if it results in physical assault.

Generally more successful is the Amiable Ignorance ploy, best used during the cocktail hour. The strategy follows one simple rule: never appear to know anything at all about the other person's institution.

Various phrases convey ignorance. For example, a low-level entry is achieved by inquiring, "Am I right in thinking that you are still working on your doctorate?" Or, one might ask, "Just who is on your faculty now?" Inquiries can also be made about whether the institution is a state college or church supported, what size computer it has, or whether touring theater companies ever stop there.

By the sheer force of Amiable Ignorance, the expert conveys that he has never heard of the school, that he never expects to hear of it again, and that he is still not certain where it is located.

Yet, by maintaining a friendly and sympathetic air, bordering at times on gemeinschaft, the expert produces in the listener the impression that the expert is a thoroughly nice person, and a concession that the expert's credentials should be taken seriously. The resulting dissonance can result in phenomena similar to those observed by Bettelheim in the German concentration camps.

Being and Appearing Relevant

As a scientific discipline, sociology confronts mounting pressure not only to be relevant but to appear relevant. Accordingly, I suggest that a number of special commissions be formed to prepare reports to prove that we can be both.

Appointing agents should use two guidelines: First, they should assume that any bona fide member of a sociological association is qualified to work on any commission. Second, they should select appointees not by political, geographical, or racial criteria, but by the relevance of their names for the task at hand.

The first guideline insures competence for the task of generating documents showing that sociology is relevant. The second guideline insures that a symbol will be present to make sociology appear relevant. This dual assurance is what the public demands today.

You are aware, of course, that even though a commission has an official title, it tends to take the name of the chairman in public discourse. For example, the National Advisory Commission on Civil Disorders (NACOD), which dealt with problems of urban riots, issued what came to be known as the "Kerner Report." But they didn't follow our second guideline. To illustrate, let us take some obvious problem areas and suggest some possible appointees from sociology to new public commissions.

Suppose that the national concern over "hippies" and "yippies" led to the founding of a Commission on Subculture of Teenagers (COST).

How might we sociologists respond under the second guideline? Clearly, someone like Herbert Simon and Harold Garfinkle should be appointed as co-chairs. They could then issue the Simon-Garfinkle Report.

Or take the problem of pollution. Who should head up the Commission on Pollution (COP)? Who but Arthur Stinchcombe and Neil Smelser?

There is no limit to the possibilities for this collective ploy. Certainly we could identify problems to establish commissions for combinations of sociologists such as Leonard Cain and Theodore Abel; or, Listen Pope and Talcott Parsons; or, Carolyn Rose and Herbert Blumer; or, Wilbert Moore and Lee Rainwater. From experience, I can testify that the Commission on Obscenity and Pornography (COP) would anxiously await a report from such distinguished sociologists as Warren Breed, Herbert Hyman, and Melvin Seeman.

Having ventilated the symbolic interactionist approach to collective gamesmanship, I must now conclude.

Conclusion

From our professorial role-set, I have examined how sociologists define and perform their roles as researchers, authors, and expert consultants. The data clearly show that no further research on this topic is suggested, required, or warranted. You may take comfort from this conclusion. But can we take anything else from the foregoing analysis?

Three years ago at our meeting in Vancouver, I forecast that 1971 would be "The Year Sociology Stood Still." That vision was projected from some disturbing trends in our professional life--trends that persist today with considerable cost to our scientific and intellectual activities.

However, what I did not sense then, but what I have tried to identify on this occasion, is the special capacity that sociologists have for coping with trials and thus turning the stress of transactions into a confidence for survival.

One note remains: the downside consequences of gamesmanship.

At best, we might view gamesmanship as a character struggle; one where the individual professor is concerned with achieving status goals while sustaining established norms.

Appropriate as this might be for many interaction contexts, one must be concerned with abuse by researchers, authors, and experts.

These roles are also entries to the arena of action. Continued ploys tend to "cool out" or make safe the very situations that require a crystal moment of engagement, chance-taking, and moral sensibility.

I have attempted to show that in the ultramultiversity a certain amount of flab, sham, and excess has been brought to our role commitments. These must be reduced. Energy could then be devoted to innovation, to the liberation of imagination in areas such as that unmentioned element of our professorial role-set, teaching.

This role, now more than ever, means learning along with our students, so that calls to action may be linked to real problem-solving, not by exhortation or rhetoric, but by identifying feasible alternatives, discovering key points of leverage, and by measuring efforts by actual results.

A great deal is at stake in a redefinition of professorial roles. The very life of the university may hinge not on our capacities for gamesmanship, as functional as the may be for the status wars within the discipline, but on a strategy of self-presentation that takes more risks and presses toward more genuine involvement.

Involvement could take many forms. The essential one, as I see it, is for sociologists to bring what they know as researchers, authors, and experts to the arena of action for clear-cut tests of competence.

Who else but sociologists are better equipped to propose and assess means of building change into resistant human institutions--beginning with our own?

When that is done, we will become confident that sociology is not standing still.

Chapter 30

The Ongoing Pursuit of Knowledge
Sociology Commencement, University of Washington
June 9, 1992

It is an honor to be here for this landmark occasion. This is the first time in the 75-year life of our department that graduating sociology majors have had their own special departure ceremony.

Going back to 1917, our first distinguished department leader, William F. Ogburn, would have called this a monumental case of cultural lag. I think we should salute you, the innovative class of 1992, for creating historical closure. Your mastery of sociology is evident. You have come to know the potency of primary group principles. You also sense the power of the latent functions of ceremony.

And now, years of study bring you to the triumph of graduation. I congratulate you. You have earned a celebration. Your efforts yield a justifiable moment of pride. It is shared by your parents, your friends, and your professors.

Let me make a confession. Forty-five years ago, in 1947, I ran from where you now sit. That is, I did not participate in any commencement exercise. In fact, until tonight, I have never attended any such observance at this university.

That neglect I now regret. It left me without a role model for a commencement speech. However, since I have never met anyone who can recall what their commencement speaker said, I shall, without fear, plunge ahead. I am pleased to be in this risk-free setting where visions can be cast despite their uncertain character.

Expect Accelerated Change

Indeed, uncertainty must crowd your mind tonight. Undoubtedly you are asking, what lies ahead? Is there anything you can count on? Not much, perhaps. But the tempo of your life will be touched by two certainties, one personal and perceptual, the other social and real.

First, before you know it the next 45 years will have slipped away. Second, social and technological change will accelerate.

The thrust of change, shaped both by technology and by social invention, penetrated my generation at many points to speed up the pace of life. Thus we were the first to experience travel by jet, food by microwave, information by computer, education by Head-Start, justice by plea-bargain, sports by sudden-death, and divorce by no-fault.

More dramatic impulses lie ahead. One wonders what new surge looms from the laboratories of genetic engineering, or from the robots animated by "intelligence" inserted by fifth-generation computers. Change is certainly on the agenda. And, given the general environment that you inherit, there is need for change. More than one forest is in jeopardy.

As we stand on the threshold of the 21st century, the social landscape is littered with pollution, poverty, debt, disease, drugs, hunger, crime, and terrorism. Racism and sexism continue to plague society. And the world is not getting safer for diversity as ethnicity erodes into ethnocentrism and war between nationalistic factions again threaten the globe.

So your generation confronts a bulging inventory of trouble. How will you respond?

I urge you to stay informed, to pursue knowledge, and to get involved. This you can do whether or not you go on to graduate school. This you must do if you are to remain true to our common sociological heritage.

Stay in the Hunt

The key word for tonight is "knowledge." This is appropriate because the pursuit of knowledge does not cease in the glow of graduation. I will touch lightly on our legacy, on the nature of knowledge, on its utility, and on its limitations.

Well, then, what did you gain from a major in sociology? I mean, can you specify some distillation beyond grades and the fun that marks a memory of college?

That's not easy. Such essence is rarely recognized at the hour of graduation. But somehow, at sometime, we gain a more meaningful measure of our university days. We come to know that it is more than a simple sum of efforts over a variety of subjects explored in all those classroom hours.

For me, given the chance development of an academic career, exposure to sociology at Washington left a powerful imprint. Four normative traits stand out, each nurtured over 75 years by our leaders extending from William F. Ogburn to Edgar F. Borgatta, with special emphasis added along the way by the likes of George Lundberg, Calvin Schmid, Robert Faris, Stuart Dodd, Tad Blalock, and Herb Costner.

Among other things, sociological training at Washington has always implored students to be empirical, to strive for precision in quantitative terms, to reach beyond description to systematic explanation, and to be modest in claims.

The harvest cannot be the same for each generation. Your returns will be even richer because you have absorbed a sociology that also emphasizes comparative, historical, cross-system analysis. You are, in fact, well prepared to become effective actors in the continuing social and political drama played out around the pursuit of knowledge in society.

But let me warn you: an educational legacy while rewarding is also demanding. Each element provides moments of trial. The tide of reality comes in with many tests.

To illustrate from my own experience, I have found that being empirical and quantitative does not automatically make us less defensive about our status or more modest in our claims.

Along with you, I have also found that knowledge is elusive and is hard earned. To appreciate that fact is a major mark of a liberal education.

In sociology, we worry a lot about how we know what we know. There are always concerns about validity and generality. Furthermore, there are always puzzles about the linkage of knowledge to attitudes, behavior, and action, particularly problem resolution.

Some of your professors even hope that the enlightenment you have gained on these matters will prompt you to go forth as informed citizens to do battle with politicians over more support for research.

To understand this array of general points is not a minor achievement. It rests on some elementary distinctions that are now part of your sociological intellect.

You have come to appreciate that knowledge can be built from direct experience and also from information, but it is not identical with these elements. Furthermore, you know that while information can be acquired through direct experience, it can also be gained over other routes. Thus, fortunately, we can have information about poverty, pornography, or prisons without direct experience.

"To experience" betokens familiarity. "To have information" is to be able to state a fact. But, "To hold knowledge" is to have the power to explain--and the curiosity to pursue further understanding.

And that is the heart of the matter: until regularities are discerned in that collection, until a theory and thus an explanation is imposed upon facts--often through artful association with values, logic, and assumptions--information remains something less than knowledge.

This is a point of emphasis in sociology. When lost, it leads to an easy leap from correlation to causation. And that can be costly, even if it produces dramatic news accounts.

This leap occurs only too often when people receive information that shows that two things seem to move along together, such as poverty and race, pornography and rape, or television and violence. Merely to note simultaneous occurrences does not offer explanation. Nor does it advance the understanding required for effective involvement.

Knowing and Doing

As you continue the pursuit of knowledge, or become an active supporter of such efforts, there will certainly be moments when you ask, "Why don't we do better when we know better?"

Yes, in an age of specialization, one can't help but puzzle over why it is that shoemakers have holes in their shoes, barbers need haircuts, physicians rarely heal themselves, or sociologists don't run organizations better than anyone else.

How do we account for the slippage between knowing and doing?

Not easily. Two elements blur the linkage. The first is that knowledge is conditional and open ended. The second is that doing is also propelled by aspirations or conceptions of the desirable. Such values can have a certitude that often resists the penetration of knowledge.

So our on-going task is more complex. Clearly, we need to know more than we now know about what we do know and what we don't know.

The knowing-doing nexus, in particular, awaits further penetration.

We have to gain a clearer understanding of the conditions under which reliable knowledge can be linked to desirable values. Short of that, we will continue to be unable to predict the ways that knowledge will be applied, as when the cure for a disease also creates the capacity to spread that disease.

You now leave the incubator of such concerns. Your investment in this great university will reward you with an appreciation of the past, new perceptions of reality, and an expanded sense of potentiality.

To the extent that you have reaped that harvest, the prospects for your compassionate involvement with society are surely enhanced.

However, henceforth you will have to guard against cynicism because, as you have no doubt sensed from sociology, being ignorant seldom prevents people from acting. Indeed, some ignorance seems to encourage action where knowledge might prescribe indifference or caution.

Sociology has also sensitized you to the complexity of social systems and to the existence of powerful dynamics that both resist and foster change.

You have learned, and now it will be confirmed, that major social concerns invariably involve the intersection of competing values, beliefs, and interests, some congruent, some incompatible.

Moreover, it will be bracing to confront the reality that there are no cost-free solutions, and whatever is attempted will most likely entail gains for some and losses for others.

But you have also learned that if undesired collective outcomes are to be minimized, decision-making must involve wider participation and greater accountability by those whose vital interests are importantly affected.

Conclusion

On that hopeful note, we celebrate commencement, perhaps with some misgiving since you shall not get these four years back again.

Our salute to this precious time calls for a conclusion.

Here, then, is mine.

The literature of classical mythology alerts us to choices shaded by bright prospects or by dark risks. The route of Pandora opens up the darkness of extensive and unforeseen troubles. The path of Prometheus boldly pursues the light. My journey of 45 years through this university commends the values found along the Prometheus passage, despite the risks.

For 75 years, sociology at Washington has been a staunch champion of the Prometheus thrust toward light. If your experience in the next 45 years is written in these terms then, no matter how harsh or strenuous the times, you will possess knowledge to encompass both rational detachment and compassionate involvement.

So, let this message ring out from this class of 1992: we will *stay informed*, we will *pursue knowledge*, and we will *get involved* in our world in compassionate ways.

Three Memorable Mentors

For 23 years, or about one-third of my life, I was a student in elementary, secondary, college, and graduate schools.

That means that I had been under the tutelage of countless teachers, some forgotten but many remembered for their remarkable tolerance and their total dedication to excellence.

I came from a generation, and from a locale, where finishing high school was okay but attending college was an extraordinary step. But I also came from a family where, despite no explicit pressure, there was precedent and there was opportunity, and I yielded to both.

Along the way, there were many teachers. My assessment of their worth, competence, and impact varied over time. It is startling to realize that experience alters judgments of how "good" a "bad" teacher was, or vice versa.

That estimate both haunted and cheered me when I became a practitioner of the art. It was also troublesome as we struggled to place more emphasis on rewarding "good teaching." The problem is how to identify it in a fair and fearless way so that it reflects both immediate and longer-term contributions.

On a personal level, the solution is to live long enough, and be fortunate enough, to have teachers who later become your colleagues. That affords insight into valuable educational traits not always visible in the classroom. This final section provides testimony on that point.

Lundberg and Dodd were outstanding teachers and generous colleagues. Blalock, while not formally my teacher, generated inspiration and direction. In fact, when it comes to advancing the precepts of science for sociology, Tad was the great enactor of what the others, including their student, merely, no, strenuously, advocated.

All three men are now deceased. That harsh fact was the occasion for two of these three talks. I trust that the words spoken about Stu and Tad, and earlier about George when he was still with us, makes it clear why for me, and for many others, they did earn the accolade *"Memorable Mentors."*

Chapter 31

The Foundations of George Lundberg

18th World Congress, Institut International de Sociologie
Cordoba, Argentina
September 7, 1963

A distinctive feature of this Congress is the presence many
students from the great universities of Argentina. I am impressed by
how you combine a respect for your heritage with critical attitudes,
and with a quest for new ideas.

It is, therefore, a pleasure to accept your invitation to talk about a
sociologist from the plains of North Dakota here near the pampas of
Argentina. You've asked me to tell you about a major figure in the
development of our discipline in the United States, George A.
Lundberg. You apparently have read something of his works, and now
you want to know more about him as a person, particularly about his
educational background and his own teaching traits.

George Lundberg is a man of many parts. His ample bibliography
portrays the reach of his sociological enterprise. But, he is also a
polemicist, a farmer, a musician, and a serious student of opera,
poetry, literature, language, hymnology, the theater, American foreign
policy, baseball, and Arctic exploration.

One hesitates to take the measure of such a man. My reluctance is
compounded because I am consulting on his current writing project
involving autobiographical notes accounting for the intellectual
themes in his professional career. In this forthcoming volume, he will
tell his own story. It will be laced with the combat of a pioneer and
spiced with a compassion for human kind. I shall try not to steal one
anecdote from it, even though such theft might indeed salvage this
minor and wholly unauthorized biographical sketch.

Elementary Education

George Lundberg was born on October 3, 1895 in Fairdale, North Dakota. On a number of pleasant occasions, I have heard him recount his efforts to obtain a formal education. From his earliest youth, it appeared ordained that he would become a teacher. However, given his starting point, the route to a Ph.D. was not a straight line, nor was the journey to a university professorship in any sense routine. In fact, the odds against collecting the credentials he finally assembled were awesome.

His parents were immigrants from Sweden struggling to master a harsh, rural environment. Physical labor was the natural activity. Reading material was scarce, but long winters gave time for reading-- even if the fare sometimes consisted mainly of Sears-Roebuck catalogues. The country school teacher, and an occasional itinerant preacher, were the main literate models that moved over the prairie. Their skills did not go unnoticed.

His elementary education consisted of eight years in a one-room schoolhouse. There he, and his older brother Albert, who later was to become a distinguished jurist, successfully competed for prizes in spelling and debate. Lessons were learned and relearned. He can to this day recite scores of poems from the works of James Whitcomb Riley, Henry Wadsworth Longfellow, John Greenleaf Whittier, and other figures of American versification.

Armed with this elementary education, Lundberg set out to pursue what was then his life's goal--to be a public school teacher. He contends that this goal was probably set when he noted that teachers kept better working hours than farmers, and that schoolhouses were the warmest place in the community during the long, cold Dakota winters.

Reinforced by a brief six-month stint at the Mayville Normal School, not to mention certificates from correspondence courses with the Dickson School of Memory and the Siegal-Myers Conservatory of Music, he took the examination for prospective grade school teachers at the County Court House. The result led to his first teaching job--an appointment at the age of 16 as the sole teacher in a one-room schoolhouse located three miles from his birthplace.

Lundberg's first taste of teaching enlarged his appetite, but it also made it clear that the possession of further credentials would be advisable. Thereupon Lundberg sought to enter the University of

North Dakota. His inability to produce a standard high school diploma caused consternation in the admissions office. After some wrangling, he was permitted to proceed and moved rapidly from probationary to full status. Forty years later, the University of North Dakota solemnly honored him with an LL.D., awarded to the man they almost barred from entry as an undergraduate.

On to Higher Education

The first world war did not make the world safe for democracy, but it did at least three things for George Lundberg.

First, his college education was briefly interrupted when he was drafted out of the sophomore class and made his first trip to Europe, serving in France as a member of the American Expeditionary Forces.

Second, it provided him with a middle initial and name--"A" for Andrew. This came about when an Army sergeant insisted that every man should have one, and this name was duly selected.

Third, and most significant, it provided Lundberg an opportunity to pursue six months of higher education in London while waiting his turn to be demobilized. Ever eager for intellectual stimulation, Lundberg became the first sophomore from the University of North Dakota to regularly attend lectures at the London School of Economics.

Upon returning home he quickly completed work for his BA. in 1920 at the University of North Dakota. He then continued his teaching career in the public schools serving in Columbus, North Dakota, and then in Garrison, North Dakota. He also taught Sunday school in both Methodist and Presbyterian churches. The extra-curricular activity for which he became most noted, however, was as leader and violinist of the "Garrison Six," a popular dance band that broke the silence of vast Dakota airways every Saturday night.

Lundberg was rapidly moving up the ladder as a public school teacher and administrator when an event occurred that changed the course of his career and moved him into the college realm and thus toward the orbit of sociology. An offer for employment with the Hope, North Dakota schools was suddenly withdrawn. The school board charged him with subversive political activity because of his membership in a native populist movement, the Non-Partisan League.

Despite a hearing before the school board, presided over by the local banker, the decision was upheld. It was late in the summer.

Desperate efforts followed to secure employment for the forthcoming year. Lundberg placed employment advertisements in various school journals. A letter arrived from Midland College in Fremont, Nebraska, and after Lundberg clarified his Lutheran identification he was appointed to his first college teaching job--Professor of Sociology, Psychology, Education, and Director of the Practice School. Among other attributes that the Midland Deans admired was the fact that here was a man who did not smoke or drink. Had they inquired into the basis for this asceticism, they would have discovered it was digestive and not doctrinal.

As an undergraduate at North Dakota, Lundberg studied sociology with John M. Gillette, to whom he later dedicated his first book, *Social Research*. The seed sown there was further nourished during several summers at the University of Wisconsin where Lundberg pursued a graduate degree in the department thriving under the impact of Edward A. Ross.

Ultimately, Lundberg became convinced that his calling was a university teaching career in sociology. Accordingly, while still working at Midland College, he applied for a teaching assistantship at the University of Minnesota in order to pursue a Ph.D. The new chairman, F. Stuart Chapin, accepted the application and made the appointment. At Minnesota, Chapin and L. L. Bernard were particularly influential in the development of Lundberg's ideas.

In 1925, the Ph.D. was granted. The dissertation was entitled, "The History of Poor Relief Legislation in Minnesota." Lundberg reports that not a single copy of that document is available anywhere in the world today. Despite this, the University of Minnesota in 1951 awarded him its Distinguished Achievement Medal, with the citation, "Pioneer in Applying Scientific Method to Sociology--Worthy of Special Commendation for Outstanding Achievement."

Igniting Controversy in a University Career

In 1925, Lundberg launched his university teaching career which was to span thirty-five years up to his formal retirement in 1961.

His first appointment brought him to the University of Washington as an Assistant Professor. He drove 2,000 miles west from Minneapolis in a Model-T Ford. On the way across Dakota, his luggage fell off the car and was lost. Several months later it appeared in Seattle by Railway Express. The remarkable retrieval was a coincidence involving the kind of interpersonal connections that have intrigued Lundberg throughout his academic life.

A farmer, not known to Lundberg, found the luggage along the road. Without opening it, he merely stored it away in his granary. Sometime later, a traveling hardware salesman from Garrison, North Dakota, an old friend from Lundberg's teaching days in that town, called on the farmer and spied the luggage. The conversation led to identification and ultimate return of the lost goods.

Lundberg's faith in rural values and sociometric linkages has never waned since that day.

After one year at the University of Washington in Seattle, Lundberg packed his bags again and traveled East to take up successive appointments at Wells College, the University of Pittsburgh, Columbia University, and Bennington College in Vermont.

During this period, he lectured at many other universities, served in the federal government, produced his major published works, achieved a store of professional honors, gained an international reputation as a vigorous spokesman for a rigorous sociology, and ignited controversy wherever he went.

The latter point is illustrated in so many contexts that it is clearly central to his sociological self. He believed in free speech and he practiced it. He also reflected upon its exercise. One occasion was particularly dramatic.

In 1943, Lundberg was elected President of the American Sociological Society (the youngest ever to that point and the first to elected by a membership-wide secret mail ballot). As was the custom, a presidential address was to be delivered at the annual meeting. Lundberg chose the topic "Sociologists and the Peace." He has told me that the talk was not an immortal masterpiece, either as a specimen of academic discourse or as a sample of oratory. He added that its only claim to uniqueness was that it was the first time that a presidential address to a learned society was interrupted by boos and other sounds of disapproval.

What sparked such a response.? The argument was strong. The burden of his remarks was that sociologists especially should guard against a vindictive and sentimental peace settlement which would do violence to known geographic, economic, and cultural principles that underlie and basically condition the possibility of community life. He attacked the legalistic, as contrasted with the scientific, approach to the problem. Along the way he also took swipes at quite a few groups, including several religious, national, and cultural groups who were already,two years before the war's end, agitating for territory, boundaries, and independent national existence. That, he concedes, probably ignited negativity.

Indeed, on reflection Lundberg now acknowledges it was probably inconsiderate of him to speak so bluntly at so critical and trying a time. He certainly does not blame the audience for their agitation. At the same time, he felt compelled to remind his colleagues that for a scientist it would be a mistaken kindness, not to say a gross immorality, to fail to report what we know or believe to be the facts.

Another indication of how Lundberg fed fires of controversy may be seen in examining the fate of his ideas in the footnotes of scholarly communications.

Over a 28-year period from 1936 on, 178 authors cited Lundberg 334 times in 186 articles in the leading journals of sociology (Six of his books were cited, with *Foundations* mentioned most frequently-- 71 times; his most frequently noted article, "Social Attraction Patterns in a Village," garnered 38 citations).

The citations were coded by whether they referred to substantive sociological content, sociological methods, or meta-sociological material. They were further coded by whether the author making the citation expressed agreement, disagreement, or was neutral with respect to Lundberg's material. The *American Sociological Review* contains the largest number of citations, 44 percent of the total, and at least one reference is made to his work there in 25 of the 28 years, suggesting a considerable "life-span" for his ideas.

With respect to the generation of controversy, the data show that in about one out of four of the total citations, disagreement was registered with the ideas expressed. The main source of contention was in reference to his meta-sociological material, but some disagreement was registered in the other two areas also.

Clearly, Lundberg has served as an irritant and he continues to arrest contentious attention in the field of sociology.

It should also be noted, however, that controversy was not the only element to mark the progression of his career. He was a builder, too, and a genius at drawing a staff together into a cohesive, dynamic team.

In the Spring of 1945, Lundberg returned to the University of Washington to deliver the Walker-Ames lectures which later were ecorded in his high voltage volume, *Can Science Save Us?* He stayed on as Professor and Chairman in which capacity his leadership vaulted the department into a vigorous program, bringing it into the front rank of sociological centers.

The force of his leadership was not found in the functions of administrative detail, which he detested, nor even in the imaginative personnel and program decisions that he instigated.

The main force was his thoughts and his manner of projecting them. No student nor colleague from that period will ever forget the power of his presence.

One colleague characterized the imprint very well, "You brought giant ideas and you taught others to lift their sights and to aspire."

Tributes Capture Traits

Upon his retirement from teaching in 1961, tributes poured in from former teachers, students, colleagues, and associates. Thus, Theodore Newcomb wrote: "Please tell George Lundberg that I loved him and learned from him in the Green Mountains of Vermont a long generation ago when I got the habit, and have been doing it ever since."

Others got the habit, too. Numbered among the many messages are cues to his character that reflect the art of the person. What traits, and how were they sensed?

Is it that he was different? Nels Anderson gave one clue: "Your ego is something I always envied, because you had something to back it up. You were sufficiently deviant never to be a stereotype, in a milieu of too many stereotypes."

Is it his communicative skill? Robert Merton observed that: "George has always been one to press for clarity of thought and of expression. This has been of even greater benefit to those who, on occasion, have disagreed with his conceptions than to those who followed his views implicitly."

Is it that he was a battler? Richard LaPiere thought so: "I congratulate you, first, for the valiant fight that you have waged these many years against the Forces of Darkness. You have fought with vigor, with logic, and exceptional sincerity; and I honor you for this."

Is it the manner in which he fought? Paul Hanley Furfey, offered the following estimate: "It seems to me that intellectual controversy is always a good way to take the measure of a man; and, as an opponent,

Professor Lundberg has always appeared in a very favorable light. He has always been scrupulously fair, he has always remained aloof from petty emotions, and he has always shown intellectual brilliance. He has always made it seem obvious that winning an argument is unimportant, but that arriving at the truth is supremely important. What better compliment could one give to a scholar?"

Is it the powerful imprint that he leaves at the point of first contact? Frederick Stephan asserts: "I have fond memories of our first association over a third of a century ago in Alumni Hall at the University of Pittsburgh. At that time, I discovered in you a deep seriousness of purpose well protected by a coating of skepticism. You brought a refreshing realism to many muddled subjects."

Is it his ability to work harmoniously with co-workers? Mirra Komarovsky testifies: "Accept a rare tribute from a former collaborator: I am ready to do it again!"

Is it his total intellectual posture? Robert Bierstedt thinks so and expresses it in a remarkable tribute: "...in the history of American sociology there are few indeed who have made more stimulating contributions to our discipline than George Andrew Lundberg. Impatient of fraud and pomposity, clear in intent and purpose, energetic in his sponsorship of science, clever in controversy, and brilliant in general--these are the things I would remark upon as I think about his scintillating career. Some day...I shall tell him how proud I am to know him, to have been his friend, to have read his articles and books (often before publication), to have argued with him, and even to have fought with him on the battlefield of the intellect. It is only the lesser mortals, the ones who seek disciples, who ask us always to agree. No one will ever say about you, George, that you were a lesser mortal. There are many of us in fact who rank you with the great ones, and who will keep you there in mind and heart."

The Teacher

These accolades make it clear that part of the art of Lundberg as a teacher was that he did not have to be in a classroom to be effective in this role. His pen was powerful, and so, too, was his personality. Add to these his gift of oral expression and the teaching skill comes to focus.

In his own judgment, Lundberg always claimed that writing and reading were superior to talking and listening as channels of education. In *Can Science Save Us?* he wrote: It is a waste of time to listen to lecture for an hour, the content of which a properly trained person should be able to get much better in fifteen minutes through reading. He often opened his lectures with a similar observation.

Lundberg may not like the lecture form, but students appreciate his lectures. He comes prepared to do a job. The tall, lean figure is impeccably attired. His mind moves like a steel trap and snaps out wit and wisdom. His tests bring out analytic skills, and while they are infrequent, you know that he personally reads each one.

Even in presenting the most abstract materials, each student feels that Lundberg is talking directly to him or to her. Some themes are oft repeated, but there is ever the fresh illustration drawn from his broadly based set of current readings.

In his famous Sociology 178 theory course, the give and take of a seminar was always present. Participation was prompted, but it must be prompt.

Mannerisms, too, are memorable. Some teachers are ear twisters, others wind watches or rub their chins. Lundberg is a pencil man, and he has a cough. A question from a student brings a brief pause during which Lundberg deftly taps a long sharp pencil over his teeth. Then comes the reply which, like the pencil, is sometimes long but always sharp. And each new batch of students would agonize over his persistent cough until they learned from experience that the interrupted sentence is miraculously retrieved and carried to a conclusion.

The art of Lundberg as a teacher in the classroom is the man himself. He generates confidence because he is confident. He instills curiosity because he is curious. He is critical and cutting, but never cruel. His arguments move by evidence, not by the eminence of their source. He is serious in intent and content, but not about himself.

In 1953, he and other living ex-presidents of the American Sociological Association were asked to record their advice to younger sociologists. Lundberg's career exemplifies the advice he offered which included the following points:

- ♦ Get literate somehow as early as possible.
- ♦ Don't waste too much time on courses and lectures.
- ♦ Get jobs on real research projects.
- ♦ Avoided the beaten paths.
- ♦ Go in for special pleading, but don't claim that it is a scientific exercise.

On occasion, Lundberg expresses regret that more of his own efforts were not directed toward more doing of science and less talking about it. But in the flow of scholarly affairs, there is a right time for everything. Lundberg seized the right moment in the development of sociology and helped turn the tide in the direction now running.

His students can now run with that tide.

Chapter 32

The Dimensions of Stuart C. Dodd

Memorial Service, Magnolia Congregational Church, Seattle

January 14, 1976

The "C" in Stuart C. Dodd could stand for many things. Years ago as graduate students we used to wonder about that.

Early on we thought it might stand for "correlation," or "causation," or even "computers." Stu's abiding concern for commensurability undoubtedly provoked such thoughts.

But he also had substantive interests, so our thoughts naturally drifted toward the possibility that "C" stood for "community," or "communication," or "consensus," or "cooperation," or "concord," or "cosmology." Each of these were key C-words in the lexicon of this man's vast interests.

In lighter moments, some hungry graduate students, and they were numerous in the late 1940s and early 1950s, even postulated that the "C" stood for the three items than one could always find in the bottom drawer of Stu's desk, items that nourished many students through many late hours in the Public Opinion Laboratory: "cheese," "chocolate," and "crackers."

But as we worked with Stu over the years, his style and his character yielded even more likely possibilities for referents to the letter "C." These included "curiosity," "creativity," "concern," "courage," "commitment," "compassion," "civility," "candor," and "charisma." Each of these traits he had in full measure.

A Career of Products Not Sums

However, it is clear that even the rich possibilities drawn from this one letter of the alphabet are not adequate to find a word that sets a tone for summing up the essence of this remarkable teacher, colleague, and friend. And even if we could agree on a list of terms for such an effort, it would be a violation of a primary Doddian axiom to try to sum up anything. Stu always insisted that systems were products, never sums, of their interacting parts. And he emphasized, with delightful fervor, that this was the fundamental principle whether for atoms or protons, biological cells or organisms, human thoughts or actions, and spiritual aspirations as well as any other form of interaction.

The rich and far-ranging career and personality of Stuart Dodd were each, then, a product of many interacting elements that Stu himself would factor out into the modes of knowing, feeling, and doing. He gave full measure to each mode during each day of his life.

Much of his motivation must have been rooted in the fact that both his father and grandfather were medical missionaries in the Middle East. There was a missionary zeal to all that Stu did, reflected even in the titles of his major research efforts--Project Consensus, Project Worth, Project Revere, Project Concord--and also reflected in his final major concern with Epicosm Models, a system of hypotheses to help understand and unify the cosmos.

Ever a student, Stu Dodd was a brilliant teacher, as hundreds can testify from Beirut to Seattle. In 1927 he founded the department of sociology at the American University in Beirut and served as its chairman until 1947. He then came to Seattle to found and direct the Washington Public Opinion Laboratory until his retirement in 1971.

From his classic controlled experiment to improve rural hygiene in Syria, through his daring conduct of polls for General Eisenhower in Sicily and Italy in World War II, and up through his innovative research on message diffusion in Seattle, Dodd pressed for the rigorous assessment of the forces that form and function as public opinion .

He contributed as a scientist, as a practitioner skillfully applying knowledge, and as an organizer to promote standards of competence in the field. In 1946, he reconciled sharp differences between Gallup and Roper and was a key figure in the Central City Conference that led to the founding of the American Association for Public Opinion Research and the World Association of Public Opinion Research. He drafted the constitution for the latter organization and served three terms as its Secretary.

A Scientific Humanist

But the impact and meaning of this remarkable man cannot be found by reference to the work that impinged on public opinion alone. Warm and gentle in manner, this vigorous exponent of rigor in the treatment of social, value, and symbolic systems left a legacy of scientific humanism reflected in nine published books and 140 articles in some 60 journals representing a score of disciplines.

Furthermore, his technical and inventive fascination with languages, scales, matrices, models, and systems, was always coupled to an active concern with movements to abolish colonialism and war, to enhance social welfare, to extend democratic participation, and to produce human unity.

The mystery is solved. The "C" in Stuart C. Dodd always stood for "caring."

Chapter 33

The Footprints of Tad Blalock

Memorial Service, Faculty Club, University of Washington

March 5, 1991

One must respond when called to celebrate the life of our dear friend and colleague, Tad Blalock.

I am going to limit my remarks to two aspects of his bountiful being. Tad touched us all with his deep *sense of social obligation* and his profound *commitment to accuracy.*

A Sense of Social Obligation

First, a few words about social obligation.

A recent issue of *Time* magazine carried a full-page account of a new idea characterized as more than a slogan but less than a coherent philosophy. It arrived under the label "Communitarianism," a word that *Time* fetchingly asserted stumbles awkwardly off the tongue, all 16 didactic letters, sounding like a fuzzy echo from a long-ago college lecture.

I chuckled over that opening sentence. It must have been prompted from a sociological source. And, sure enough, it was. A group of eastern intellectuals, headed by Amitai Etzioni, have launched an intellectual movement with a new quarterly journal entitled *Responsive Community.* The statement of purpose declares that the rights of individuals must be balanced with responsibilities to the community.

This may be a worthy intellectual movement, but it certainly isn't a new idea. Tad's life testifies to that. Long ago, he incorporated community responsibility into each pulse of his everyday life. I have never known a person with a more fierce sense of social obligation.

I first encountered this dedication when Tad was on the Council of the American Sociological Association during my tenure as Executive Officer from 1972-1975. Tad was the burning conscience of the Council. Let me briefly illustrate how this was manifest in four areas:

♦   More than any one, Tad mobilized efforts to foster achievement by minorities.

♦   When other senior figures faltered, Tad gave unstinting effort, and thus legitimacy, to endeavors that would enrich undergraduate education.

♦   When others bickered, Tad committed his book royalties to founding a program on the Problems of the Discipline, a mission that still energizes fundamental exploration in sociology.

♦   Tad was the spur for an "Open Forum" in the newly founded Footnotes so that serious issues could be addressed by various voices. He set the model with powerful essays to compel sensitivity and stir action.

I have to admit, however, that there was one point where I had to contest Tad's spirited leadership.

He never liked the idea of holding Council or Annual meetings in resort areas or in fancy hotels. He thought we should meet in drafty dormitories or down at the railroad YMCA. I tried to tell him that the hotel rooms were complimentary, and that the devoted efforts of council persons deserved some amenities.

He never quite believed that. But, then, as I remember, he also advocated that we all take cold showers.

Which, somehow, brings me to the second quality that Tad's life personified and animated: his unrelenting pursuit of accuracy.

Commitment to Accuracy

Others have spoken or will speak of his multi-faceted contributions to measurement. I merely want to confirm his commitment to accuracy in all matters by a single anecdote. After all, Tad did appreciate the linkage of parsimony to accuracy.

At the time of his retirement dinner, I had the privilege of serving as master of ceremonies. Such an occasion affords fun through hyperbole. I thought it fair to warn Tad that I would surely address the evening with a series of half-truths. His response was immediate, Oh, that's all right, just be sure they are accurate.

With that in mind, let me conclude my notes on this celebration of his life.

And Departing Leave Behind Us

I can still see Tad strolling down that great beach before his home off Foulweather Bluff.

About a hundred years ago, Longfellow might well have passed such a place as he formulated a Psalm of Life. You remember that poem. It contained verses that must have been meant for the likes of Tad.

> *Lives of great men all remind us*
> *We can make our lives sublime,*
> *And departing, leave behind us*
> *Footprints on the sands of time;*
> *Footprints, that perhaps another,*
> *Sailing o'er life's solemn main,*
> *A forlorn and shipwrecked brother,*
> *Seeing, shall take heart again.*

Thank you Tad, for deep, caring, and accurate footprints. They will continue to bring heart.

Afterword

A Grand View of Social Science
By William R. Catton, Jr.
Professor Emeritus, Washington State University, Pullman
Reprinted from *Sociological Inquiry*, 62 (February, 1992): 1-10
and used by permission of the author and the journal.

"A search for knowledge" is the way my dictionary defines "inquiry."

That was clearly the meaning intended when Otto N. Larsen chose the word as part of the new title for the former Alpha Kappa Deltan, the journal of the national sociology honor society. Appearing for its first thirty years under that more cryptic title derived from the initials of the honor society's Greek motto, the journal was not easily identified by non-members as a sociological publication or as having anything to do with the quest for knowledge of societal phenomena. The name change was a means of facilitating communication.

Larsen was in Copenhagen, Denmark, in the autumn of 1959 when he received from Alvin Scaff a letter telling him he had been elected editor by the United Chapters of Alpha Kappa Delta at the annual meeting in Chicago. The journal was small and somewhat obscure, so the prospect of being its editor seemed at first a dubious distinction, but Larsen was willing to try to enlarge its significance. When he later changed the journal's name, it reflected this determination. Effective communication is essential for any field of scientific research; sociology is no exception. Adapting and editing *Sociological Inquiry* for enhanced service to that function constituted an important step in the development of a career whose "off camera" impact on the fortunes of our discipline was to become enormous. As is often the case, however, Larsen entered upon that career path almost inadvertently, as we shall see.

Was there indeed a special function this particular journal could serve? Larsen speculated that perhaps "*the Deltan*" (as he at first continued to speak of it) could usefully provide thematic treatments of timely and vital special topics pertaining to the sociological discipline. He felt for example, that awareness at that time among American sociologists about sociological work being done outside the U.S. was scant. He quickly formed the intention of devoting the first issue he would edit to a report on Scandinavian sociology.

Who was this new editor? What was he doing in Copenhagen? How had he become the kind of person he was? What had shaped his particular sociological outlook? What was he destined to accomplish in the years ahead?

Some Background

Otto Larsen was born to Danish parents in Tyler, Minnesota, in January, 1922. As an infant, he moved with his family to Junction City, Oregon. There he grew up and went through high school, after which he attended a two-year college in Des Moines, Iowa. Grand View College was just forming its Alumni Association in the year Larsen entered as a freshman. The flavor of what students called "the Grand View experience" is indicated by the fact that the first 132 members of the alumni association included seven Hansens, seven Petersens, six Christensens, six Jensens, six Strandskovs, five Nielsens, four Larsens, and four Thompsons.

One prominent possibility for students at Grand View was preparation for entrance into seminary and a career in the Danish Lutheran ministry. Larsen duly considered this, but it was sociology's good fortune that other factors happened to divert him from this path. In a paper he wrote for a philosophy course at Grand View, he penned a sentence that would have been worthy of Robert Merton's 1965 book, *On the Shoulders of Giants:* "Loyalty to our fathers does not consist in standing where their journey ended, but in pursuing the path their vision discerned." As we shall see, separating ethnicity from ethnocentrism was to become a compelling aim for Otto Larsen, sociologist. The effort was to have profound benefits for social science.

Following his two years in Iowa, Larsen returned to the west, where he attended the University of Oregon in 1942-43, taking, among other courses, sociology of religion. This did not yet alert him to his future career as a sociologist. He was of military age. The country was at war. While at Grand View he had written for a student publication (just after U. S. entry into World War II) that "no sacrifice is too great to check the 'black plague' of the twentieth century" but that "the destruction of Hitlerism is not an end in itself." He joined the Army Air Corps after his year at Oregon. During his military service from 1943 to 1946 he found himself located for a while in Missoula, Montana, and for a while in Denver, Colorado, and both locations permitted him to continue university studies. His military service ended in the year after the war ended. His family had moved to Seattle, so Larsen entered the University of Washington, where he received his B. A. degree in 1947 (the year in which he also married Greta Petersen).

The G.I. Bill that enabled many American veterans to further their education in these early postwar years was accompanied by a peculiarly American hubris. Having achieved the explosive release of nuclear energy in time to end the war by resorting to phenomenally potent new weaponry, visions of Pax Americana coalesced with those images of the good life expected in the post-war world that had been held up to American readers by institutional advertising during the war. Larsen was a member of the cohort of veteran students among whom, for some, the aura of supreme confidence got focused upon the idea that social science research in service to humanity was the means of future progress. George Lundberg's little book, *Can Science Save Us?*, was among many influences that persuaded some, Larsen included, that social scientific inquiry was a noble calling.

With a Little Bit of Luck

Following graduation and marriage, the next order of business seemed obviously to be getting a job. Having edited a student publication while he was at Grand View, it seemed plausible to Otto Larsen that he should apply for a position he saw advertised, city hall reporter for the newspaper in Aberdeen and Hoquiam, Washington. At this point his future achievement for sociology might have been lost. Fortuitous (and seemingly unrelated) facts intervened. The Norwegian ethnologist, Thor Heyerdahl, had already before the war begun to speculate about the striking similarities he had observed between major artifacts in the islands of Polynesia and artifacts of the South

American west coast. The anthropological profession generally scorned his hypothesis that Polynesians might have had South American origins. It became apparent to Heyerdahl that credence for his ideas could be gained only by demonstrating that people could actually have sailed west across the Pacific on a balsa log raft of the type known to have been built by South American tribes. In 1947, fortunately for us, Heyerdahl was experiencing difficulty finding a suitable sixth person for his Kon Tiki expedition crew. Along came a red-bearded Swede, Bengt Danielsson, a graduate of Uppsala University who happened to have an asset possessed by none of the other five members of the subsequently famous expedition--he spoke Spanish. This, plus Heyerdahl's conviction that a solitary Swede who was plucky enough to want to make the voyage with five Norwegians "could not be squeamish," caused Danielsson to relinquish a research assistantship he was to have had at the University of Washington, working with George Lundberg. Lundberg offered the vacated position to newly graduated Otto Larsen. As it turned out, the Aberdeen-Hoquiam newspaper's loss was sociology's gain.

A Comparison and Contrast

One of the impressive facts from the early history of American sociology is the achievement of quite universal insights and very important conceptual contributions by a man whose entire academic career was spent at one university. It was the same institution where he had studied as an undergraduate and as a graduate. He was Charles Horton Cooley, who coined the terms "primary group" and "looking-glass self" and who effectively discerned the social basis of human nature. Personal observations within the town of Ann Arbor and on the campus of the University of Michigan sufficed as his "data-base."

Like Cooley, Otto Larsen remained affiliated for the entirety of his academic career with the same university where he earned his Bachelor of Arts and Ph.D. degrees. In Larsen's case it was the University of Washington in Seattle, a much larger and more cosmopolitan city than Cooley's Ann Arbor. And the world would become Larsen's database. Between 1949 and 1962, Larsen advanced at Washington from teaching fellow to instructor to assistant professor, associate professor, and professor, holding this rank for twenty years, including periods as director of the Institute for Sociological Research and as department chairman. Unlike Cooley,

Larsen's rootedness at one university did not preclude horizon-extending temporary appointments at others, either during summers or during leaves of absence. He taught at San Diego State, the University of Colorado, and the University of Hawaii, and spent a year as Fulbright Professor at the University of Copenhagen. In addition, he was invited to lecture on various occasions at seventeen other U. S. universities as well as a dozen foreign universities.

For much of his time on the faculty at the University of Washington, some of Larsen's departmental colleagues were also Washington Ph.D's. Once, in a departmental faculty meeting, when another colleague whose degree was from the University of Chicago began to worry aloud about whether the U.W. department was becoming "inbred," Larsen quietly looked around the room and noted with a wry smile that the Chicago Ph.D.s outnumbered the Washington ones. Was this department becoming an "in-bred Chicago-west"?

By taking several leaves of absence from Washington, Larsen was able to devote his talents to several non-university roles of considerable importance for sociology (and for social science in general). He served a three-year term as executive officer of the American Sociological Association (in the other Washington, 1972-75) when able leadership was needed for surmounting organizational stresses arising from national political turbulence due to the undeclared Vietnam War. He also served as chairman of the board of the Social Science Research Council in New York, 1978-80, and again in Washington, D.C. 1980-82 he was director of the Division of Social and Economic Research at the National Science Foundation. His influence continued during the 1983-86 period in the role of senior associate for social and behavioral science with NSF. These were years when it was touch-and-go as to whether NSF could continue as a social science funding source, and Larsen was a steadfast defender of sociology and its sister disciplines.

From time to time he was a consultant to several federal government agencies--the U.S. Civil Service Commission, the National Institute of Mental Health, the Commission on Causes and Prevention of Violence, the Commission on Obscenity and Pornography (where his commitment to the importance of empirical research importantly bucked "we-already-know-answers" sentiments of national political leaders, and where his expertise on mass communications media was of clear relevance), and the National

Endowment for the Humanities. His influence (and some of the influences upon him) can be seen in his service on a number of national boards and committees. He served on an advisory board for the National Opinion Research Center at the University of Chicago, various committees, boards, or panels of the National Academy of Science, the American Council of Learned Societies, and the Social Science Research Council. Through the years he also chaired or was a member of various committees of the American Sociological Association--not the least of these having been the local arrangements committee for the 1958 annual meetings of the ASA--the last annual meetings the association ever held on a university campus, at the University of Washington. Increasing size of the organization precluded a campus venue for subsequent meetings.

Teaching and Publication

Larsen was both creative and effective as a teacher. He was admired and respected by students at all levels, and he was a motivating influence and informative "coach" at times for a crew of pre-doctoral fledgling teachers of introductory sociology. A colleague who foresaw how being exposed to foreign mass media might enhance his already effective capacity for imparting sociological principles pertaining to mass communication wrote a vigorous recommendation when Larsen applied for the Fulbright grant that took him to Denmark. This colleague wrote that he knew of no one "who can establish rapport so readily in so wide a range of interpersonal situations as Otto Larsen" and went on to describe his qualities as a teacher: "He is friendly and enthusiastic, arouses and holds the interests of his students, and presents both ideas and information in an understandable and sometimes really exciting fashion." Having had opportunities to observe closely Larsen's office consultations with individual students, the colleague wrote: "Students find him very helpful, and they respect him. In short, he gives himself fully and effectively to all phases of the teaching task."

Often, with students as with faculty colleagues, Larsen indulged in good-natured jest. But he was also deeply serious about knowledge, and he put into his books, his lectures, and his journal articles solid efforts that always reflected the fact that he cares intensely for the advancement of learning.

Many of his published journal articles and book chapters have dealt with mass media, a subject he began to teach when Joseph Klapper left the Washington department. Larsen has been consulting or associate editor of communication journals, as well as having edited at one time or another two other sociological journals besides *Sociological Inquiry*. As the executive officer of ASA, he took pleasure in instituting Departmental Alumni Night as a feature of the association's annual meetings, and he was also responsible for launching its distinctive professional newsletter, *ASA Footnotes*, which he edited throughout his term at the national office. All through his career he has been vitally interested in communication, both as a subject for social science study and as a process that is as essential for social sciences' advancement as for other scientific disciplines. This interest is reflected in the books he has authored or co-authored: four editions of an introductory textbook, two editions of a manual of exercises for teaching basic sociological concepts, an especially timely book on *Violence and the Mass Media* (1968), a pair of books for and about the application and advancement of sociological knowledge--*Social Policy and Sociology* and *The Uses of Controversy in Sociology*. He has most recently (in retirement) written an important account of the pressures for and against support of the social sciences at NSF, *Milestones and Millstones,* 1992.

Between 1959 and 1989, Larsen delivered almost two dozen papers at regional, national, or international conferences. From 1949 to 1989 almost three dozen of his articles appeared in scholarly journals, and he wrote an assortment of chapters for books edited by others. He came to be well-known and respected far beyond the boundaries of his own discipline.

Missionary Efforts

Speaking in Washington, D.C. in April, 1969 to a convention of the American Society of Newspaper Editors, after a year in which newspapers had built myths about the previous summer's racial events, Larsen deliberately sought to make members of audience uneasy about their own profession. He tried to dissuade them from the self-righteous notion that media complicity in the ills of society was confined to television. His topic was the question of whether mass media treatment of violence was in some ways a hazard to the health of our society. Forthright about his attentions toward this audience, Larsen began his talk by noting how his father, a preacher in a small-

town church, had often felt while preparing his sermons "that the
special kind of hell he wanted to raise seemed more suitable for
persons absent than for the congregation present." Ultimately, said
Larsen to the editors, his father had abandoned the pulpit, partly from
weariness over "nourishing the self-righteousness of those present."
The newspaper editors were admonished not to suppose their
profession was immune to temptations so famously afflicting
electronic media. What is the dominant newspaper story, Larsen
asked, "when the students stir on campus, or when the blacks revolt in
the ghetto"? It is all too often "an account of incidents of violence,
largely isolated from antecedent conditions, conveying little
understanding of either the root causes or the possible consequences
of unrest." He challenged his audience at the end by asking: "Are you
really certain that the current practices of your newspaper have not
made some contribution to the image of the world apparently so
prevalent among today's youth who want to smash it?"

The 1980s were a time of troubles for the social sciences in a
different way than the 1960s and 1970s had been. There were serious
threats to the financial survival of social science research. When a
particle beam physicist, Edward A. Knapp, took over as director of
the National Science Foundation early in its fourth decade of
existence, it appeared that the answers to U.S. insecurity were going
to be sought in technological might that could counter what were
assumed to be the prime threats facing the U.S.--Soviet military
power and Japanese entrepreneurship. Budget emphasis at NSF was
directed toward the physical sciences, consistent with such a premise.
But Otto Larsen was at NSF as director of social and economic
research, and he rose to the challenge. His influence helped persuade
Knapp to reject "the Dr. Strangelove view of science." Knapp came to
want to understand the social sciences, at least after touring the
University of Michigan's Institute for Social Research with Larsen--
who insists that even if "we might be called the soft sciences we have
the hard problems."

The Reagan Administration had come to power apparently
determined to eliminate social science research support by NSF and
made an initial cut of seventy-five percent in the funds budgeted for
social science. Some of this was restored by Congress. Knapp was
willing to admit that he knew less about the social sciences than other
sciences and said he was working hard to understand them, "to see
where they were quantitative, where they were qualitative, where real

data can be used, where they are productive in terms of scientific output." He said he thought physical scientists ought to spend some time learning about the successes, the failures, and the criticisms of the social sciences because "if, in fact, the social sciences could be quantitative and accurate, then the kinds of questions that could be asked and the kinds of answers that could be given are extremely important." Larsen offered this advice to social scientists: "Take a physicist to lunch," meaning we should seek opportunities to discuss our research with those in the more venerable sciences and thereby dissuade them from stereotyped notions of our disciplines' worthlessness. Since Larsen practiced what he preached, the social sciences suffered far fewer losses than they might have in a time of adversity.

Congress, too, was targeted for such enlightenment. For example, in expressing support for the fiscal year 1984 authorization for NSF, Representative Carl Pursell (R-Michigan) said he was "particularly interested in the financial support provided for behavioral land social sciences. Research support in this area is essential in addressing the questions of improved human productivity." He believed it was necessary to face "the fact that increases in human productivity are tied as closely with behavioral factors as with technological advances."

Fun with Sociology

In 1956, for an annual departmental party at Washington, involving a "let's not take ourselves too seriously" type of program, Larsen arranged for a friend of his who had "perfected the funniest Swedish accent that I have ever heard" to be introduced as professor from Uppsala University to give a talk on "The Situation in Europe." The friend regaled the audience of sociologists and graduate students with a series of fantastic stories mixed with enough serious description of Sweden to persuade everyone of his legitimacy, only to conclude by abruptly dropping the fake accent and acknowledging he'd never been in Sweden and didn't even understand the Swedish language. The whole gag went over well and revealed to the audience the limitations of their supposed sophistication regarding "roles."

But even as an undergraduate, Larsen had been impressed with the fact that serious sociological research was fun. Perhaps more in those days than now, it was possible for students to become involved in the collection of data. When real research was being done without benefit of grant money and computers, it may have been easier for students to be eye-witnesses to the emergence of new knowledge and to internalize the very idea that questions lead to hypothetical answers and that hypotheses can be tested against observations. Larsen's first publication as a sociologist was a paper he co-authored with George Lundberg based on interviewing he did for his mentor in a community near Seattle. There was a thrill in realizing one's efforts could be informative to professional readers, and Larsen began to realize he would indeed be a sociologist.

As the years passed and his career advanced, he retained this wide-eyed student's feeling of astonished amazement with the joys offered by academic life. In February 1960 he was in Stockholm, Sweden, and described in a letter to a friend the experience of "this little old Dane boy from Junction City, Oregon." It was "quite an international binge" he was having, he said. He and Greta were going out to dinner that evening at a Hungarian restaurant with some Swedish and Dutch friends, after which they would be going to an exhibition of Spanish classic art at Sweden's National Museum.

The fun he was having always fed his perceptions of the possibilities for sociology to grow and inform. He found contact with sociologists from the Scandinavian countries (during his Fulbright year) very impressive. "Their long philosophical tradition is not," he felt, "being wasted as they seem very adept at basing their empirical research, for which they are well-trained, on a well thought out theoretical base."

His year in Scandinavia clarified his self-conception and at the same time it enhanced his understanding of an important sociological concept--ethnocentrism. Here is an excerpt from a paper he wrote (almost two decades later) for a Danish American journal: Since every culture encourages ethnocentrism, this raises a   critical question about the pursuit of a heritage: Can we be ethnic without being ethnocentric? I am uncertain about the answer. I think we can if we allow others the legitimacy we accord ourselves in the pursuit and promotion of a heritage. But it will probably take more than that if we are going to have a world that is safe for diversity. To combat ethnocentrism and yet hold our ethnicity, we may have to develop an appreciation of ethnicities beyond our own. However, it is not easy being a cultural relativist, as any of us senses as we begin moving about in the world.

Having written these thoughts, Larsen went on to become director of the Division of Social and Economic Research at NSF, where part of his task became the mission of disabusing politicians and persons in "the hard sciences" of their ethnocentric disregard for the "soft sciences." But he also found ethnocentrism in the attitudes of social scientists toward each other's disciplines and worked to overcome this. He had embraced the phrase President John F. Kennedy had used in a speech at the University of Washington, about making the world safe for diversity. But he now saw a need for making the world of research safe for unity. The social sciences must respect each other if they are to earn respect for themselves.

In a report to the United Chapters of Alpha Kappa Delta as the organization's president, ten years after renaming the journal, Larsen described his experience on a sabbatical visit to Greece, handicapped by not knowing the language. His working vocabulary, he said, "hardly extended beyond three words: *anthropon, katamanthanein, diakonesein*. These terms were not exactly useful in negotiations concerning transport, food, or housing." They roughly translate as "mankind, research, and service," so they express the ideals of our honor society and knowing them did somehow impart to Larsen some confidence in coping with the challenge of exploring new territory.

It is to be hoped this account of his career and personality may assist in making that confidence contagious.

Name Index